ADVANCE PR
Goodbye t

"Clayton's characters come to life
He has been seduced by Soho's sle.
are we." —Marc Almond

"That dirty old whore Soho has no better pimp than Clayton
Littlewood. Both funny and touching, *Goodbye To Soho* hums
with the still sad music of humanity."

—Tim Fountain, playwright (*Resident Alien and Rock*)

"As scurrilous and entertaining as ever - but this time there's a
deep vein of melancholy running through the fun and gossip, a
glimpse of grief that makes the hectic jollity of the Soho streets
all the more affecting." —Rupert Smith, author of *Man's World*

"Like Christopher Isherwood's Berlin, Clayton Littlewood's
Soho comes to life right off the page, with all its humour and
madness and in full technicolour."

—Jonathan Kemp, author of *London Triptych*

"Beautifully composed vignettes of outsiders, outcasts, fantasies
and refugees, observed by a ravenous, compassionate, amused
voyeur of the first rank."

—Nicholas de Jongh, theatre critic/playwright (*Plague Over England*)

"I've come to know, and love, Clayton's cast of Soho characters
so much that I truly hope this is not "Goodbye"."

—Michael Tonello, author of *Bringing Home the Birkin*

"It might sound strange to be comforted by the daily trials of
prostitutes, trannies, prisoners and street sweepers, but that's
what Clayton does - brilliantly."

—Stewart Who? (Writer/Editor/DJ)

GOODBYE
TO SOHO

Love from
a
Dirty White Boy

Clayton
x x
x
April 2012

PRAISE FOR
Dirty White Boy: Tales of Soho

"Touching, funny and poignant." —Sir Elton John

"Funny, perceptive, sexy, exquisitely observed." —Stephen Fry

"Clayton Littlewood's book is tender, warm and full of humanity." —*New Statesman* (London)

"A collection of witty and piquant vignettes." —*The London Paper*

"His novel truly shines." —*Gay Times* (Book of the Year 2009)

"A 21st-century Samuel Pepys of the Soho subculture."
—Holly Johnson

"Downright hysterical." —*QX* magazine (London)

"Clayton's genuine interest in the people he writes about makes *Dirty White Boy* such a compelling read." —*Polari Magazine*

"A sense of historic Soho (Rimbaud and Verlaine, Quentin Crisp) percolates through the book." —*One80* magazine

"Original anecdotes and real-life stories told with a Hogarthian incisiveness—a sort of unofficial tourist guide evoking a vivid portrait of an area that is like no other."
—*West End Extra* (London)

"*Dirty White Boy* is a warts 'n' all year of seedy beauty, faded glamour and real danger. ... It is honest writing without preconceptions. Clayton stayed true to himself, and so his book stays true to Soho." —*reFresh* magazine (London)

I'm sitting on my ... looking out onto Old Compton ... a face ... up in front ... black top coat, black hair, ... a fey flutter of ... Sebastian, Sebastian ... street, Meard Street ... the door that reads: "... prostitutes live here." At first, ... suicide, Sebastian is ... When we first ... als would point at him and, ... recount strange stories about ... figure, he was a drug addict ... was a connoisseur of prostitutes (... more than a thousand). ... crucifixion ... hippies (he painted pictures ... been through).

GOODBYE TO SOHO

Clayton Littlewood

Press

Published in the United Kingdom by:
DWB Press Ltd.
Email: dwbpress@aol.com
www.dwbpress.com

A CIP catalogue record for this book is available from the British Library.

Cover Painting: Maggi Hambling (Sebastian XI, Oil on Canvas, 2011, 48 x 36 inches). © 2011 by Maggi Hambling.
Cover design: Joe Pearson and Graham Rees.
Text design: The Book Design Company (www.thebookdesign.co.uk)
First author photo © 2012 by Jamie McLeod (www.jamiemcleod.co.uk).
Calligraphy by Lois Froud (www.halo-is.com)
Second author photo on page 261 © 2011 by Gabriella Meros (www.gabriellameros.com)

Littlewood, Clayton
Goodbye to Soho/Clayton Littlewood.—1st ed.
ISBN 978-0-9570291-1-8
Goodbye to Soho 2. Gay business enterprises—Social aspects—England—London 3. Soho (London, England) I. Title
Memoir/London interest
For more information on ordering please contact:
Turnaround Publisher Services
Email: orders@turnaround-uk.com
Tel: 020 8829 3000

Printed and bound by CPI Group (UK) Ltd, Croydon, CR0 4YY

This book is dedicated to Sebastian Horsley
and Chico Thomas

IMAGINE A COLD, BLUSTERY, WINTER EVENING, RAIN FALLING QUIETLY but steadily on a London street. Consider the street: restaurants, delicatessens, cafés, sex shops, water emerging from drains, creating miniature black lakes, the street busy despite the weather.

Now picture the life on this street. A cultural melting pot. Couples sheltering under large umbrellas; shapeless raincoats, in-shape hoodies; a homeless man carrying a plastic bag over his shoulder; an old Chinese woman with a limp, bent over with age, covering her head with her hands.

Finally, imagine one of the shops on this street: a man inside, sitting beside a window, staring intently at the screen of his laptop, concentrating; looking outside every few minutes as if for inspiration; scratching his head as if unsure how to proceed.

Now watch as he smiles. As he takes a deep breath. As he places his fingers on the keyboard.

That man is me. The street is in Soho. And my Soho stories are about to begin again...

January 2008

January 2nd, 2008: The Day Begins

Dirty White Boy. 50 Old Compton Street, Soho.

We've just opened and there's hardly anyone on the street.

Suddenly a tall Amazonian-looking woman sashays into the shop; Dior sunglasses, hair pulled back in a ponytail, holding a black Chanel handbag in one hand and a silver-tipped walking stick in the other.

'You've gotta see this guy in the gym!' she says in a loud, androgynous Cockney voice, oblivious to the couple of customers browsing the rails. 'He's blond and cute and he's got a bum like a beach ball.'

I put my magazine to one side, grin. 'I think I've seen him.'

'Now, you know I don't usually go for the chickens, but darlin', please!' She takes a seat on the little red chair by the window, places her handbag on the floor and crosses her legs. 'So...,' she says, leaning forward, 'here's what I found out. He's a part-time model. He's straight. An' he's got a stud just here.' She points at her tongue. 'I said to him, "How about seein' if that stud of yours can work a bit of magic down here?"' She uncrosses her legs, opening them slightly for effect. 'Poor little thing. He didn't know where to look.'

It's eleven o'clock. Soho's just starting to come to life and Angie's one of the first on the street, a tour de force of tranny energy, humour and anecdote—the signal for the day to begin.

Jorge walks up the stairway.

4

'Jorge, honey! I was just tellin' Clay, there's a guy in the gym you're gonna love!'

'Really?'

'Mmm-hmm,' she affirms, removing her sunglasses and shaking out her auburn hair, which cascades around the white fur collar of her bolero jacket. 'Look, I don't mean to cause divorce proceedings or nothin' but you are gonna *die* when you see him!'

I turn to Jorge, smile. 'He is quite good-looking.'

'Quite?' Angie shrieks as she opens her handbag and pulls out a lipstick. 'Darlin', I'm still wet!'

She glides toward the dressing room mirror, examines her face and applies her lipstick in one well-practised movement. Then she stares at herself and sighs. 'If only I were twenty years younger—the dirty bastard would 'ave me up all night, I'm sure.' She moistens her lips, runs a finger along them, then pulls her black sports top down slightly, pushing up her voluptuous breasts until they're positioned to her liking. 'Oh, why can't I get a boyfriend?' she moans to no one in particular.

'What's that?'

'I said,' she repeats, swishing back, 'why can't I get a boyfriend? I'm on the Stairmaster every day! Working my butt off! An' what do I get? Tranny fuckers! That's what!' She walks back toward the window where Jorge's now sitting, working out yesterday's takings. 'Did I ever tell you about the scaffolder from the gym?'

Jorge looks up from his paperwork. 'No, I don't think you did.'

'Gorgeous. Absolutely gorgeous. Big arms. Big knob. Honey, he's got everythin'! An' he's bin sniffin' round me for weeks.' She repositions her glasses in her hair. 'So he invited me over for dinner.'

Jorge stands, picks up his paperwork and walks behind the counter, looking for the calculator. Angie raises a dark, perfectly plucked eyebrow. 'Are you listenin'?'

'Yes, but I have to finish this.'

She huffs and turns to face me instead. 'So, anyway, I get round there an' he goes straight to the bathroom. An' I thought, Hello? Wot's goin' on 'ere? Then he walks out, bollock naked, an' starts waving his hard-on at me!'

'No!'

'Oh, you 'aven't 'eard the best of it. So I said, "What're you doin'?" An' he said, "What do you think I'm doin'?" An' I said, "It's lovely, darlin'—but can you put it away now?" An' he said, "Come on, let's fuck. But don't tell anyone. Let's just keep it between you and me." Like I was his dirty little secret or summat! So I just picked up me handbag an' I said, "Listen, darlin', you may've fucked every tranny in town but you ain't fuckin' this one! Keep your little tranny fetish to yourself!"'

'What did he say?'

'He didn't get a chance to say anythin'—I left!'

'You didn't!'

''Course I did! His hard-on dropped quicker than a whore's knickers!' She takes the seat vacated by Jorge and fishes inside her handbag, pulling out a compact mirror, which she uses to examine her eyes. 'Darlin', I may be "on the meter" but I don't give it up that easily. I had to fuck a lot of boxes to get this box an' I ain't givin' it up to every Tom, Dick 'n' Harry! Anyway...' she sniffs, 'I found out he's bin shaggin' that vile Brazilian tranny from the gym an' there's no way he's puttin' it in me after it's been in her.'

'You're terrible.'

'An' get this,' she adds, 'Last week I found out he's turned gay an' he's become a hooker! Livin' in Earls Court with a porn star, he is. I was really upset about that, actually. I said to him, "You sad fuck!"'

'Why? Was he straight before?'

'Well, what's straight, darlin'? Oh, it's the story of my life. They go from me, to being gay, then "on the game". I'm like a bleedin' steppin' stone.' She closes her mirror case. 'An' I'm fed up of it. I really am. I wanna man who wants me. I wanna "Angie fucker" not a "tranny fucker".' She twirls a lock of hair around a finger and looks up at me expectantly. 'Does that make sense?'

Angie is 51 but looks 20 years younger, a sought-after model as an effeminate boy and, later, as a beautiful woman. Over the years I'd watched her in the clubs holding court, her voice both attracting and repelling in equal measure. She had star quality— and if it's measured in its outrageousness, its survival, its 'don't fuck with me' attitude, then Angie was overdosing with it. Over the years, with age increasing and clubbing decreasing, our paths crossed less often. Not that she was even aware of my existence. Angie was destined for higher things, part of the A list, and I was definitely not. So when I first met her in Soho, I already had a sense of who she was. I was prepared—or so I thought.

Her first words to me were: 'Girl, where can I get a good butt plug round here? It's for the fanny, luv. I've just had the cock chopped off and I need to dilate.' What followed was an hour's worth of theatre. The story of her life. The ups, the downs, the film roles, the boyfriends. It was a performance without self-congratulation or self-pity. It was as if she was saying, this is me. I'm loud. I'm in your face. Take it or leave it. Oh, and if you're still around in 10 minutes we may just end up friends. And we have.

'I said'—Angie tuts—'does that make sense?'

'Oh, sorry... Yes. Yes, it does.'

Having off-loaded, she looks across at Jorge and notices, for the first time it seems, that he's concerned, scratching his head as he tallies the previous day's takings with the daily target. 'What's wrong, honey?' she asks.

'These figures...' He looks in my direction. 'That was the worst Christmas we've had.' He places his pen on the counter and sighs. 'Oh, well... It'll turn around.'

Angie, sensing that her audience has dwindled, reaches for her handbag and her walking stick. 'Well, at least you've got each other,' she reminds us sympathetically as she makes a move to leave. She lets the sentence linger for a moment. 'Okay, boys, Angie's off!'

'Where're you going?'

'Seein' me surgeon.' She looks down at her breasts in dismay. 'I'm still not happy with 'em.'

I decide now's not the time to ask what's wrong with them and I walk her to the doorway. I reach up, kiss her on each cheek and watch as she leaves, brandishing her walking stick, a-swishin' and a-swayin' as only Angie can.

January 4th, 2008: My Trip to the Coffee Shop

I'm in Costa, the coffee shop across the road, on the corner of Old Compton Street and Dean Street. It's quiet inside, the few customers either reading the papers, surfing the net or chatting with friends. I scan the menu. Approach the counter. As I do, the assistant, as if sensing my presence, turns to face me.

'Good morning, sir!' she sings, clasping her hands together as if in prayer and nodding her head in deference.

She's Chinese, androgynous, with an unusual face, almost 'Toblerone' in shape, and though she's polite, the servile manner she adopts is slightly unnerving. I look down at her name tag, quickly raising my eyes again when I realise I'm also examining her left breast.

'You want coffee please?' she asks, bowing like a concubine.

'Umm... A cappuccino would be nice.'

She clears her throat. 'You like it large?' She blushes, hiding her mouth behind her hand as if the word *large* is somehow impolite.

'No. Er... A small one will be fine,' I reply, trying to ignore the sexual overtone.

I hand her some change and watch as she counts it carefully, her lips moving in a foreign tongue. Then she tears off a receipt and presses it into my hand, thanking me three times, nodding furiously, taking little steps backwards until she bangs into the coffee machine.

Feeling slightly uncomfortable, I look out the window toward the shop, but after a few seconds I have this overwhelming urge to look at her peculiar face again. I turn around. It's inches away. I let out a queeny squeak. She titters and pushes the coffee toward me, her smile so pronounced now that her eyes have all but disappeared.

I thank her. Grab a serviette. Leave.

As it's still early, the street is quiet too: a family leaving Patisserie Valerie, an early-morning road sweeper, someone loitering suspiciously outside The Groucho. I take a sip of my coffee, cross the road, heading back to the shop. On the crossroads is a familiar face. One of Soho's grande dames, dressed in a black fur coat and a matching hat. Like an ancient Romanov in exile.

'Hi, Michele!'

She's staring at the coffee shop but breaks her gaze to scrutinise me, a crooked smile creeping over her face that gives the impression few teeth lie behind it. Although we've chatted a few times before, whenever we meet I'm forced to reintroduce myself.

'It's Clayton. We've met before.'

'Have we, dear?'

'Yes, the last time was in Soho Square.'

'If you say so, dear.' She nods, looking back toward the coffee shop as if I've just interrupted her favourite TV show.

Although the street's predominately youth oriented, the old return, often unnoticed, to remember, to reflect. They see a different Soho. The ghosts. It was on this street that Michele first cross-dressed. Although she probably didn't make a particularly convincing woman in her youth—her jawline too pronounced, her features too masculine—now she's in the winter of her life she's acquired the look of an eccentric granny and passes without comment. I watch her for a few seconds, then leave her to her world, making my way back inside the shop to mine.

I'm sitting by the window now. On my little red chair. Laptop open. I take another sip of coffee. Wince as it leaves a slight burning sensation on my tongue. There's a knock on the window. It's Maggie, one of the madams from the brothel upstairs. She mouths, 'It was my birthday yesterday!'

I mouth back, 'How old? Twenty-three?'

'Almost.' She laughs. And she escorts a well-dressed businessman up the stairway.

I go back to my laptop. Rest my fingers on the keyboard. Start typing.

January 12th, 2008: Bum Business
Somerfield on Berwick Street.

I'm laden down with shopping bags, a French stick tucked under one arm, a box of cornflakes under the other; the handles of the bags are cutting into my palms.

Outside the supermarket it's the usual Soho milieu: a sprinkling of shady characters loitering in Walkers Court, a busty girl in a tight-fitting top smoking outside a doorway with a sign that says 'Model', a heavyset businessman perusing a sex shop window.

I walk down Peter Street, cross Wardour Street, continue down Meard Street. My arms are starting to ache now, my fingers turning numb with the weight of the bags. So I place them on the ground and re-grip, the pit-pat of raindrops bouncing off my jacket.

As I lift the bags I notice a figure approaching. He appears to be smiling so I smile back in anticipation, but being shortsighted, I don't recognise who it is until the figure is halfway down the street. Green umbrella, beige suit, yellow silk scarf floating behind him in the breeze: it could only be…

'Leslie!'

'Hello, ducky!'

'I haven't seen you since—'

'The big meet!' he says, with a twinkle in his eye. 'Oh, it were all very *Brief Encounter*.'

'How did it go?' I ask eagerly, placing the groceries on the ground again. 'You didn't call or anything.'

'Oh, I couldn't, dear,' he says, peering from underneath his umbrella at the overcast sky. 'Me nerves 'ave bin all over the place. Playin' up somethin' terrible, they 'ave.'

'Why's that?'

'Well, it's not every day you fall in love.'

'You're in love?' I gasp. 'With Charlie?'

'Of course with Charlie! Who do you think I'm in love with? The bleedin' bin man?'

'That's great! I mean—it must've gone well, then?'

'You could say that,' he chuckles behind a cupped hand.

My eyes widen. 'You've had sex, haven't you?'

''Ow dare you!' he shrieks. And he reaches over and slaps me playfully on the wrist. 'I'm not tellin' you!'

'Oh my God, you have!'

As it's stopped raining, he lowers his umbrella and leans on it with one hand, running his fingers through his hair with the other. 'Well, ducky, if you must know, contrary to popular belief, sex is not confined to the under-thirties. Men of my generation are more than capable of finding satisfactory fulfilment in the bedroom department.' He licks a forefinger and strokes his still arched eyebrow. 'And, I might add, it's without the aid of rubber toys and a handful of pills, or whatever it is the scene uses these days! Charlie and I don't need such accoutrements to enhance an evening in.'

As Charlie is a regular customer at the shop, and knowing his fondness for one particular item of clothing, I gently tease Leslie by saying, 'I bet he makes you wear his thongs, though.'

He hits me gently with his umbrella. 'Oh, you filthy homo! There may be a bit of dressin' up involved, but as I am still very slender in the leg, it's all very tasteful, thank you very much!' We stop talking for a few seconds as a couple walk past. 'Right, I'll have no more talk about the bum thing. There's no need to be discussing bum business in public.'

I laugh and say, 'When are you gonna bring him in the shop, then?'

'Er... Not just yet, ducky,' he replies hesitantly. 'We've decided to take things slowly to begin with.'

'Slowly? It's been forty years since you've seen him! Any slower and you'll be dead!'

Leslie throws me an icy stare. 'I'm fully aware of the time frame involved. And if one of us is unfortunate enough to drop dead while we're in the honeymoon period, then... Then at least we found each other in time.'

I feel myself blush, embarrassed by my crass comment.

'Anyway...' He smiles thinly. 'Apparently, I owe you an apology.'

'What for?'

'My behaviour.' He clears his throat and looks down at a shoe which he points like a ballerina. 'I reacted quite badly over this...affair and Charlie feels... Well, it was Charlie who pointed out that if it wasn't for you we'd never have found each other again.' He pauses. Looks me in the eye. 'And he's right.'

'Leslie, there's really no need—'

'Quiet! I'm apologisin'!' he snaps. Then he sighs, as if in pain. 'So, I want to say "sorry" and I want to thank you for what you did.'

'Ahhhh... That's nice of you to—'

'Well, that's that, then!' he says abruptly, sweeping his scarf over his shoulder. 'Now, ducky, I really must be on my way. It's the Bloomsbury Association's monthly meeting tonight and I promised I'd bring one of me Victoria Sponges.'

'Hopefully I'll see you both in the shop soon, then.'

'I'm sure you will.' He opens his umbrella again. 'I'm sure you will.'

And I watch as he walks slowly but regally to the end of the street, until he's finally out of sight.

January 18th, 2008: Wolfy

A rather stressed looking man with a mop of unruly black hair, wearing an excessively tight black T-shirt, bursts into the shop and starts charging around the rails.

'I need clothes. I like plain. Fitted. Black. Has to be black. But plain. And fitted. Do you have anything?' He rushes toward the counter. 'So do you have my size? In black? Fitted? But plain? For me? In my size?'

'Well, we—'

'Yes, but I want plain. It has to be plain. But very fitted. Look at my body.'

'We do. But—'

'Plain? Black? And fitted? Yes? You have it? Yes?'

Working in a shop in Soho you get to meet a variety of people—not all of them sane. But that's part of Soho's charm. Though it can make selling clothes a bit problematic.

'I am from Copenhagen,' the man says, extending his hand. He pulls it back a second later just as I'm about to shake. 'And I have very rich family, so I do not need to work. But I do work. I am caterer. Do you think I make good caterer? I have boyfriend. We keep arguing. I do not think he loves me. And it is my fortieth birthday in June. He is going to spoil my birthday if he does not love me.' He looks across at Jorge. 'Will you come to my birthday party? It is going to be dinner party. In June. I am cooking.' He looks back at me. 'You are both invited. Yes. Dinner party. Dinner party.'

At a loss now, I signal to Jorge, who's much more experienced in dealing with these situations. He walks confidently over.

'Hi, I'm Jorge!'

'Dinner party. Dinner party.'

'Er, yes. So—'

'I am Wolfy. But I need black. Plain. And it has to be fitted.'

'Well, we have black, plain and fitted,' Jorge replies quickly but calmly. 'But are you looking for a jacket, a shirt or a pair of trousers?'

'Yes!' he shouts, and he slams his hands down on the counter. 'That is exactly what I am looking for!' Then he rushes right back out of the shop, as fast as he came in, promising to return very soon.

January 21st, 2008: Breasts

We're in bed, in our little studio flat below the shop. Jorge's asleep beside me, his arm around my waist. The only noise is the click-clack of stilettos on the street above and the distant sound of drilling.

I try to sleep but the more I try, the more my dream state dissipates and reality seeps in. So I slip carefully out of the sheets and tiptoe across the tiled floor toward the kitchen. I press the light switch and the fluorescent bulb flickers on and off before illuminating the small room in a ghostly light.

I step inside.

To my right is a cold, menacing passageway that leads under the street. The passageway has dark, damp caves on one side and whenever I walk down there to check the electric meter I always feel like Jodie Foster walking nervously toward Hannibal Lecter's cell. To my left there's a small sink and, one step down, a humidifier which hums softly. The only other sound is a steady drip, drip, drip of water from a leaking pipe above my head which splashes into an overflowing saucepan on the floor. I reach up and turn the mains tap to 'off.' The dripping stops.

An hour later I'm dressed, sitting in my usual spot on my little red chair by the window, sipping coffee, waiting for the day to begin. All of a sudden there's a flash of white outside and a pair of matronly breasts burst past my line of vision. Seconds later they're in the shop, charging toward me like a pair of angry rhinos.

'IS YOUR WATER ON?' yells Sue, one of the other madams from upstairs.

'I think so...' I squeak, my nose peeping above a yard of cleavage. Then I remember the tap. 'Oh, er... Sue, I think, when I, er... When I switched the water off this morning I think I might have...'

The breasts inch closer, rearing up, ready for battle. 'YOU'VE TURNED OUR BLEEDIN' WATER OFF!'

'I'm sorry Sue. I—'

'I GOT TWO GIRLS NEED A SHOWER AN' WE GOT PUNTERS WAITIN'!'

I contemplate asking her to stick to hand jobs until I can get a plumber in, but as the breasts are now aimed right at my face like a pair of heat-seeking missiles, I decide against it.

'I—I'll just go and turn it back on, then—'

'WELL, BLEEDIN' WELL 'URRY UP!' she barks.

Then, quick as a flash, the breasts swing around (I duck underneath) and propel themselves back out the door, past the window, bouncing their way back up the brothel stairway again.

January 22nd, 2008: Mr Topper's

I'm walking down Moor Street. Ed's Diner on my right, a glass-fronted door coming up on my left. 'Mr Topper's. Haircuts for Men and Women. £6' screams the sign above my head.

I look inside. Oh, good, it's almost empty. So I push open the glass door.

Suddenly I'm bombarded with hard techno music, the bass line thumping like a musical migraine. Undeterred, I hang my gym bag on the coat stand and scan the empty seats, taking one by the window.

I check my watch, more out of stress than necessity. I have to be out of here quickly and get back to the shop. The chores of the day are already mounting up in my mind. Meanwhile, two Australian blonde female assistants (they're always blonde in Mr Topper's) are discussing the burning issues of the day: clubs, clothes and cosmetics, while their customers, draped in grey sheets, stare blankly into the mirror ahead.

A copy of QX magazine lies on the chair next to me. I flick through it impatiently until I get to a column by a rather portly drag queen professing to be an authority on the music biz. Her 'What's Hot' suggests she's not.

'You wanna go for a drink after work?' one of the assistants asks the other.

'Where do you wanna go?'

'Barcode.'

'Oh, not Barcode again!'

'What's wrong with Barcode?' asks Aussie Blonde 1.

'Do we 'ave to go to gay bars all the time?'

'Why? D'ya wanna get laid?'

My eyes peep above the portly pic.

'Nah, it's not that...' says Aussie Blonde 2 offhandedly, as if she's had her fill for the week. 'It's just that it's the only place we ever go!'

Aussie Blonde 1 runs a hand through her platinum locks while she thinks of a suitable reply. When one particular lock fails to stay in the desired spot she takes a can of hairspray from the counter and proceeds to spray-coat it with the intensity of a graffiti artist, until her customer starts to develop the first signs of emphysema.

'We could buy some charlie?' Aussie Blonde 1 ventures with a half smile, admiring the strand of hair which is now glued to her head like a limpet.

'Can't afford it.'

'What d'ya wanna do, then?'

'I dunno. 'Ave you seen that *I Am Legend*?'

'Yeah. I got a pirate copy. I'll lend it you,' says Aussie Blonde 1 as she brushes loose hair from her customer's neck, the majority of which ends up on his trousers. 'There!' she announces, holding up a hand mirror so the customer can see his newly shaved head from all angles.

After this discussion of sex, drugs and pirate DVDs, I'm intrigued as to what else is on today's agenda, so, forgetting I'm in a rush, I make my way over to the vacant seat. After we've exchanged details of what I'd like done, I pretend to examine the different snips of hair that carpet the floor while my ears start to flap to the techno beat.

'Pass me those small clippers?' Aussie Blonde 1 asks Aussie Blonde 2.

'Oh, you can't use those. They're Karen's.'

'She won't mind.'

'She will! She 'ates anyone using her clippers.'

'Well, she won't find out, will she?' says Aussie Blonde 1, reaching toward them.

Seconds later, after blowing on the blade and wiping it on her sleeve, she starts to trim away merrily, humming Madonna's "La Isla Bonita" (with the techno beat backing). At that moment in walks a third blonde.

'Hi, Karen!' Aussie Blondes 1 and 2 sing in unison.

I sit bolt upright, my eyes following Karen through the mirror as she takes off her jacket, hanging it up on the coat stand. What if she spots her clippers? A bead of sweat drips down my back. The two Aussies are quiet now, Aussie Blonde 1 trimming away with her head bowed while Aussie Blonde 2 drags her customer over to the wash basin.

I look from Karen to Aussie Blonde 1 and back to Karen, my eyes darting backward and forward like a Wimbledon spectator in a neck brace. Aussie Blonde 1 watches Karen out the corner of her eye and I imagine uneven tramlines careening around my head. Then Karen walks over to her section. She looks down at her equipment. I hold my breath. Has she noticed? The suspense is overwhelming. I want to stand up and shout, 'She took your clippers! I've nothing to do with this!' But instead, I slink a couple of inches lower in my seat and pretend to reexamine the floor.

Seconds tick by. Aussie Blonde 1's on the second verse now, though she's starting to stutter. 'I, I, f, f, fell in love with San Pedro.' Karen doesn't say a word. The atmosphere's tense. Like a cat fight's about to erupt any minute. Then:

'WHERE'S MY CLIPPERS?'

'Warm wind carried on the... Sorry?' Aussie Blonde 1 gulps.

'I said, "WHERE'S. MY. CLIPPERS?"'

Aussie Blonde 1 rests them on the back of my neck. Still on! I'm now imagining them slowly trimming their way into my scalp.

'Oh—your clippers!' Aussie Blonde 1 squeaks, biding for time, as if she's only just understood the question. 'You mean these?' She brandishes them in the air like Harry Potter's wand. Karen glares at them. Then her face turns into a grimace. Her eyes start to narrow. She puffs out her already quite considerable chest. We all stare at the clippers. Anything could happen. It's a real Hitchcock moment. I haven't drawn breath for five minutes. The hairs on my balls start to rise. What will break the spell?

'Oh, that's okay, babe. You can borrow 'em!'

I faint and fall off the chair.

January 24th, 2008: Customer of the Day

The first customer of the day is an Israeli belly dancer.

He's wearing a red skirt with silver bells attached to the hem and pink ballet slippers. His triple-processed hair is held in place by a green diamante-encrusted head band. (I'm not making this up.)

He tries on a baby-blue crushed-silk shirt by Cavalli which he ties at the front, bikini style. Then he gyrates around the shop, showing me the various moves associated with male belly dancing. Then he stops. Looks in the mirror, frowns and says, 'You don't think I look too gay, do you?'

January 26th, 2008: Angie's Date

'Whatta day!'

Angie's just stepped in. Dior sunglasses perched in her hair, matching handbag, walking stick, a black couture two-piece with a figure-hugging crop top.

'Hi, Ange!'

She lets her fringe drop over an eye, pouts and bats her eyelashes. 'Helllooooo.'

I offer her my seat. She takes it without a word, rests her walking stick against the wall and starts to fan her breasts with *Hola!* magazine. 'Gurl, I am worn out! I've been to the gym. Food shoppin'. An' I've just walked all the way back from Regent's Park.'

'What were you doing in Regent's Park?'

'Seein' me surgeon again.' She peers down her crop top, examining each breast as if they're soufflés in a gas oven. As she doesn't look too happy, I decide to try to lighten the mood.

'So...,' I say cheerfully, 'what are you doing later?'

'I got a date,' she replies nonchalantly.

'Really? Who with?'

She narrows her eyes suspiciously. 'That's for me to know and you to find out.' Then she relents. 'A guy I got chattin' with on a tranny site.'

'I didn't know you did the Internet thing.'

'Oh, yes, darlin'! You get to see all the bits. It's like havin' yer puddin' before the main course.'

'So is it a "date" date?'

'Yes! It's a "date" date! His name's Stuart, he works in the city, an' he's a real butch number.'

'Where're you meeting him?'

'Maison Bertaux.' She looks down at her sparkly Cartier watch. 'Oh, God! I gotta go!'

* * *

Fifteen minutes later Angie sweeps back in, incensed.

'Never. A. Gain!' she fumes, waving her walking stick perilously close to my face. She takes a seat on the little red chair again.

'What happened?'

She removes her sunglasses and shakes out her hair, the way she does, up and down, side to side. 'You don't wanna know.' Then she pulls the collar of her crop top forward and peers inside again as if she's checking babies in bed. Satisfied that they appear to be sleeping soundly, she continues. 'So I get there. An' I order a coffee. An' while I'm waitin', this old bat taps me on the shoulder. Oh, a right ugly cunt she was. An' I looked at her an' I said, "Look, luv, I've already paid!" An' she says, "Hi, I'm Stuart!"'

I cover my mouth with my hand.

'I said, "You 'ave gotta be jokin'! Do you really think I had me cock chopped off so I could date a dinner lady?"

I bite my lip.

'Clay, I am never going on an Internet date again!'

February 2008

February 2nd, 2008: A Mouthful

It's amazing what you can hear when you're standing in a shop doorway. Take five minutes ago…

Big Jim the policeman is walking across Dean Street.

'Hi, Clay! How's business?'

I shrug. 'So-so. Hey, what was going on outside last night with all those police?'

* * *

Flashback.

3 am. We're asleep downstairs. Suddenly,

BANG! BANG! BANG!

'What's that?' cries Jorge, and he jumps out of bed.

'I dunno!' I reply. I immediately think back to last week's 'smash and grab' raid at the opticians just a few doors down. Please, no!

BANG! BANG! BANG!

We rush upstairs, fearing the worst.

'What is it?' I hiss as Jorge peers out the window.

'It's the police! They've got a guy pinned to the ground.'

* * *

Back to the doorstep.

'Oh, that!' Big Jim laughs. 'Well, you won't believe this but we had a call from the girls upstairs.'

'Really? Why?'

'There was a fight going on.'

'Someone was attacking them?'

'No. Nothing like that,' Big Jim laughs again. 'There were four guys queuing up and one of them tried to push in.'

'They were queuing up? I thought business was really tough at the moment.'

'Well, not for them.' Big Jim grins. 'They've got this new girl up there. She's called "the Gobbler". And the word's got out she gives the best blow jobs in London. She's making a fortune.'

I think I'm in the wrong job.

February 3rd, 2008: Pam's Fags

11 am. I'm pushing up the grates to the shop, getting ready to open up. There's a tap on my back. I turn to find Pam looking up at me, grinning inanely.

Pam is the local homeless 'celebrity' and wherever I am in Soho, Pam is there too. If I'm walking past the Coach and Horses, Pam will step out of a doorway. If I'm having a coffee outside Caffè Nero, her radar will home in on me. If I'm collecting a burger at Ed's Diner, Pam will be standing outside with her hand out. Today she's dressed in her usual attire: camouflage trousers, donkey jacket, 'barn owl' NHS glasses, sporting a number one haircut.

'You're gonna be really proud of me,' she says.

'Why's that, Pam?'

'I've got seven pounds in me pocket and I haven't bin in the amusements all day.'

'Is that where you've been spending all your money?'

'Not all of it!' she replies, shuffling nervously from foot to foot. 'Sometimes I 'ave a dog bet.'

'So all the money I've been giving you has been going on dog racing?'

'No!' she replies indignantly. 'I save seven pounds for me room for the night and then anything over seven pounds goes on the dogs. I'm not that stupid!' She frowns, as if I am. 'Anyway, I fink I'm over me gamblin' addiction. Now it's just the beer an' the fags.'

'Well, one step at a time, I suppose…'

'An' I've learnt summat about the fags.'

'What's that?'

'If you buy a pack of twenty, you end up smokin' twenty. But if you only buy a pack of ten, you only smoke ten.'

'So you only smoke ten?'

'No, I smoke fifteen.'

'Bye, Pam.'

February 4th, 2008: A Bona Holiday

Another quiet morning in Costa. A couple of queens gossiping by the window, an old man in the corner reading the papers, the gentle whooshing sound from the coffee machine.

As I wait for my coffee, I look toward the doorway, thinking about the day ahead—the chores, the deliveries—not really concentrating on what's outside, not really taking in the person who's just walked in, not until he's standing right in front of me.

'Leslie!'

'Thought I was dead, did you?' he smirks, flicking his beige silk scarf over his shoulder.

'No, I—'

'Lyin' little homo!' He signals the assistant, arches an eyebrow, and nods in my direction. 'She only thought I'd kicked the bucket!'

The assistant smiles nervously, while I try to answer. 'I didn't, I—'

'Listen, ducky, the flesh may be saggin' but I can still do the can-can! Now, get me a coffee.' He brushes past the old man in the corner and pulls out a chair. 'An' I want a—'

'Pick-me-up, not a keep-me-up. Yes, I remember.'

* * *

Leslie's already seated when I return, straw hat on a nearby chair, elbows on the table, resting his chin on his clasped hands, reminding me of an old schoolmistress watching a pupil in detention. We sugar our coffees, the only sound the tinkle of the metal spoons against the cups. Then Leslie breaks the ice.

'Soooo...' he drawls, tilting his head to one side, clutching his scarf as if it's a string of pearls and I'm a mugger. 'How's the rag trade?'

'Okay...I 'spose.'

'And what about that bloggy thing of yours?'

'My MySpace blog? Well, I'm still doing it.'

'And the book?'

'It's finished.'

'There you go, see!' He reaches over and taps me on the hand. 'Ducky, there're more important things in life than makin' money, y'know!'

I tell him about a play that I'm trying to write and that he's in it.

'Moi?' He bats his eyelashes and opens his mouth in mock horror. 'Wot yer got an old queen like me in it for?' He elbows the old man sitting next to him. 'She's only gone and put me in 'er play. An old queen like me!'

'Well, I thought the story about you and Charlie was really touching...' I take a sip of my coffee. 'How is he, by the way?'

'He hasn't been in the shop then?' Leslie asks guardedly.

'No, he hasn't.

'Oh, he's fine, dear. Fine. He's at the flat at the moment. I said to him before I left, I said, "Listen, lambkin—"'

'Lambkin?'

'I said, "I'm just poppin' out and I want that roast out the oven by four!"' Leslie reaches for his coffee. 'I was just off to buy 'im some truffles from Fortnum's when I saw you... Oh, 'e loves 'is truffles.' He takes a sip of his drink. Winces. 'We can get through a whole box just watchin' a weepie.'

I try to suppress a giggle. Then I say, 'Charlie hasn't been in the shop for ages. The last time he came in was...God—just before Christmas. He came in to buy some underwear.'

Leslie puts his coffee down. 'Yes. Well.' He tuts. 'He would, wouldn't he? 'Im and his underwear. Honestly, he's got drawers full of the stuff. You can't move for undies! Now, I like a silk undergarment, but some of the things he's got... 'E gave me one for me birthday and I said to him, I said, "If you think I'm mincin' round town with a piece of string bitin' into me bum 'ole, you've got another think comin'!"' He reaches for his coffee again. ''E's always been an avid collector, has our Charlie.'

The old man at the table next to us stands up. He looks shocked. He's just about to leave when Leslie grabs his arm. 'You should be wearin' a hat on a day like this. Keep the sun off yer eek!'

The man nods nervously and edges toward the door.

'You'll get cancer!' Leslie shouts. Then he leans toward me again and continues. 'Oh, I'm always well creamed when I go out. Oh, yes. Never let the sun on the visage. Not with my skin, dear. Well, you can't with skin like mine, ducky— I'm an English rose! Which reminds me, we're thinkin' of taking a little trip abroad. Somewhere with a few ruins so Charlie can do the day trips while I sit under the brolly with me crosswords.'

'That sounds nice.'

'Hmmm. It's the toilet arrangements I'm worried about. All that hoverin' over a hole.' He twists his head to one side, nose aloft. 'Oh, I hate all that! I 'ave to 'ave good plumbin'! It's the first thing I do when I get to a hotel: check the lav. I've even been known to bring me own bleach.'

He goes on to tell me about all the holidays he's been on where he's experienced problems. In India, it was the air conditioning. In France, an amorous couple in the room next door. In Germany, food poisoning from a sausage salad. In Sitges, his friend Dolly used all his Factor 30 ('peelin' like an adder, I was!'). The Isle of Wight, strangely, he recommends. Though his last visit was spoilt somewhat when he got into an argument with a nun in the Botanic Gardens ('right next to the agapanthus!')

As I listen, his hands flap this way and that like a campy silent movie actress, and I'm reminded of how amusing I find him, how I'm never really sure whether his personality is put on for my benefit or it's a hat he wears all day.

'Anyway, what about you, ducky? Any holidays planned?'

'I don't think we'll be taking a holiday anytime soon. Not with the shop the way it is... Hey, I was thinking—how about we go out for dinner one night. You and Charlie and me and Jorge?'

'Oh, bugger that—I'll cook!' Leslie says, reaching for his hat and preparing to leave. 'Why do you think Charlie's back? It ain't just for me slender legs, ducky. Oh, no. I'm a dab hand at the cuisine. Me pot roasts are legendary!'

February 5th, 2008: Customer of the Day

Old Compton Street's deserted, the weather's turned Soho into a ghost town. Just the woman with the striking makeup and waist-length plaits sitting outside Costa and the old Chinese woman pulling a battered tartan-plaid trolley full of clothes.

I'm behind the counter. Jorge's at the back of the shop, trying on a shirt in the dressing room. A cute guy in his early thirties staggers in.

'Your shop's racist!' he opines.

Here we go.

He staggers closer, reeking of booze. 'If it was called Dirty Black Boy it'd be shut down!'

'But it's not called Dirty Black Boy.'

'Yeah, but if it was it'd be racist!'

Then he smiles, revealing a graveyard of broken teeth. 'You know I'm just joking, don't you?'

'Yes. You're very funny.'

He leans to the right, almost falling over, and looks down

toward the dressing room. 'Your mate's gotta a cute ass. It needs a good rimmin'!'

'Have you by any chance just graduated from charm school?'

He looks at me, puzzled. Then he pulls a wallet from his pocket, opens it, and shows me a photo. 'That's my daughter.'

'She's very pretty.'

He drops the wallet on the floor, bends down to pick it up, and struggles to get back up again. Then he blurts out, 'I wanna Dirty White Boy T-shirt!'

I take one off the rails and gift wrap it. He hands me his credit card and I swipe it through the machine. It's declined. I look at the name on the card: 'Kwan Wong Hok.' Which is strange, given that he's about as Asian as my arse. I hand back his card and he staggers out of the shop and promptly throws up in the drain.

Dirty White Boy. Where posh people shop.

February 11th, 2008: The Year of the Rat

It's Chinese New Year and the crowds spill out of Chinatown onto the streets of Soho.

Paper dragons breathe fire on sticks. Overweight mothers push Big Mac kids.

Chinatown and Soho—the crowd starts to blend. And the Old Compton Street habitués come to an end. (It's the Year of the Rat meets the queers in a pack.)

The melting pot melts with surprising ease. Queens cruise by in Abercrombie tees.

The first hint of sun brings the first hint of pec. A heavyset lesbian couple aggressively neck.

A little Chinese girl, a badge with her name. The old leather queen who always dresses the same.

Firecrackers explode and we jump in our seats. Chinese New Year on Old Compton Street.

February 12th, 2008: Sue & Maggie

Sue and Maggie are chatting outside.

Given the rarity of the occasion I'm desperate to rush to the window and have a good nose, my ears already flapping like Gladys Kravitz. Unfortunately I'm in the middle of serving a rather fussy old queen. Eager to get back to my perch, I decide, somewhat shamelessly, to compliment him on the age-inappropriate jeans he's toying with. I whisper an apology to baby Jesus as I swipe his credit card.

Before he's even had a chance to put his card back in his wallet, I'm already peeping from behind the pillar, trying to listen to the muttering madams. But it's no good—I can't hear a thing. And so I decide to take drastic action and I step outside.

Luckily the girls are so engrossed in their conversation they haven't noticed my arrival, so I'm getting snippets of this and that but not enough to piece together the full story. Something about another punter who hasn't paid.

Edging closer, I try to make my approach appear genuine by looking at my watch, tutting, and scouring the street as if waiting for someone. Seconds later, Elton, our part-time employee, walks toward me.

'And where've you been?' I ask, exasperated, while at the same time trying to signal to him with my eyes and a nod of the head that I don't really mean it. Understandably, he looks at me strangely. 'I said, where've you been?' Nod. Nod. Eye roll. Eye roll.

'It's my day off. It's Saturday,' Elton replies, looking at me as if I've lost the plot.

The girls glance in our direction.

'Oh, it is, is it?' Nod. Nod.

'Er... Yes.'

'Not in my book!' Eye roll. Eye roll.

'IT'S SATURDAY!' shouts Sue.

Now all three are staring at me. I look from one to another.

'Oh, of course! Silly me.' And then, highly embarrassed, I slink back inside the shop.

Being the neighbourhood snoop is not always an easy task.

February 13th, 2008: Publicity

Someone came in this afternoon and informed me that last week our shop was on *Newsnight*, the BBC Two daily news analysis, current affairs and politics programme.

Apparently the cameramen were going up and down Old Compton Street and focused in on the shop sign and the underwear in our window. And the topic for discussion that night? 'Barebacking' in the gay porn industry.

February 14th, 2008: Mr Muscles

Soho Athletic gym.

11 am. There's no one around. The café bar is empty. The only sound is the receptionist washing glasses, the manager ringing up till receipts and the distant sound of club music floating through from the gym.

I pull out my wallet. Sign in. Pay for a towel and head purposefully toward the changing room, eager to get my workout over and be out of here as quickly as I can. Then:

'OI, YOU!'

I turn to find a tall, well-defined woman pounding away on the Stairmaster, her hair pulled back in a ponytail and swishing from side to side. 'AN' WHERE DO YOU THINK YOU'RE GOING?'

'Angie!'

'Don't you "Angie" me!' she scolds as I draw near. 'I've bin in that shop three times lookin' for you!'

'I do have a life, you know!'

'Hmmm...' she murmurs suspiciously. She doesn't appear to be out of breath, though the Stairmaster's showing that she's been running for more than 45 minutes.

Moments later we're sitting in the café.

A meaty guy with a shaved head and a tattoo of a green lizard snaking around his calf ambles in. Angie nods at him.

'What do y' think?' she whispers.

'What's to think?' I reply. 'Is he straight?'

'Supposedly... Anyway, we've gotta date next Wednesday.'

'Really? Does he know?'

''Course, darlin'! Why do you think he wants me?'

'But I thought you were over the tranny fuckers?'

As if on cue he turns around and looks Angie up and down, his eyes resting on her legs, transfixed. Angie re-crosses them. 'Hi, there, Kelvin,' she purrs. 'An' how are you today?'

He grunts back, throws her a Neanderthal leer and swaggers off toward the changing room.

'Not big on conversation, is he?'

'I'm not lookin' to shag Einstein!'

'I know, but aren't you at least looking for someone a bit more stimulating?'

She points between her parted legs. '*This* is the only thing that needs stimulatin'.' She stands, towering over me. 'Clay, I've given up waitin' for Mr Right. There ain't no such thing.'

February 15th, 2008: Street Art

I'm standing by the shop doorway watching a young guy throw up on the pavement.

'Are you okay?' I ask. (A stupid question, I know.)

'Urrrggghhhh!' he rasps back, head down, vomit spreading across the pavement.

I watch as the little puddle starts to take shape, forming two lines, like reindeer antlers, and I'm torn between asking him if he needs help or if he could move nearer to the drain so passersby won't step in his artwork and walk it into the shop. Three retches later, he staggers toward the opposite side of the doorway, presumably thinking that throwing up against our wall will provide artistic symmetry. This is verging on rude.

'Excuse me. Would you mind leaning over that drain over there?'

He looks up, his face contorting into something from *28 Weeks Later*, drool forming from lip to lip.

'Urrrggghhhh!' (I take this to mean 'Here's fine, thanks!')

A minute later, his stomach finally empty and our shop wall glistening in the sunlight, he stands up again and takes a deep breath. As he does a young girl walks across Dean Street and calls his name. 'Ricky! There you are! I've been looking for you everywhere!'

She rushes over, wraps her arms around him and proceeds to give him a big, open-mouth kiss.

February 17th, 2008: Where Is It?

There's a man standing in front of me, admiring the jewelry in the display case.

After a few minutes he looks up and says, 'Do you know where I can buy a Prince Albert that glows in the dark? My wife's a bit shortsighted, you see.'

February 18th, 2008: Carlos Acosta

Whenever Carlos Acosta walks into the shop my heart skips a beat.

Carlos is a principal dancer at the Royal Ballet. Feted for his dazzling leaps and artistry, he's been compared to Rudolf Nureyev and Mikhail Baryshnikov. A Cuban, Carlos often drops by to visit Jorge, also Cuban, and they talk about Castro, leaving Cuba, the family members they've left behind, while I hover in the background like a bit-part actor in an epic movie. When he came in yesterday, however, I was alone. As he walked toward me my throat immediately went dry.

'Hi... Er, umm, Carlos. How are you?'

'Hi, Clayton. I'm good.'

'How... How's the dancing going?'

Oh, Clay, what a stupid thing to say. How's the dancing going? He's just finished *Swan Lake* at the Royal Opera House. You make it sound like he's auditioning for *Riverdance*.

'Yes, it's going well,' Carlos replies. 'You speak Spanish?'

'Ummmm.'

'Don't worry. We can talk in English.'

What I don't want to tell him is that my Spanish is limited. I can order a beer, or, at a push, a vodka and coke, and I have, on a few occasions, been able to ask for a blow job—phrases that have always stood me in good stead on weekend trips in Madrid but are hardly conducive to discussing Carlos's pas de deux.

'So what are you working on at the moment?' I ask.

'I'm about to start *Apollo* on Monday...'

I'm already lost, falling into his big hazelnut eyes, watching him so intently I can make out small beads of sweat glistening on the edge of his broad nose.

'It's a very difficult piece...'

As he rests his hand on the counter, it's so close to my arse that I imagine he's about to sweep me up in his arms, high above his head, spinning me around, while I, with that fixed ballerina smile on my face, point my toes and extend my arms, the audience watching us with bated breath.

'I'm only dancing it twice...'

He carries me over to the left of the stage. The orchestra have stopped playing now. We've rehearsed this so often we can do it in our sleep. He times his steps perfectly and lays me gently down on the stage. Then he's off again. Grands jetés. Round and round. Faster and faster, while I rest my head on the stage, trying to catch my breath.

'There's a two-week break...'

He spins back in my direction. We're nearly through now. That diet of fruit an' fags is finally paying off. Then he stops. Reaches down. He pulls me up onto my tippytoes. There's not a sound in the theatre. We wrap our arms around each other. He presses his body into mine. And we kiss. The curtain falls.

'I have to rest up between dances, though...'

The audience erupts. The curtain rises again. The whole theatre on its feet. The applause echoing around the Gods. I look across at Carlos. The spotlight's on his face. He's perspiring, breathing heavily, but still manages to blow kisses to the adoring crowd. Then he bows low, pointing his feet. Oops! Where's my manners? I grab the sides of my tutu and do the deepest curtsey you can imagine, one leg tucked behind.

'You should come and see the production. I think you'll love it...'

A second, third, fourth encore. The chemistry is electric. They'll talk about this one for years. Our names engraved in the Hall of Fame. Oh, Carlos! The audience are still cheering. Carlos directs their cheer toward me. I blush and curtsey again. A stagehand runs across the stage and presents me with a big bouquet...

'Clayton? Would you like to come?'

I think I just did.

'Sorry? Umm, what?'

'To my next show.'

'Oh, er... Yes. Of course. I'd love to.'

And then he says goodbye and leaves.

Once he's out of sight I take a deep breath (it's been an exhausting routine), brush the creases out of my tutu (I mean my trousers), reach for my little black book and write it all down.

February 19th, 2008: Finland

3 pm. I'm sitting behind the counter, keeping myself busy by staring into space, when a young sandy-haired guy staggers in.

'I'm drunk and I'm from Finland!'

I smile politely.

'What should I do?' he slurs.

'Drink a pint of water and in the morning you'll feel a lot better...'

He turns to leave.

'... although I'm afraid you'll still wake up Finnish.'

He burps and staggers out.

February 20th, 2008: Fingers and Thongs

Despite his age, his hands are ageless.

'I've got the hands of a virgin nun,' Leslie says, looking down proudly at his splayed fingers, as if each one is laden with precious jewels. 'Just like Nanette Newman.' He starts to sing. 'Hands that do dishes can feel as soft as your face, with mild green—'

'They're very well manicured.'

'Well, they should be!' he reproves me. 'They get buffed every night!' He rests them on the table, gazing at them lovingly. 'Oh, I can't abide dirty nails. Never 'ave.' He glances in my direction. 'It's true! I couldn't have a dirty-fingered friend. What would the neighbours think?'

I examine my own beneath the table. Decide to keep them there. 'Anyway, you were telling me about your holiday—'

'Oh, yes!' he says, repositioning himself in his seat and crossing his legs. 'So the chambermaid took us to our room an' she said, "Room!" An' I looked round an' I said, "What do you mean, room?" An' she just stared at me. So I said, "Listen 'ere, Consuelo. I asked for a view of the sea, not the bleedin' car park!"'

'What did she say?'

'She could only say one word, ducky! Honestly, you'd think in a continental resort they'd employ someone who could speak the Queen's English.' He licks a forefinger and runs it up and down an eyebrow. 'Now, I don't know about you, dear, but in my book "sea view" means a balcony, a small table, fresh flowers—'

'What was the room like?'

'Oh, bijou, dear! Oh, it were bijou!'

'And what did Charlie say?'

He re-crosses his legs. 'Don't talk to me about Charlie! Fourteen thongs he brought with him! Fourteen! I said to him, I said, "No one wants to see your bulgin' basket." What that poor pool boy thought, Gawd only knows!'

I ask him about the excursions.

'Oh, I didn't bother with all that. Well, there's never a decent loo when you need one.'

'So what did you do?'

'Minced round town and bought a few postcards. Left the ruins to Charlie. Oh, he loves all that. Pickin' up bits of rock and vaderin' the old pots. I'm fine in the deck chair. A deck chair by the pool with a decent shade and I'm away with the fairies. But the heat, ducky! Oh, it were awful! Drownin' in me own juices, I was.'

'And the food?'

He pulls a face. 'Well, you know what the Spanish are like… It's all stuffed this and fried that.'

'Poor you,' I say sympathetically. 'It sounds like you didn't enjoy it.'

'Oh, no, we 'ad a great time! Bookin' for next year.'

The story over, I signal for the waiter. 'Do you want another coffee?'

'Not for me, ducky,' Leslie replies, pulling a small tub from his jacket pocket and carefully applying Vaseline to each nail. 'I've 'ad two already. Any more and I'll wet the bed.'

Seconds later the waiter brings the check. As he puts it down Leslie gasps and clasps his hands to his cheeks. The waiter looks perplexed, not quite sure what he's done, and backs away. I lean forward. 'What's the matter?'

'Did you vada the nails?' Leslie hisses. Then he swivels around in his seat and addresses the customers at the table nearby. 'An' in an establishment like this! 'Ands of a leper!'

The coffee bar goes quiet, cups poised at lips, eyes darting back and forth. I quickly help Leslie out of his chair, pay the bill, and usher him out onto the street, keeping my hands well and truly hidden.

February 22nd, 2008: Driving On

There's a homeless woman often in these parts.

Her hair is shoulder-length and mousy brown, hair that was probably once a source of pride. Now it hangs limp, dull and lifeless. Her face is ravaged, pockmarked, hardened despite her young age. The type of face you see on those adverts warning you about the dangers of drugs. And then there're her teeth. The two she has. My eyes are drawn to them. It's hard not to be. They stand, defiantly, on either side of her lower jaw, like pillars supporting a menacing cave.

I've given her money before and now every time she sees me she stops. And I can read her face: Does he wanna fuck me? Or does he feel sorry for me? Trick or treat? And she always makes a big show when she sees me. Telling me how much she's missed me. Cracking jokes. Speaking to me as if we've known each other for years.

After two years, I recognise the tactics. With some of the homeless on this street it's over-friendliness. With others it's aggression. And then there are those who are just so wasted they don't even care. But her tactic is to treat you as an old friend. So whenever she approaches I say hello while trying not to come across as too friendly, not wanting to encourage her too much, because—well, because I've been caught out a few times on this street and I've been told I'm viewed as a 'soft touch'.

She spots me today as I'm coming out of the 24-hour supermarket on the corner of Frith Street. She immediately stops walking.

'Hi,' she mumbles, her eyes haunted.

'Hi,' I reply, cautiously.

'My boyfriend's been taken away by the police. They took him away this morning.'

'Oh. I am sorry.'

She takes a step closer. 'He got caught selling smack.'

'Do you know what police station they took him to?'

'No.'

I'm not sure what she wants me to say. I want to walk off but I can't just end the conversation like this. Her eyes search mine. And then I see it again. That look. Does he wanna fuck me? Shall I ask for money? Offer him my body? And now I know what it is about her that I'm drawn to. It's morbid curiosity. Like that urge you get to slow down when you drive by a crash and you just want to see it all: the horror. And then you drive slowly on. Head forward. Praying that it'll never happen to you.

'Clay!' a friend shouts from across the road, breaking the spell.

I wave back. Trying not to look too eager to get away, but thankful for the excuse.

And as I walk off, her smile fades and she shrinks back. Back to her life. While I walk slowly on—head forward, but uncertain, back to mine.

February 23rd, 2008: The Silver Screen

Midnight.

I'm about to close my laptop and go downstairs to bed. I take one last look outside the Dean Street window. It's like staring at a giant cinema screen: the car headlights whizzing around the shop, the projector beam; the noise from the street, the soundtrack; the people outside, the actors. A magical movie with stories about to unfold.

That's when I spot her: a new face. Outside Soho Books. Drawing on a cigarette. Short, sharp, impatient drags as she surveys the street, checking her watch as if waiting for a friend.

A long black limousine crawls slowly by. It stops right next to her. An electric window slowly lowers.

She crushes the cigarette under heel. Steps forward. Leans in. One hand resting on the window ledge. Talking. And then she pulls back, slightly. Laughing. Showing 'the goods.' Her shoulder-length platinum-blonde hair tumbling forward, obscuring my view. Then the car door opens and she steps in. Her long toned legs slowly disappearing; black seamed stockings, stilettos, a bejeweled hand reaching out, pulling the door closed. The car glides slowly away. The flickering headlights, the street lamps, the flashing neon: mise-en-scène for my own film noir.

I rush to the Old Compton Street window and watch as the limousine turns right into Greek Street, moving smoothly, carefully, until the taillights disappear, the second act about to begin.

* * *

I imagine the car continuing on its journey, crawling down Shaftesbury Avenue, turning right into Great Windmill Street, crossing Brewer Street, entering the NCP car park, up one floor, two floors, driving to the far wall, reversing into an available space at the far end. Then the engine's switched off.

She turns to face the driver. 'Okay, so what do you want? A blow job?'

There's a pause.

The driver's voice is that of an aging smoker. 'How about a fuck?' he says, his face silhouetted in the dim interior light.

She opens her handbag. Removes a lipstick and a compact and applies the gloss, swiftly, expertly. 'Okay... But that'll be thirty.'

'But you're clean, though?'

She hesitates. 'Yes. Yes, I'm clean.' She drops the lipstick and compact back in her handbag, hesitating again as she glimpses her meds: Lopinavir, Atazanavir. She snaps the bag shut.

There's an awkward scrambling. Trousers unzipped. Pants

pulled down. And then he rams into her. Aggressively. Without feeling. She holds on to the car seat, sinking her head into the upholstery; closing her eyes, she blocks it out, blocks it out as the car moves rhythmically. She thinks back, as she always does at times like this: back, back. Back to his Mediterranean skin. Back to his forearms, muscled, tattooed. Back to his chest hair, swirling, swirling. Back to a vision of a man so vivid she can imagine it is him on top of her now. And yet still this other man rams. And he rams. And he rams. And he rams. Until the vision is rammed out of her and all she's left with is... Emptiness.

* * *

I close my laptop. Stand.

The street's virtually empty now. A couple of young girls in a deep embrace. A dealer waiting for one last customer. And then, just as I'm about to head downstairs, I spy the limousine cruising past. It slows. Stops by the red pillar box. And out she steps.

She glances in my direction. It's a freeze-frame moment. Did he see me? Does he know?

Then the car pulls away, the same route, the same pace, and she leans back against the doorway again, reaching into her handbag, pulling out a cigarette, a lighter, taking a deep drag, a long, deep drag, the smoke spiraling upwards, upwards, upwards. Like the last of the Hollywood Greats. Like a goddess from the silver screen.

February 24th, 2008: Chico

Soho

For some a door to freedom—all kinds of freedom

For some a door to prison—so many kinds of prisons

The room I'm in is large, the size of a school gymnasium, with rows of tables and chairs, all numbered. Guards line this room. Unfriendly guards. And in the corner of this room, by the entrance, is a small canteen inside which a woman, the same woman who stamped my visitor's pass and checked my ID in the visitors' room 30 minutes before, serves teas, coffees and home-made scones. She's cheerful. Annoyingly so. I try not to let her drag me into a conversation while I wait for the two watery coffees that I've bought with the handful of change you're allowed to bring in here.

As I carry the coffees back to the allotted table a whistle blows and the prisoners, all wearing blue sweatshirts and jeans, enter from a door at the far end. Finally I spot him. He's the last to come through. He scans the room. I wave. He sees me, waves back. Walks toward me, smiling pensively. And as he nears, my mind drifts back to the days when he was a very different person.

* * *

Chico was like champagne. Whenever he burst into the shop it was as if someone had shaken the bottle, popped the cork and sprayed his camp, infectious, bubbly nervous energy all over us. I would stop blogging, the hookers hooking, the pimps pimping. The customers would peep from behind the racks of clothes like frightened rabbits, everyone watching this most charismatic of characters as he lit up the shop with his shrieks and shenanigans. Of all the interesting and eccentric people we've met at the shop, Chico was the first. An Afro-Caribbean ex–Diana Ross impersonator, he'd swan in every weekend with an escort on his arm and shower him with gifts, spending money like a lottery winner—laughing, flirting, cracking jokes, always dressed in the chicest outfits, a queen with money and taste. You couldn't meet a nicer person, and I loved everything about him.

I remember one night Jorge and I went for a drink with him in the Village. We'd known each other for a few months by then. We were sitting in the back bar. The drinks were flowing. Chico was holding court, a crowd gathered around. He seemed so at ease. But as the evening ended, with just the three of us left, he suddenly broke down. Sobbing. Uncontrollably. And that's when his story started to unfold.

You see, all this time, Chico had been grieving. He'd nursed his boyfriend through a painful illness, and when he died Chico was left with a lot of money to spend and a lot of love to give. But, unfortunately, he gave them both to the wrong people. The bravado. The shopping. The escorts. It was all a front. Chico was a broken man.

Anyway, the night over, we hugged, Chico wiped away his tears, we said our goodbyes and we made plans to go out the following weekend. But that was to be the last night we had together. Chico never came back to the shop. I called his mobile, left messages, but he never returned my calls. Chico vanished.

Two months later (I think it was a Sunday morning because I remember it being very quiet), we were sitting in the shop reading the papers when a young guy walked in. He asked if we were friends of Chico's. When we confirmed that we were, he pulled a dog-eared newspaper cutting from his back pocket and placed it on the counter. I looked at Jorge. Jorge looked back at me. We both looked down at the article. It was Chico. An unflattering, haunted mug shot, but Chico nonetheless. I scanned the headline. He was in prison. For rape.

Of course, we couldn't believe it. Chico's about half my size. And a bottom. There was just no way. So I trawled the Internet, tracked him down, wrote to the prison. And so our visits began.

I remember the first time we visited him. The look on his face. He didn't think anyone knew where he was and he certainly wasn't expecting me and Jorge to turn up. It was so strange seeing him in there. From the wild, over-the-top, fun-loving queen, he'd become a frail, frightened shell of a man, his lower lip trembling, his hands shaking. It was such a transformation.

Over the next few visits he told us everything. How he'd lavished his money on escorts. How he'd been trying to convince himself that they wanted him for all the right reasons. How they started to ask for more and more money. How, when he refused, they called the police and accused him of rape. It was like a Greek tragedy. And bizarrely, we were all he had left.

So the visits have continued. And Chico has slowly reverted to the person we first met. He's started studying. Going to the gym. He's met someone inside called Maz. And as the months have gone by, months that are turning to years, we've shared stories. We've laughed. Cried. Planned the night out we'll have the day he is released. And gradually his confidence has started to return.

* * *

He takes a seat. Number 51. 'Oh, honey, I'm so glad you could make it.'

'How're you?'

'I'm okay...' He shrugs. 'You know how it is...'

The first few minutes are always the most difficult. The first and the last.

'You look great,' I tell him cheerfully. 'And you've lost weight too. You still going to the gym?'

'No. I should be.'

'Well, you look in good shape.'

'Do I?'

'Yeah, really!'

I hate myself for saying this. For not being able to find the right words and telling him what I think he wants to hear. Because the truth is, he looks haunted. His eyes jump this way and that like a trapped animal's. And his lower lip is drooping, cracked, as if he's severely dehydrated. I don't remember it looking like this before.

'Ahhhh, thank you, honey. You always say the sweetest things. I don't feel in great shape, though.' He reaches toward his back and pulls a face. 'I think I've pulled a muscle or somethin'. I've got a lump here somewhere.'

These visits always follow the same pattern. After the first few awkward moments we start to open up, and then the next two hours fly by. Right up to the last five minutes, when, for some reason, it becomes awkward again, and I have to force myself not to be the first one to stand up when the guard shouts, 'Okay, time up!' I'm that eager to get away. But of course, you can't give Chico any indication that you want to leave. The whole point of these meetings is to keep him positive, make him laugh, take his mind off it all.

'Hey, just one more Christmas to go now,' I tell him as the visit draws to an end. 'And it'll go really quickly now, you watch.'

'Clay, I jus' wanna get outta here. I can't take it much longer.'

'I know, Chico. I know.' I reach for his hand. 'But you'll be back in the shop soon.'

And as we say our goodbyes, the conversation becoming awkward again, I try to imagine Chico bursting into the shop, filling the room with his laughter and his light. But the weird thing is, as I walk away through the three sets of doors, through the security checkpoint, back to the visitors' room to collect my bag, I have a strange feeling, and I'm not really sure why, that I'll never see Chico in Soho again.

February 24th, 2008: The Road Sweeper

Seven minutes past midnight.

I'm by the window. All the lights off inside so no one can see in. And I'm listening to Hercules and Love Affair on my laptop.

Outside, the night road sweeper brushes the pavement: empty beer bottles and discarded G.A.Y. flyers. He sweeps them into a small pile, then reaches toward his cart for his shovel. As he does a drunk walks through the pile and staggers on, oblivious. The road sweeper looks down at the scattered rubbish. Runs his fingers through his hair. Sighs.

On Old Compton Street crowds make their way home. Rowdy gangs, boisterous boys, gregarious girls. Like an embarrassing office party that you wish you could leave.

I stand up. Watch from the doorway.

Just by the door a group of businessmen congregate. They crack jokes about the gay couples, unconsciously deflecting the curiosity that draws them here. Patting each other on the back with each comment. Hugging. Whispering in each other's ears. Lips touching skin. Like lovers exchanging tender words. Ironically, the most homoerotic presence on the street.

I go back to my seat. Think about the past week. How much longer we can stay open. What we'll do next. While I'm mulling this over, the businessmen turn into Dean Street. They kick at the resurrected pile of rubbish as they pass, laughing. The road sweeper shouts back at them. They ignore him. Carry on. Then the loudest of the group kicks at a bottle and slips, landing on the pavement. He picks himself up, curses the road sweeper and storms off to join his friends.

The road sweeper leans on his brush, dejected. He stares at the rubbish strewn across the pavement again and shakes his head. Then the flicker of a smile. What's he seen? Then I spot it, there amongst the flyers. A £20 note that must have fallen from the businessman's pocket.

As one door closes...

February 25th, 2008: A Bed for the Night

I've been writing a weekly "Soho Stories" column in *The London Paper* and we've been hoping that the extra bit of publicity might bring some customers into the shop. Well, this afternoon I thought it'd worked...

I was sitting behind the counter flicking through a magazine when a voice shouted, 'Do you write that column in the paper?'

I looked up and grinned. 'Yes, that's me!' I replied, puffing my chest out proudly.

'I slept on you last night!'

It was the local homeless guy.

February 25th, 2008: Growing Up

10 pm. I'm in Comptons, a gay pub on Old Compton Street, and it's heaving, full of bearded bears and burly boys. It's a 'spit and sawdust' type of pub, the crowd friendly and attitude free.

I order a drink, vodka and coke. And take a seat by the window so I can spot Jorge, who's due here in a few minutes. I feel relaxed tucked away in the corner, watching the crowd as they laugh, as they gossip, as they cruise. And as I watch them it takes me back to the excitement I felt on my first-ever visit to a gay pub.

* * *

When I was growing up in Weston-super-Mare, a small decaying Victorian seaside resort, there was only one gay pub in the town, The Britannia, and it was only gay on the first Sunday of every month. This made the monthly trip to The Britannia a big event and nothing has ever quite beaten the excitement I felt on entering that dismal pub, next door to a theatre, all those years ago. I was just 17 when I first went in with my friend Mike Hopkins.

Mike was an enigma. He was the first gay man I'd ever seen in the flesh. I'd be sitting in a coffee bar, or browsing in the local record shop, and I'd catch sight of Mike mincing down the High Street, laughing in a really high-pitched voice, without a care in the world, wearing red trousers, which, I'd been told, were a definite 'sign'.

I'd secretly follow Mike around town, both fascinated and repelled. He was everything I'd been warned about and everything I wanted to be. It was only a matter of time before we became friends.

In those days it was the done thing to call each other by girl's names and your assigned name was usually related to your job. I worked in a sewing machine repair shop and therefore became known as Sally Sewing Machine. Mike, who was unemployed, was known as Dolly Dole Queue, and my other friend Rob

Brown, who worked on the 'Pick and Mix' in Woolworths, was christened Wendy Woolworths.

Every month, locked in Mike's bedroom, the three of us would crimp our hair until it melted, gel the remainder into rock-hard spikes, and then spray the living daylights out of the whole ensemble. Then, with faces caked in makeup, we'd make our way to The Britannia, like teenage Avon Ladies off to a gay prom night.

Just managing to get inside the pub without being beaten up, however, required a battle plan worthy of the SAS. As I was only 17, still four years away from being legal, this made any sexual encounter not only a criminal act, but considering the roughs in town, fraught with danger. About the same time that a new virus was being identified in the US, I was already discovering that the lure of gay sex could be a deadly pursuit.

The Britannia was a strange bar, dodgy on one side and, given its proximity to the theatre, theatrical on the other. Every now and again there'd be a 70s 'end of the Pier' act inside: a faded soap star or an aging camp comedian would recount showbiz stories to a mesmerised audience, throwing back his arms with dramatic gestures, ordering strange drinks that I'd never heard of, like vodka martinis, and regaling us with tales about the pubs in Soho. And the three of us would sit there, sipping warm cider, watching in awe, like three camp handmaidens, feeling like we'd really hit the Big Time.

But not only was The Britannia dangerous to enter, once you were on the theatrical side, if you spotted someone you knew on the dodgy side, it was a case of hiding behind a pillar for the night so that your secret wouldn't be exposed. Because this was a secret world. Normal life would have to be returned to at some point, but, in those days, it was a case of never the twain shall meet.

Looking back, the clientele were not exactly the crème de la crème. They were as old and decrepit as the bar. An elephant's gay graveyard. The three of us were the only things in there under 60. In fact, the clientele were so old that it felt like we were a new breed of gay man, discovering ourselves early in life, rather than upon retirement. It was no wonder we had so much attention.

Sex was playfully experimental, an experiment that could, then, still be conducted without fear. We'd had little straight sex education at school, so obviously knew absolutely nothing about what gay men were supposed to do. I remember on my second visit to The Britannia I was asked by an old queen if I liked watersports. 'I'm the fastest in my school at backstroke,' I replied cheerfully.

But if it was tough for the three of us, imagine being a lesbian. There was only one out lesbian in the whole town, Julie Poolie. She'd be at The Britannia every month, in Gateways apparel, fresh from repairing her boat, knocking back drinks as if the town was about to run dry. She'd spend the evening lunging at any straight girls who'd been dragged along for the evening.

Then, one night, I had my Quentin Crisp Portsmouth vision. A man came in who looked butch. I mean, really butch. I'd never seen a gay man wear camouflage trousers, or any kind of uniform, before. It was such a revelation that gay men could dress in anything but effeminate clothing that from then on I knew I had to leave that town. There was another world waiting. There was another life to lead.

A month later I was on a coach to London, my parents waving goodbye at the seafront coach stop, convinced I'd be back in a week. But I knew I could never let that happen. This town would destroy me unless I left.

So I waved goodbye until my parents were out of sight, then slowly sat back down in my seat and cried. I was free. My second life was about to begin.

And the first place I headed for when I stepped off that coach? Soho.

February 26th, 2008: The Best on the Market

The first hint of blue sky creeps tentatively above the rooftops of Soho and the sun filters through, the muted colours of the street slowly disappearing. It's as if Soho's coming back to life. Pulcinella's having a repaint. The delivery vans are trundling past more regularly. And the first tourists of the year, the Scandinavians, have arrived.

Inside the shop it's a hive of activity. Jorge and Elton are manically unpacking the new Spring/Summer collections, steaming and folding: a production line of designer goods about to be priced and displayed before we're forced to sell them at half price in June.

Amidst all this to-ing and fro-ing, an androgynous voice shouts, 'Hellloooo, boys!'

We all look around. It's Angie, leg draped around the doorway in a Sally Bowles pose. She's dressed in her signature look: Jackie O sunglasses, a black Chanel suit, silver walking stick and a new designer handbag with silver clasps the size of knuckledusters.

'Hi, Angie,' we reply in unison.

She sweeps toward us. 'Wot's going on?'

'We're trying to get this stuff out.'

'Well, don't let me stop you!' she says, removing her glasses and taking a seat on the chair by the window.

'How'd the date go?' asks Jorge as we fold.

'What date?'

'The caveman,' I remind her.

She purses her lips. 'Let's just say Mr Muscles wasn't quite the daddy I thought he was.'

'Why's that?'

'Darlin',' she coos in a breathy Marilyn-like voice, 'a lady does not kiss 'n tell.' She reaches inside her handbag for a compact, opens it, checks her eyes and, satisfied, snaps it shut again. 'Good job I ain't a lady then, innit?' She leans forward. 'Honestly, my love life—it's a bleedin' joke.' Her voice goes up 10 decibels, almost to a squeal, as it does when she's telling a salacious story. 'All that trouble I went through havin' the cock chopped off an' he only wanted me to use a strap-on!'

I can't help but laugh.

'I said to him, "Listen, darlin', I spent twenty-two grand on this fanny. It's one of the best self-lubricatin' ones on the market. An' if you think I'm gonna strap a dick to it, you gotta another think comin'."'

'And he looked so butch.'

She sniffs. 'The bigger the muscle, the bigger the mary, in my book.'

Jorge stops folding. 'Well, I think you're doing really well putting yourself out there.'

Angie peers down the front of her black T-shirt, examining her breasts, as she does quite regularly now. 'Yeah, well,' she mutters, not entirely convinced, whether at Jorge's statement or her breasts, it's hard to tell. 'There'll be no "puttin' myself out there" for a while. Not 'til I get these sorted.'

I decide now's the time to ask her what's wrong with them.

'Never you mind!' she fires back. Then she stands up and sashays toward the doorway, making full use of her walking stick.

'Where're you going now?'

'To the market to get me lunch.'

Then, just as she's about to leave, a tall, distinguished-looking mixed-race gentleman in a light-tan suit brushes past. Angie stops. 'Helllooooooo, big boy,' she purrs coquettishly, swishing her hair over one eye in a sultry pose.

'Er... Hello,' the gentleman replies nervously. 'And, er... You are?'

She holds out her hand, waiting for it to be kissed, and says in a posh voice, 'Royalty, dahling!'

The gentleman hesitates, takes her hand, brings it to his lips.

'Ohhhh, a gentleman!' Angie sings, this time in broad Cockney. 'Don't see many of them roun' 'ere!' She blows him a kiss and sweeps out, leaving a crowd of bemused passersby in her wake.

'Who was that delightful creature?' the gentleman asks in disbelief, watching her from the doorway.

'The Queen of Soho,' I reply with a smile.

And I don't think even HRH would argue with that.

February 27th, 2008: Charlie Reveals All

Outside, it's grey and dismal. Soho's virtually empty. The depressing atmosphere invades the shop.

All of a sudden Jorge says, 'Look who's outside!'

I follow his line of vision. An elderly man in a brown raincoat and a porkpie hat has his nose pressed against the main window, staring at our underwear collection.

'You're back!' Jorge cries, as Charlie rushes in, making a beeline for the thongs.

'Yes! Yes!' he replies excitedly without looking in our direction. 'That I am.'

I jump out of my seat, eager to catch up on all the latest news about him and Leslie. 'Charlie, how are you?'

'Oh, I'm fine, thank you, dear...' His voice trails off as he runs a finger along the underwear section. 'You have the new L'Homme Invisible underwear collection in, I see,' he says, his voice quivering with excitement as he pulls a see-through number from the rails, squinting as he holds it up to the light. 'I haven't seen one like this in a long time.' He examines the pouch, strokes it, and places if carefully back on the rail. Then he turns to face Jorge. 'Do you, by any chance, have their simulated-sequin, high-gloss, zebra-print thong that I've read so much about?'

'No, not yet,' Jorge replies, shaking his head. 'That'll be part of our Winter collection.'

'Would you be so kind as to save me one? I'd be very grateful.'

'Of course.'

He pulls another thong from the rail. 'Oh, I love this!' he says, holding the thong against his legs. 'Gold lamé. I haven't seen one like this before. What do you think? The large or the extra large?'

'Ummm…'

'Because if I go for the extra large, one's bits could potentially fall out.'

'Er…'

'And I'm not sure if it'll fit Rodney.'

'Oh, are you buying it for a friend?'

'No—this is Rodney,' Charlie explains, matter-of-factly, pointing at his crotch. Jorge's eyes widen but Charlie continues on obliviously.

'But if I were to go for the large, then the goods would be cradled quite comfortably. Yes. Yes, I think I'd better go for the large.'

'Would you like to try it on?' asks Jorge.

'Oh, no, dear! I'll do the unveiling at home.' He places the thong on the counter, taking a step back to admire it.

When he walks back to the rail, I seize my chance. 'So, Charlie, how's—'

'Oh, and look at this!' Charlie says hungrily, holding up another lacy piece, this one encrusted with Swarovski crystals in the shape of a dragon. 'This is just divine!' He hands it to Jorge to wrap. 'I'll take this one as well.'

'Well, you certainly have a good eye, Charlie!'

'I am an homme du monde when it comes to underwear, my dear.'

'You are. So, that'll be…with discount… Fifty-eight pounds, please.'

Charlie takes his wallet from his coat pocket. 'Now, if I pay on my Visa card then by the time the bill comes in I can pay it all off with my pension. Yes, yes, that's what I'll do.' He hands Jorge his credit card.

'You're spending your pension on thongs?' Jorge asks, incredulously.

Charlie looks puzzled. 'What else would I spend it on?'

I take a step closer. Clear my throat. 'So. Charlie. How's—'

'Oh, these are beautiful!' he cries, pulling a pair of Zegna flip-flops from the shelf. 'I'll take these too for wearing round the house. They'll go wonderfully with the gold lamé.'

As Jorge wraps the purchases, trying not to laugh, I try one more time. 'So, Charlie, how was your holiday?'

He looks puzzled. 'What holiday?'

'With Leslie. In Spain.'

'Holiday with Leslie? I don't know what you're talking about.' He sounds perplexed, his eyebrows furrowed.

'But I thought...'

Charlie scratches behind his ear. 'I think there's been some mistake...' He looks concerned now. 'I haven't seen Leslie since...since the night he visited me in hospital. I assumed you knew.'

'But Leslie said—'

'My dear, I can assure you that Leslie and I are not in contact. I've called him. On many occasions. But he won't return any of my calls. And I certainly don't know anything about a holiday.' His eyes travel down to the floor. 'It's such a shame... I thought perhaps that after all these years he would let bygones be bygones and we could start afresh... As friends if nothing else.' He looks up and sighs with resignation. 'But it appears not... I think he just wanted to see if I was all right.'

'Why would he lie?'

Charlie thinks for a moment. 'Your guess is as good as mine. Leslie is a law unto himself. It's part of his fascination...' He reaches for the bag that Jorge's just finished packing.

'But he talks as if you're together.'

'Does he, really?' Charlie sounds surprised. He looks from me to Jorge and back again. 'What can I say? I've never known where I am with Leslie. He's always been so...so hard to pin down. Mind you, who am I to talk? After what I put him through. Maybe this is just Leslie's way of getting his own back. I really don't know. I've tied myself up in knots thinking about it.' He adjusts his hat. 'I just hope that one day he picks up the phone. It was so nice seeing him in hospital.' Then, just as he's about to leave, he says, rather sadly now, 'Goodbye, my dears.'

March 2008

March 2nd, 2008: The Dandy Is Coming!

I'm sitting on my little red chair looking out onto Old Compton Street. All of a sudden a face pops up in front of the window. A shock of coal-black hair, white powdered cheeks, a fey flutter of painted fingernails. It's Sebastian.

Sebastian Horsley lives on the next street, Meard Street, the house with a sign on the door that reads: 'This is not a brothel. No prostitutes live here.' Artist, writer and failed suicide, Sebastian is a Soho legend.

When we first moved in, the locals would point at him and, in hushed tones, recount strange stories about this mysterious figure. He was a drug addict (heroin). He was a connoisseur of prostitutes (he'd slept with more than a thousand). He'd subjected himself to a crucifixion in the Philippines (he painted pictures of what he'd been through). It was like arriving in Transylvania and being warned about Dracula.

Of course Soho has always attracted the bohemian, the eccentric and the dandy. Rimbaud and Verlaine, Oscar Wilde, Quentin Crisp, they were all attracted by the lure of sex, Soho's cosmopolitan feel and the touch of danger that lurked within. But now there was a new dandy in town.

I first saw Sebastian back in February of 2006. But there was so much to write about back then, I was on a roll. So although I knew that one day he'd feature in my diary, the timing wasn't quite right. It was almost as if I was 'saving' him. Waiting for our stars to collide. And then one night they did. I gazed out of my window and there he was, dressed as if from another age, and I thought, OK, here goes. And, of course, Soho being the village that it is, eventually he got to hear about it.

Dear Clayton (he wrote, in response to my first email)
I don't mind you referencing me at all, my dear. I would only mind if you did not reference me. My reputation is terrible, which comforts me a lot, but I do hope it doesn't harm yours.
The important thing is that nothing reported about me is ever humdrum. And of course, I don't care what is written about me so long as it isn't true.

With much love,
Sebastian x

We've been friends ever since.

* * *

Today he's wearing an inky black-velvet three-piece suit, a white shirt with the longest pointed collars you've ever seen, the double cuffs adorned with diamante, and a pair of stout, black-calf, high-altitude platforms. He sways toward me, across the shop floor, arms outstretched.

'Darling! I've just heard that you won't be coming to New York for my book launch!'

'Sebastian, I'm sorry. I would love to, but—'

'Is it too expensive?'

'Well, er—'

'Can't you walk, you lazy bastard? I have a group of Sohoites coming along and I was rather hoping—'

'I just can't afford it. The shop's not doing too well at the moment.'

'You're not closing, are you? Tell me you're not closing!' he beseeches me, and he takes my hand, pulls me out of my seat and wraps his arms around me. 'Oh, you mustn't, my darling. You're part of Soho now.'

'Nah... We'll be fine,' I reply, a touch unconvincingly. 'Anyway, tell me about your launch. I read the review in the *New York Times*. And you got a whole page in the *LA Times*. They love you already!'

He covers his mouth with his hand like a naughty schoolboy. 'Mmmm... My notoriety goes ahead of me like a leper's bell in hell.'

'Maybe you'll do a Quentin and never return.'

'Well, my dear, I've always felt American in my artificial heart. You see, we are all English at puberty and then we die American.'

I must look confused, because he adds: 'You see, in America they love a loser who becomes a winner as much as we love a winner who becomes a loser. As Saint Quentin once said, "It is because of our hearts. The English have shriveled hearts. The Americans, plump, peachy, warm ones."'

He tells me about his trip and what he'll do when he gets there.

'It is not enough to conquer, one must know how to seduce. You see, strangers are just people you haven't fucked yet. Enemies are just people you have failed to charm.'

'Will you be staying in New York?'

'I was rather hoping to go to LA. I know everyone goes to New York but LA appeals to me. I'll be misunderstood there. Plus, I'd rather like to appear in a porn film. Do you think I have the legs?' He grins, pulling a trouser leg up to his knees.

Then Jorge shouts from behind the counter, 'Sebastian, how are you going to pack your top hat? It's two feet tall!'

'Darling!' he shouts back. 'I shall wear it on the flight and arrive in style! And when I descend the steps of the plane, instead of announcing, Wilde-like, "I have nothing to declare but my genius," I shall announce, Whoresley-like, "I have

nothing to declare but my genitals. My heinous, genius, penis."
Bon mot voyage!'

I love Sebastian. He is a star and his visits are always an occasion. I admire his honesty. His intellect. His 'two fingers up at the world.' Sebastian has made it the object of his life to become a work of art, just as Quentin Crisp did. And that takes courage.

He languorously extends his slender, snow-white fingers, his nails crowned with gleaming crimson varnish, and entwines them with my own. His touch is marble-cold and surprisingly sensuous. 'Clayton, my darling, are you a Gemini?' he purrs.

'Yes, I am.'

'Of course you are. All my friends are Geminis. They are the only ones who truly understand me.' He looks me directly in the eye. 'But now, tell me about your book. How, if one may ask, is it going?'

I tell him it's finished. Then I have a thought. 'Would you write a quote for the back?'

His face lights up. 'Of course I would! I'd be honored. I shall think of something suitably nasty while I'm away.' He giggles at the thought. 'Oh, Clayton, wouldn't it be fun if our books end up in the same remainder bin? Would you prefer to be a top or a bottom?' He giggles again. 'Anyway, my darling, I really must be going.'

He gets as far as the doorway, then spins back around. 'Oh, I almost forgot! I got up at five o'clock this morning and there outside my door was a video in a brown paper envelope. Oh, someone's sent me a porno, I thought, and I immediately got my knob out. But it was from you. And it was *The Naked Civil Servant*. And the line you wrote, "In case you want to brush up on some lines before you go." Oh, what a Gem(-ini) you are, Clayton. Like a precious stone, your gorgeous personality derives its value from its scarcity. Goodbye, my darling.'

We hug, kiss each other on the cheek and I wish him luck,

wondering what they'll make of him in America, wondering if he'll ever return.

March 3rd, 2008: Quentin Crisp

To be taunted at school was a common occurrence, and though I wasn't singled out especially there was one particular taunt that cut deep. 'You look like Quentin Crisp!' It was the ultimate put-down. Even at home I remember recoiling whenever I saw him appear on television, frightened that my parents would look at him, then look at me, look back at the television and say, 'So, that's what you are!'

Now I live in the street in which he spent most of his time. He worked around here, socialised here and, as a youth, prostituted himself here. Living below a brothel myself, I feel tied to the same sights, smells, noises, and the whole mish-mash of cultural references that drew Quentin to this area. It feels like his ghost still walks this street. And sometimes, when I'm sitting by the window late at night watching Sebastian glide by, I think of that other Soho dandy and the magical day I once spent with him.

* * *

A long time ago, I was in a pop band called Spongefinger. With the confidence of youth (but with zero talent to back it up), I thought I was a star in the making. Thus, having written a pop song titled "Last Night I Dreamt I Was Julie Andrews", I did the natural thing and got on a plane to New York to deliver the song personally to Julie, who was appearing in *Victor/Victoria* on Broadway. The day I arrived I found out that she'd been replaced by Raquel Welch. Totally heartbroken, I did the next best thing, I picked up the telephone book and thumbed through the C's. Ah, here it is! Crisp. 2-5-4 0-5-0-8.

'*Oh… Yesss,*' said the strange, strangulated voice coming out of the phone. I sat there nervously clutching the receiver.

'Hello, Mr Crisp, you don't know me, but my name's Clayton

and I've come all the way from London to meet Julie Andrews and, well, the day I arrived I found that she'd already left.'

'*Oh... Yesss. What a lousy musical,*' said The Voice.

'Well, I was thinking that if I couldn't meet Julie, perhaps... I mean, you're the other person I really would like to meet. You see, I've got this song for Julie and I was wondering... Could I give it to you instead?' I was getting flustered now, realising how preposterous this must sound.

'*Why don't you meet me in the Cooper Square Restaurant on East Fifth and Second Avenue at eleven am. I am meeting some people from the outer reaches of Boston at ten am and should have finished by then,*' The Voice replied, as though being a stand-in for Julie Andrews was a daily occurrence. '*I will be sitting by the window like a Dutch prostitute awaiting your arrival. Goodbye, Mr Clayton.*'

Looking back on my diary entry for July 12th, 1997, I sound like I was about to meet the Queen, which in some ways I suppose I was.

July 12th, 1997: Meeting Quentin

Just going to meet Quentin. What should I wear? Smartish? Casual? Sexy? Should I kiss him? Do I curtsey? Shake hands? Do I bring flowers? What am I going to talk about? Have I got enough money for the bill?

From the outside, though the Cooper Square Restaurant is glass-fronted, its clientele appear out of focus. It was like watching one of the last episodes of *Dynasty*. On closer inspection, the hat was the giveaway. It could only belong to one person in this city of baseball caps. So, willing myself forward, taking a deep breath (as I was not expecting to breathe again for a good 10 minutes), I breezed through the diner's doorway and walked straight up to The Voice with the flowers I'd just bought. He caught my eye straightaway, as gay men always do. That look. The recognition.

'Mr Clayton, do join us for eggs.'

He was dressed just as I imagined, in a black jacket, a fedora, a white shirt with large collars and a silk cravat held together with an ornate brooch. The clothes had seen better days. His nails were dirty, his makeup hastily applied. And yet, offset by his pale, dame-like appearance, he was still a star. St Quentin. HRH in exile.

I watched as he held court with his Boston entourage, who gushed and fawned over him like a gay Gloria Swanson. Line after line, cliché after cliché, I'd heard them so many times before. He must've realised that I wasn't as easily pleased with the scraps he was throwing to his hungry audience, because he said, mischievously, 'It won't be long now.' And I watched him again as he milked the crowd for every drop of admiration they could bestow.

I had read somewhere that he said people are rarely with him; 'they are in my presence or interviewing me.' I was determined that this would not be the case with us. But how could you possibly meet Quentin and not want to ask, 'What was it like then? How did you get through it? Are you an angel sent to guide us?'

As he delicately ate his eggs, we talked of London, Old Compton Street and the area I lived in at the time, Notting Hill. 'Do you keep in contact with any of the crowd from the Black Cat?' I asked as casually as I could.

'How would I know who they are?' he replied. 'I only ever knew them by their stage names.'

I thought of people I knew from my past and the people I know now. Would I know them in a few years?

The conversation drifted from London to its inhabitants, Sting and his 'Stinglettes', Boy George ('I didn't understand a word of his album'). I noticed the book on the table beside him, titled *Call Me*, that he'd been given earlier by the author, P.P. Hartnett.

'Will you read it?' I asked.

'Of course not! It'll go in the trash!' (Nonetheless, in his review Quentin would call it 'the kinkiest book in all the world'.)

We were cautious with each other, I felt. He'd seemed much more relaxed earlier with his ladies-in-waiting. Did I remind him too much of home? Did my being English make him more cautious? Was I a harder audience to conquer? Just when the conversation was beginning to run dry, in burst Larry.

'Hi—I'm Larry. Larry Vide. President of the New York Prime Timers. That's the society for mature gay and bi men and their friends!' barked the mountainous man who looked like Lurch from *The Addams Family*. 'You guys ready? Taxi's waiting!'

Larry helped Quentin out of his seat.

'You will be accompanying us, won't you, Mr Clayton?' Quentin said with what appeared to be a 'Save me!' look on his face.

'I'd love to!' And I dived into the back seat of the cab.

Larry sat in the front, gave the driver directions and then pulled back the dividing panel. 'Clay. You don't mind me calling you Clay, do you? You English too? We're off to the Lesbian and Gay Center. Quentin's giving a talk to the Prime Timers. He does it every year, then we get him a meal after.' He added, whispering, 'We pay.' I glanced at Quentin, who was adjusting his hat and appeared not to notice. 'Part of the deal,' Larry mouthed at me, tapping his nose as though I was somehow in on it. 'Always a good crowd, isn't there, Quent? Although we had a few deaths last month. Still, fewer sandwiches for me to make! Ha! Ha!'

'You don't mind coming, do you?' Quentin whispered.

'Of course not! It's an honour.'

'An honour for me too, to be thought of as an understudy for Miss Andrews.'

We laughed and for a second I visualised waking up in Quentin's bed, the morning after, covered in dust and mauve hair dye, with Quentin under the duvet beneath me. I coughed. Turned away and watched the skyscrapers race by.

'Stop! Stop! Here we are,' Larry said to the taxi driver. Then he pulled back the dividing panel again. 'You wanna become a member of Prime Timers, Clay?' and before I could reply he said, 'If you wait 'til you're sixty we may be oversubscribed! Look at me! I started Prime Timers when I was sixty-three! It's given me a new lease on life. Hey, wait 'til I show you our July event list. You're in luck too! Tonight's Leo's Ecstasy Night, where he shows his ecstatic porn films followed by a late-evening supper. You can leave your clothing at the door at Leo's place too,' he winked. 'I'll get him to give you the address later.'

The Lesbian and Gay Center on West 13th Street is always busy, with events to cater for every need. Walking around it was like visiting a school reunion and trying to remember where the gymnasium was. Old and crumbly, full of lecture halls and amateur dramatic stage sets. Larry led us into the Prime Timers hall, where Quentin was to deliver his talk. I noticed the flyers on the notice-board providing the Prime Timers with some useful tips.

Pepperminty Comfort
After-dinner peppermint has a chemical that's been shown to reduce flatulence and its accompanying discomfort

Fruit and Oral Sex
If your partner objects to the taste of your seminal fluid, you may want to skip the spices and bring on the fruit

Marty Leff will offer sexercises and other fun, fanciful, fantastic, fallic frivolities! And don't forget the bountiful buffet, too. Call to reserve and get address. Limit 17. Donation $3

I was still reading the notices when Larry's voice bellowed through the hall.

'Gentlemen and gentlemen! We are most fortunate to have with us today Mr Quentin Crisp, who is going to address us with his usual entertaining flair. So take your seats quickly, everyone.' There was a sound of scraping chairs and then Larry's voice again. 'Now, before we start, just a quick reminder about Leo Falk's Ecstasy Night tonight. That's porn and supper at Leo's starting at six pm. He'll be serving exotic food like turkey stew and there'll be a chance to enjoy each other's bodies after you've eaten. All clothing will be bagged and tagged, and sleepovers are possible.'

The crowd looked visibly excited by this news and there was a lot of laughter around the hall.

'Leo's is always a good venue,' said a blind man next to me as I took a seat. 'He encourages the sleepovers. We never did them until the venue moved to Leo's. Are you coming?' he asked, squeezing my knee.

'I'm not sure yet... Is it always turkey stew?' I squeaked, trying to steer the conversation toward food.

'Well, Leo usually starts off with an ecstasy punch. And sometimes there's a buffet. Although it doesn't usually get eaten. It's a cold buffet, though, because most of us are naked and we can't afford spillages, can we?' He snickered, squeezing again.

I scouted the hall, looking for Leo, imagining he would be the one with the broadest grin in anticipation of the night's events. I wondered if he knew what a spicy buffet can do to seminal fluid.

'Clay, you're on stage!' Larry shouted above the noise. 'We've put a chair next to Quent. Go on! Get up! We're about to start!'

I stared at him for a second, not quite understanding what he meant. Then I looked across at the stage and noticed a chair next to Quentin, who was adjusting his microphone, trying to decide whether to attach it to his cravat or his shirt collar.

What am I doing? I thought as I clambered up on the stage. What do they want me up here for?

'How nice to have company,' Quentin said. 'It does tend to get lonely up here. Could you nudge me if I nod off?'

'Are you nervous?'

'Oh, no,' he replied. 'Not at these events. I just tend to ramble on until I've run out of steam.'

'Well, you do seem very calm,' I gushed, suddenly feeling totally in awe of him.

'I am very calm. But then again, I should be. I'm eighty-eight. If I'm not calm now, when will I be?'

The next hour flew by. All the anecdotes and lines again. The same stories, rehashed and served up again. But when you've lived to be 88 I suppose the new lines don't come as easily. This was an icon on autopilot. Like watching a fading Margaret Thatcher on *Question Time*. The crowd at times looked a bit uninterested—or had they too heard it all before? Then the questions started to be directed at me.

'Hey! You Quentin's son?' asked a polar bear at the back. Somebody hadn't done their research.

'Mr Clayton's an old friend from London,' said Quentin, sensing my nervousness.

The word 'London' echoed around the hall as though it was some mystical land.

'You live with Quentin?' asked another.

'No, Quentin said he could never live with me—I'm too untidy.' This allowed Quentin to take over with another set of Crispisms. Then, almost without warning, it was over. He had literally run out of steam.

Suddenly there was a mass scramble for the sandwiches that Larry had discreetly been arranging at the back of the hall. A queue quickly formed. I fetched Quentin a plate full and left him on stage quietly eating. He appeared rather tired and the talk seemed to have drained him.

Then Larry came bounding over. 'Great talk, Quent! Hey, Clay, wanna check the bathroom?'

I felt myself blush.

'Clay, I know what you're thinking, but there's time for that later. Have you seen the Keith Haring paintings in the bathroom? Come on, follow me!'

I left Quentin on the stage while one of the Prime Timers served him a beer. 'Will Mr Clayton be coming back?' I heard him say faintly in the distance as I followed the hyperactive Larry out of the hall.

The toilets were incredible. The walls and ceilings were covered in huge black cocks all entwining and entering orifices. It looked quite mystical. If you forgot that they were cocks, it was like being in a mysterious jungle surrounded by erotic snakes and huge creepers. Larry took some pictures and I tried to pose standing on the toilet seat while an eight-foot member dangled above me.

'You look great,' said Larry. 'Try to look a bit more sexy!'

'Shall we go and check on Quentin now?' I asked nervously.

When we came back into the hall Quentin was still sitting onstage, no longer eating, in a world of his own, almost like he was meditating. The crowd, meanwhile, were drifting out slowly, the odd one or two nodding or saying goodbye to him as they left. It was like the end of school assembly with the headmistress still on her podium surveying her brood as they made their way into the world.

I touched Quentin's arm. 'I think Larry wants to take us to a restaurant. Shall we go?'

How long would he have stayed there if no one had come for him? He looked at me for a moment as if trying to place me. It was as if he'd aged 10 years in the past hour. Then he smiled. And we made our way slowly outside to find Larry waiting for us.

We must have looked a strange sight as we walked slowly down the street: Larry, six feet tall, with his craggy face, wild thatch of dyed black hair and boundless energy; me in my tight green army top and matching camouflage trousers, holding Dame Quentin's arm as we passed the Chelsea boys who stopped to stare.

It took a while to get to the restaurant. When we stepped inside we found it was virtually empty, though there seemed to be a rowdy group of older queens at the back.

'There they are!' Larry said, leading us to their table. 'Clay, meet Leo. Leo Falk. Leo, this is Clay from London.'

A small old man, bleached blond, tapped the seat next to him and reached out to shake my hand, eyeing me up and down.

'I've heard all about your Ecstasy Night.' I said.

Leo shook my hand vigorously. 'Well, then you must come. We've already reached the limit, but here, take my card and whoever's on the door will let you in. It's West 56th Street near 10th Avenue. There's my number. It's porn and supper and jack-off by ten pm.'

Quentin, seated opposite me, held his hands up to his face, mouth open in horror, like Edvard Munch's *The Scream*.

I could feel Leo putting his card in my back trouser pocket, letting his hand linger inside a few seconds. Quentin leaned over and whispered, 'Networking.' Leo just grinned back at me as though we were 'on a promise.'

Dinner was dominated by Larry, Leo and another huge inferno of a man called Fred Morgenweck who delighted the group by reading from some scraps of paper which turned out to be the latest porn story he was writing. Fred ran the creative writing workshop that met every other Thursday night. He bombarded me with questions.

'Clay, give me your address—I'll mail you a copy! I'll even put you in my story if you want. Hey, Clay, you circumcised? How many men are circumcised in England? You like foreskin, Clay?'

The meal ended. I asked Quentin, 'Do you miss anything about England?'

'Yes. Gas fires. You can regulate the heat in England.'

In the cab on the way home I felt a strange sensation that I'd never see him again.

'Will you ever go back to England?' I asked.

'Not if I can help it. I go back less and less these days, and one day I'll never go back again.'

I remember thinking, I don't suppose it would be right for him to die in England. Or New York, for that matter. Quentin lives in a world of his own, somewhere in between, watching over us like a glittering star.

I had one last thing to do before we left each other on the street corner—give him my song.

'I don't have anything to play it on,' he said. 'But I shall have to accept. When I die you'll find it under my bed if you want it back.'

I leaned forward and kissed him on the cheek.

'Goodbye, Mr Clayton,' he said. 'Do you know that Holly Woodlawn is the only person who hasn't spoken badly about Andy Warhol?'

And then he walked slowly, quietly away.

March 10th, 2008: Mr Benson

Café España on Old Compton Street.

I'm with David Benson, a friend I met on MySpace.

I first saw David 10 years ago in a West End theatre, in his Edinburgh-Award-winning one-man show, *Think No Evil of Us: My Life With Kenneth Williams*. So when I saw him on MySpace, I thought, I have to be his friend! I immediately sent him a friend request.

His show had made a big impression on me. Every inflection was honed to perfection: the voice, the mannerisms, the wit, the put-downs, his discussions with a table full of imaginary dinner guests—a style rarely seen onstage since Ruth Draper in the 40s. It was a mesmerising performance that took me right back to a night in the 1970s.

The 70s were the so-called golden age of British television, and Saturday nights were the one evening of the week when all the family would be at home, glued to the box. On this particular night Kenneth Williams was on. He was in his prime—the epitome, for most people, of what a homosexual looked like, acted like and stood for. I remember being curled up into a little ball on the settee, going bright red, my pale and pimply face starting to blend in with the velvet cushions, figuring that if I were to suddenly leave the room it would look suspicious. Thinking, Please, no one look at me. I'm not like that. That's not me!

And now the impersonator of my reappraised hero is sitting opposite me. I watch him closely, hanging on his every word, as he discusses theatre tradition, his heroes Harpo Marx and Fred Astaire, switching voices, one minute Kenneth, the next Frankie Howard, then Quentin—the gravelly voice, the tilt of the head, the arched eyebrow, reminding me of that magical day in New York. It's so close to the real thing, it's uncanny. It's as if Quentin himself is sitting opposite me, back in the Cooper Square Restaurant on the Lower East Side. I glance outside and there's Quentin's old haunt, The Black Cat (now Swank). It's kind of surreal.

The time flies by, as it does when you're a starstruck fan. We knock back our drinks. Pay the bill. Say our goodbyes. As he leaves and makes his way down Old Compton Street in the rain, I snap myself out of my dream. Putting the key in the lock of the shop, I suddenly have a thought. Maybe I could ask David to play Leslie in this play I'm writing.

Hmmm, I wonder…

March 11th, 2008: Stockpot

We're inside Stockpot, queuing up by the doorway; a group of four teenagers ahead of us. We spot Deborah, our favourite waitress. She looks happy to see us, rushes over and kisses us.

'Just you two?'

I nod.

She points to the small table by the counter. 'Over there okay?'

'That's great. Thanks, Deborah.'

I take the seat against the wall, Jorge facing me.

I take off my jacket, place my gym bag on the floor and look around. The little restaurant is packed: two elderly ladies lingering by the entrance, a young guy with a goatee scanning the menu, two bears in rugby shirts with unkempt beards, huddled up, deep in conversation.

Then, as I reach for the menu, I notice, directly in my line of vision, a Soho regular, the tranny with the cheaply made long blonde wig. She's in her sixties, I would imagine, and can often be seen, whatever the weather, walking up and down Old Compton Street in a tight miniskirt and black opera gloves. Unfortunately, with the thick glasses and dour expression, the look is less Bridget Bardot and more Olive from *On the Buses*. Still, the street being the place it is, she's often ignored.

Tonight she's wearing a fake-fur jacket and an ankle-length black cotton skirt. The skirt is decorated, randomly, with sequins, stars and half moons. It reminds me of the hippie skirts the girls used to wear at the alternative club I used to go to as a kid called Hobbit's Hole. A red scarf and a pair of scuffed nondescript shoes complete the ensemble. But what makes the scene interesting is that as she's eating she's nodding her head in time to the background music: Missy Elliot's "Get Ur Freak On".

Jorge follows my eyes. 'She's always on her own,' he observes. 'Have you noticed?'

He's right. She is. But I think there's a reason for this. She's an oddity on this street because she's straight, I suspect. She walks up and down the street, eating in all the local restaurants, having coffee outside, dressing inappropriately for her age. It's not a look she 'lives' with; it's a fetish. She's a part-time tranny, getting off on trying to pass, adopting the 'dowdy tranny' look that straight guys seem to veer toward. I picture her out of drag: a studious bank manager, married, with grown-up kids. Whenever I see her, I'm reminded of the trips I used to make to Provincetown when I first started dating Jorge.

Provincetown is a picturesque little seaside town on the tip of Cape Cod. It was there that Jorge opened his second Dirty White Boy shop. (The first one was in Rehoboth Beach, Delaware.) The shop was situated just opposite Spiritus, the pizza bar on Commercial Street where everyone congregates at the end of the night. It was the perfect location for me to watch the different groups which invade the town throughout the summer months.

On one of my visits it was Womyn's Week (so spelled because there is no 'men' in *womyn*) and the town was packed with sixties truck-driving lesbians. On another visit it was Family Week (lesbians with their Asian kids). Then there was Baby Doll Week (men dressed up as Shirley Temple). And Bear Week (hairy gay men). Not forgetting Single Men's Week (gay men with name badges who, after their daily 'How To Meet a Man' seminar, would cruise up and down the street with mournful eyes looking for 'the One'). But the best week of all was the straight cross-dressers' week known as Fantasia Fair (nicknamed Tall Ships Week by the locals). During Fantasia Fair the town is full of bad drag and each night there's a 'talent' contest at the Town Hall, which the cross-dressers take very seriously and the local gay men attend for a giggle. So whenever I see this Soho tranny I always think of Tall Ships Week. But, anyway, back to the meal...

We order (chicken special and glasses of tap water), and I see that she has finished her meal. I watch as she pulls a £20 note from a black, 50s-style, patent leather purse. (It seems that even down to the purse, her look is trapped in her mother's era. Maybe her whole look actually is her mother.) Once she's paid, she stands and I quickly look away, not wanting to appear rude, thinking that I've been quite discreet. Until she reaches the doorway, that is.

She stops, turns around and says, 'I hope I won't be appearing in your blog!'

March 14th, 2008: The Winds of Change

Change is on the way. You can feel it. It's in the air. I don't mean the weather. The weather's improving day by day. The cold winter wind no longer whistles down Dean Street; the queens have already ditched their winter woollies; the tables outside Costa are regularly full. No, it's not the weather. It's the economy.

If you could sit where I'm sitting and look outside, you'd see the streets are still busy: bears on the cruise, city boys in the mood, tourists munching on takeaway fast food. To the casual observer you wouldn't think anything was amiss. But there's a difference: no one's shopping. There's not a shopping bag in sight. And it's all over the papers. "The Boom Is Officially Over." That dreaded word *recession* creeping into the headlines. Three hours we've been sitting here, and not one shopper. It's as if Soho's in the grip of postwar austerity.

We're still getting visitors. Lots of them—friends, people who have been reading the blog, local traders complaining about the downturn. But no one shopping. I can't remember when we last had a big-spending American.

Every night Jorge calculates the takings, tallying last year's figures with this, worry etched on his face. At night we lie in bed not saying a word, staring at the ceiling. But we can't give up. Not yet. All our life savings are tied up in this shop. We have to get through this. We have to. What else can we do?

March 15th, 2008: Off the Air

The day after meeting up with David Benson, I was invited onto BBC late night radio to read a few of my stories. So I called David and asked him to join me.

Things were going well. Listeners were phoning in. We had a camp *Around the Horne* type of banter going on. Then we read a story about Leslie which had the words *cock* and *bumhole* in it. We were immediately taken off the air.

We apologised profusely, and we were invited back last night. And it happened again! This time we said the word *buggery* and were escorted out of the building. So ended our radio careers.

Oh, well. Back to blogging.

March 19th, 2008: The Dandy Returns

I'm sitting by the window. Flicking from site to site on my laptop. Suddenly:

You have email!

I open my inbox and click on the email. It's a press release. From Sebastian.

On Tuesday, March 18th, British author Sebastian Horsley was denied entrance into the United States by immigration officials.

Travelling to New York to promote his new memoir, *Dandy in the Underworld*, the UK artist flew from Heathrow Airport in London to Newark's Liberty International Airport in New Jersey, where he was detained by customs officials upon arrival. The flamboyant Horsley, dressed in his trademark style, complete with top hat, three-piece suit and finger-nail polish, was immediately pulled aside for questioning. When immigration officers did an Internet search on Horsley which revealed the author's often provocative and outspoken beliefs, Horsley was held for several hours of questioning and ultimately put on a plane back to London. Reached by his publishers while being detained, Horsley said in a statement, "I've got good news and bad news. The good news is, they all know about the book. The bad news is, they all know about the book."

I immediately dial Sebastian's number.

'*I'm not in!*'

'Sebastian, it's me, Clay!'

There's a pause followed by a rather mournful '*I suppose you have heard the news.*'

'Yes, it's all over the papers.'

'*Hmmm. The book launch that never was.*'

'What happened?'

'*Apparently, my dear,*'—he sighs—'*I am suffering from moral turpitude. Odd, is it not? Because I have never drunk turpentine in my life.*'

'But what proof—'

'*The book, my darling. The book!*'

'So they just sent you back?'

'*No, first they dragged me into a room and said, "Raise your right hand. Do you swear on the Bible to tell the truth, the whole truth and nothing but the truth?" So I said, "Well, I've been kissed more often than a court Bible, so 'yes', I suppose." And that, my darling, was the end of that!*'

'That was it?'

'*Well, I was just honest with them. They asked me if I had ever used illicit substances, and I said, "Yes. Brown rice. Oh, you mean heroin and crack? Then the answer's 'yes' and I am proud of it! And if I had to live my life again I would take the same drugs, only sooner and more of them!" Then they said, "Have you ever solicited prostitution?" And I said, "Yes. Mary Magdalene set a saintly precedent." Then they skimmed through the book and I was dispatched on the next flight home.*'

'They're not allowed to do that, are they?' I ask, incredulously.

'*They said that if I refused to leave they'd throw me in prison.*

Although the thought of buggery, porridge and Class A drugs did sound like fun. In fact, I was almost tempted to ask if there was a waiting list.'

'Oh, Sebastian,' I half laugh. 'I am sorry.'

'Thank you, darling. But I suppose it was a relief in a way. They seemed to have missed the more scandalous charges against me. I was only accused of racism, misogyny, homophilia, homosexuality, sodomy, drug addiction, whore-mongering, pimping, perversion and prostitution. So I think I got off quite lightly, don't you?'

'Well, to think what they could have sent you back for.'

He chuckles. *'It was such a shame, though, because I had a beautiful speech prepared. My opening line was—'* He clears his throat. *"Good evening. My name is Sebastian. I know you all want to fuck me but you'll have to wait until I finish this speech."'*

I laugh. 'But you're getting even more publicity now!'

'I suppose so.' He sighs. *'God bless America, hey? Land of the free, but sadly not the home of the depraved. Oh, well. Not to worry. The freaks will have our revenge. Anyway... Shall we have lunch soon, my darling? I have been missing your company quite dreadfully.'*

'Yes, that'd be lovely.'

March 19th, 2008: A Letter

The postman walks in and hands me a letter. The address on the back reads: HMP Littlehey, H-Wing, Perry, Huntingdon. Cambs.

I open it.

> Hi, Guys,
> Chico here!
> Thanks so much for the postal order. You guys have helped me so much. I will never forget that as long as I

live. And guess what I did with the money? I bought myself some trainers! Oh, honey, I could not wear those nasty prison shoes for one more second. You know what a fashion queen I am. The trainers are fabulous. I feel human again. I've been swishing past all the cells. Now I just need to get a pedicure and a manicure and this queen will be back on top!

Hey, and guess what? I've applied for the early release scheme—and it looks like I might get it! Isn't that great? And I've started the appeal process. So one way or another I am going to get out of here. I've just called my sisters in the States to tell them the news. I'm soooo excited!

Oh, and Clay, sorry to hear about the radio show. Maybe they will call again. And this time keep it clean! (no 'cocks and bumholes'). And Jorge, stay strong and hang in there. It'll get better. I'm praying for you every day.

I miss you guys. I'll put a Visiting Order in the post. Please come and see me soon.

Love you both,
Chico

March 20th, 2008: Colombian Roses and Paintings

I sat in an unpretentious café at the corner of Dean Street and Old Compton Street called Torino's. There were dark Italians huddled in earnest discussion and several pale young artists and poets searching halfheartedly for jobs.
—Daniel Farson, *Soho in the Fifties*

It was in this spot, my spot, that Farson wrote about Soho and his friendship with an up-and-coming artist by the name of

Francis Bacon. It was here that they would while away the hours discussing literature, history and art. Much the same as Jorge and I do with Raqib Shaw, 50 years later.

Tonight, though, we're meeting in Raqib's Islington studio to see his new paintings. Raqib's sitting opposite me. He's dressed in a blue patterned silk Lacroix shirt with a 10-inch jewel-encrusted bracelet on his arm. His olive skin (on account of his Kashmiri background) is flawless. His jet-black hair is stylishly parted. He's laughing, that eccentric laugh of his that's half human, half macaw.

Although our worlds are very different, for some reason we connect. The drink flows and the conversation moves with ease. Raqib asks us about the shop, how we're coping, how he must pop in again soon. Then he tells about his upcoming exhibitions, about having his body cast by Madame Tussauds for a life-size sculpture and how the galleries are already talking huge figures for the pieces. He talks in figures that are beyond my comprehension but at the same time he comes across as someone for whom money holds little importance.

Then he stops. Studies me through narrowed eyes. 'Claytee,' he says, leaning forward, champagne spilling from his glass. 'Sweets... I hope you don't mind me saying...but I read some of your writing and I've noticed that you're not quite letting yourself go.' He leans back in his chair, nods, as if confirming what he's just said. 'You're too aware of what people are thinking, my dear.' He reaches over and taps me on the leg. 'Don't give a fuck about them! Ignore them! Just let it flow out, Claytee, my sweet. Just let it all flow out.' He smiles warmly, nods again and then carries on chatting with Jorge.

I shift uncomfortably in my seat. Wounded. He's right, of course. Sebastian (the other genius I've met) once told me that there are two kinds of people: those who portray themselves in a positive light in the hope of seeking approval and those who lay themselves bare. I feel like I've just been exposed as the former. A few minutes pass while I think this through before I'm able to rejoin the conversation, which by now has moved on to relationships.

'I just want to be touched!' Raqib suddenly cries out, wrapping his arms around Jorge. 'That's all I want. I haven't had sex in fourteen years!'

'But you never leave the studio! What do you expect?'

'I can't leave, Jorge-san,' Raqib replies, using his pet name for Jorge.

'Why not?'

'I have to paint!'

'But you could take a break now and again, surely.'

'I do, Jorge-san! To visit your shop—and if you close, then I'll never leave my studio again!'

'You need a night out, Raqib. That's what you need. We'll take you out with us one night. To a bar. It's all about baby steps.'

A few minutes later our friend Lois, aka DJ HaLo-iS from Hard-On, the gay sex club, arrives.

'*I* know!' says Jorge excitedly. 'We'll take Raqib to Hard-On!'

I look from Lois to Jorge to Raqib. 'That's hardly baby steps.'

'No! I want to go!' Raqib squeals. 'Claytee, we'll go to Gaultier next week and I'll buy some leather bits.'

As we plan our visit the doorbell rings and more friends arrive. More bottles are opened and a plate of cookies is quickly consumed.

When Raqib first came into the shop, his star was already on the rise. But now, now it's soaring into outer space. Back then his paintings were very sexual. *The Garden of Earthly Delights* (which took inspiration from Hieronymus Bosch's 16th-century triptych) was full of lobsters fucking mermaids, cocks with spiraling sperm trails, phallus-headed underwater birds, and animal-headed man-beasts. It was surreal, pornographic and decorative, and it sold at Sotheby's last year for £2.5 million.

Now the work has moved on again and the rate at which he's

producing it is phenomenal. Admittedly he has 12 assistants working for him, but still, the guy's only 32 years old and nowhere near his peak. But what's different this time is that the work is even more detailed (if that were possible) and violent: monkeys impaled on swords penetrating their orifices, decapitations, flagellations, ritual disembowelment, Krishna-like figures engaged in fraught sexual combat, glorious butterflies hovering above the desecration. The works are covered in semiprecious jewels, using an original technique whereby pools of enamel and metallic industrial paints are manipulated to the desired effect with a porcupine quill, with every motif outlined in embossed gold.

I'm standing in front of one of the paintings now, not sure whether there was something in the cookie or it's the intricacy of the work that's making me feel giddy. I imagine it hanging in a museum for years (centuries?) to come, feeling slightly embarrassed that I don't have a sufficient art history background to fully appreciate what I'm seeing.

We move from painting to painting. They're getting bigger and bigger. One, taking up a whole wall, must be 20 to 30 feet long. Some finished, some partly so. You could stand in front of one of these for hours and still not take it all in.

The studio's very quiet now. Like a church. Everyone's talking in low voices. It's hard to describe the atmosphere, but I suppose stoned, spaced, spiritual and respectful sums it up nicely.

Suddenly Raqib shouts, 'Come on, everyone! It's flower time!'

We all float downstairs to his apartment. Then it really hits me. There's an overwhelming smell: roses everywhere. The apartment is covered in them. Red, white, orange, hundreds of them, all flown in from Colombia. Roses and lilies. It's breathtaking. Tree branches snake across the ceiling and around the walls. Barbed wire twists and turns around the room with little handmade birds pierced through the barbs, dripping blood.

There's a whole wall lined with shelves of Victorian tea sets and antique vases. Chaises longues. Chandeliers. Velvet drapes. The room lit by candles, ambient music in the background. It's like being trapped inside a Turkish Delight ad and I half expect a group of belly dancers to suddenly appear offering Tantric sex and hubbly bubbly pipes. (There *was* something in that cookie!) An hour later we say our goodbyes and drift back to our little flat in Soho.

The next day, we wake reeking of pollen and wolf down our breakfast as if our lives depended on it.

March 21st, 2008: The Crotch

There's a man sitting outside Costa. He's been there for at least an hour now, chair facing in my direction, sipping his coffee, coffee that must have gone cold long ago. He's chatting with a friend, his head turned to one side and his legs spread wide, the way men's legs are when they sit. Even at this distance his crotch appears to be on the large side. Bunched up. The fold in his jeans standing up in a peak. Creases stemming from the mound, illuminating it, like a sundial. As I stare at his crotch, thinking about what Raqib said, I let my mind drift back, back in time, until it's not really his crotch I'm staring at anymore, it's a memory. Something exciting. Something unknown. Something waiting to be discovered...

* * *

I'm eight years old. I'm at the school fancy dress party. My mum's dressed me up as Mick Jagger in harlequin tights, a white frilly shirt hanging loose. My hair is long and tousled, my face powdered, and I'm wearing red lipstick. Even at this young age I'm aware that I'm different. All the other kids are dressed up as firemen, soldiers, sailors. I look down at my outfit. I don't want to look like this. I mean, I do, but, I don't want to stand out. I'm not sure why.

Then I see Mr Brock, the music teacher. Big, tall Mr Brock.

With his dark cropped hair and moustache, his black tight-fitting trousers. And his big crotch. I can see it now as if it was yesterday. At eye level. Walking toward me. The folds. The creases. The mound. As he nears I want to reach out and touch it. I can remember the feeling so vividly. But I daren't. Something tells me it's not right.

Now he's walking past me. Big, tall Mr Brock. It's a real 'now or never' moment. I'm excited. I clear my throat. Gaze up.

'Excuse me, sir!'

He looks down impatiently, waiting for me to continue.

'Can you, er…'

'What do you want?' His face is stern.

'Can you, er… Can you help me take my lipstick off?'

He arches an eyebrow and glares at me. 'Do it yourself, boy!'

'I, er… I don't know where it is.'

'It's on your lips!' he barks back as he brushes past. 'Where do you think it is?'

Then it hits me. I've hinted at something that wasn't right. I feel like I'm about to cry. My first feeling of rejection. And it hurts. Even though I'm not quite sure what it was I wanted, it still hurts. I reach into my tights, pull out a paper hanky and wipe my face. I don't want to be Mick Jagger anymore.

I stand there, wondering what to do, wondering where to turn, watching Mr Brock gradually fade away into the crowd. So, too, the man sipping coffee stands and waves goodbye to his friend, and the memory that just seconds ago was so vivid, so clear, gradually fades away too.

March 22nd, 2008: The Key to Heaven

OK. Back to the shop…

I'm standing by the doorway when I notice two Japanese businessmen trying to get into the brothel next door. Knowing the girls don't open until midday, I ask if I can help.

'No, it is fine. We havu key,' says the taller of the two.

'A key?'

'Yes, but it is not worku,' he says, getting flustered as he tries to force it in the lock again.

'Who gave you that?'

'We buy it. Hundred poundu. The man say we have any girl we want upstair.'

'Which man?'

'That man!' says the businessman, pointing at a man running down Dean Street.

Saturday morning in Soho.

March 23rd, 2008: A Letter to Chico

Dirty White Boy

50 Old Compton Street

London

Dear Chico,

Hey darling! Just a quick note to tell you I thought of you today... The Iceberg jackets came in and I said to Jorge, 'We have to save one for Chico.' You are going to LOVE it. It is so you.

And what GREAT news about the early release and the appeal. Looks like you'll be back in Soho soon! What did I tell you?

News here isn't so great. Remember when we were always so busy? Well, not anymore. Everything's come to a full stop. We're soooo in debt. The only good thing is we're not paying rent at the moment. We told the landlady we're not paying any more until she fixes the damp problem. Honestly, Chico, the walls in the basement are permanently wet! And it's making the shop stink. Anyway, the landlady came around last week and she said, 'I don't see any damp.' Didn't see any damp? It's like the hull of the Titanic down here!

Luckily things are still good between me and Jorge

(he sends his love, by the way). Every night once we've closed he cooks these fabulous Cuban dishes on our one-ring stove and then we cuddle up in bed like two poor church mice.

How are things going with you and Maz? Hope it's working out. Are you still sharing a cell? Are you still studying? Write to me soon and tell me all your news.

We miss you. Soho's not the same without you. But it won't be long now!

Big kiss,
Clay (and Jorge) x

March 24th, 2008: Visitor of the Day

I'm in my usual spot, Jorge on his stool behind the counter. No one's been in the shop in hours. I glance in Jorge's direction. He shrugs back. No words needed. We both know what this means. The creditors are circling like vultures and they're circling lower by the day.

Then a voice says: 'Which one of you two writes that column in *The London Paper*?'

We both look toward the doorway to find a man who looks to be in his late sixties, with unkempt hair, wearing a striped boating jacket, polyester tracksuit bottoms and scuffed Nike trainers. He walks toward us.

He addresses me. 'Is it you?'

I clear my throat nervously. 'Er… Yes. It is.'

'Oh, I knew we'd get on!' he says excitedly. 'We're going to be really good friends.'

Oh, dear.

He steps closer, looking at me suspiciously now. 'Do you know who I am?'

He looks a dead ringer for Charles Hawtrey, but as he's dead I throw the man a look that says, I'm just trying to place you.

Meanwhile, he takes his hat off and steps closer still. Suddenly he thrusts his face forward. 'COME ON!'

'I...er... Have I seen you on TV?' I ask cheerfully, hoping that covers everything from the 1940s onwards.

'Oh, you do recognise me! How marvelous!' He reaches out to shake hands. 'The name's Simon. Simon Tiarks. I was very big in the seventies. I've done loads of drama.' He reels off six programmes in quick succession. 'Now, this brothel of yours...'

'It's not mine, exactly.'

'Of course not! But you write about it, don't you?'

'I have, on occasion,' I reply, cautiously. Where is this leading?

'Well, I used to go up there in the seventies. I used to wear big platform boots. And when I went up there the girls would say, "Oh, Mr Platform's back."'

'That's, er—'

'I don't use brothels now, of course. Oh, no. I've got a girlfriend. I don't have time for all that jiggery-pokery. Her name's Roslyn. She's an opera singer.'

'That's—'

'I'm off to meet her in a minute, actually. How long will you be here?'

'We're open 'til nine.'

'You promise?'

'Er...yes.'

'Oh, good. I'll bring her in.'

He makes his way to the door. Then stops and with a click of his fingers swivels around. 'Have you heard of a man called Tim Fountain, by any chance?'

'Didn't he write that play about Quentin Crisp?'

'Yes! That's him!' He nods his head so fast it looks like it's about to fall off. 'He's slept with over five thousand men, you know!'

And with that, he marches right out the door.

March 24th, 2008: A Twirling Roslyn

Three breaths later.

Jorge's serving a customer and I'm still on my seat, gazing outside, when I spot Simon again, this time with his arm wrapped around a woman about the same age. She's 'wearing' a bright yellow coat. I say 'wearing' because it's draped over her shoulders so that I'm not entirely sure if she has arms. They spot me and Simon starts waving furiously.

Act 2

'Clayton, this is Roslyn. I've told her all about you and how we met.'

Roslyn, who has a Dame Shirley Porter look about her, glides toward me and, as she glides, a hand slowly appears from beneath the coat, which she extends limply as if waiting for it to be kissed. I stand up, contemplating a curtsey.

'Pleased to meet you,' I say. Her hand moves closer, and somehow I end up shaking just two fingers of it. Roslyn looks down in disdain.

'This is Roslyn,' repeats Simon.

'I'm Roslyn,' says Roslyn.

I'm tempted to say, 'You must be Roslyn,' but what comes out is 'So... I hear you sing opera.'

Roslyn's eyes twinkle. 'I used to sing *Pagliacci* but now, whenever I think of Pagliacci, I think of that buffoon of a candidate for mayor. One weeps, Clayton. One weeps.' She dabs at an eye with a hanky.

I feel Simon's eyes boring into me. 'Don't tell her about the brothel,' he mouths, pointing above. All of a sudden he whips a wallet from his pocket and pulls out a dog-eared black-and-white postcard with a picture of a young boy sticking a finger up at the camera.

'Guess who?' he asks, holding the postcard to the side of his face.

'Er, you?'

'Bravo, Clayton!' sings Roslyn. 'Bravo!'

'Clayton, you're right—it's me!' Simon turns the card over and points at a telephone number. 'Call them if you don't believe me!'

'No. No. I believe you.' I examine the postcard again. 'You were very cute.'

'And you know what? You can still buy this postcard on Shaftesbury Avenue. Do you want the name of the shop?'

'Er, yes… That would be, er, nice. Although I'm not sure I'll get a chance to—'

'Here.' He hands me a business card. 'Tell them Simon sent you. You'll get a discount.'

Suddenly Roslyn starts to twirl for no apparent reason. By her second twirl one leg gives way and she totters toward our L'Homme Invisible underwear display (imported from France, very reasonably priced). I grab her arm to try to prevent her falling on the mannequin and ending up with a mouthful of polystyrene genitalia.

'Darling, we must depart,' Roslyn wheezes as she straightens a stiletto. 'Clayton has garments to sell.'

'Goodbye, Clayton,' says Simon, ushering Roslyn out the door. Then he brings his mouth to my ear and whispers, 'I've still got those platforms I used to wear to the brothel. They're under the bed. Don't tell Roslyn!'

To be continued (apparently).

March 25th, 2008: Coffee and Kitten Mules

11 am. I'm outside the little coffee shop on the corner of Old Compton Street and Frith Street, writing in my notebook. It's the perfect spot to sit and watch the ebb and flow of Soho life. Within seconds Pam spots me and trots over.

Now, anyone who has ever seen Pam in action will know that she has been blessed with extrasensory powers. She is able to detect a potential pound coin at 50 paces, and once her nose has sniffed out said coin, she homes in on it like a shark to menstrual blood. Here she comes now.

'I've missed you,' she sighs, gazing down at the change on the coffee table as if it's the coins she's addressing.

'Ahhhhh. That's nice of you, Pam.'

She tears her eyes away from her long-lost loves and stares at me. ''Ave you got two pound?'

'So much for small talk!'

'Wot?'

'Whatever happened to "Have you got a pound"?'

'Well, I ain't seen you for ages, 'ave I?' she fires back with twisted logic.

Feeling suitably chastised and in one of my 'what goes around comes around' moods, I fish the £2 coin from the table and hand it to her. Without so much as a goodbye, she beats a hasty retreat, chasing after a lone businesswoman on Frith Street like a lesbian Benny Hill.

A few minutes pass.

I take a sip of my coffee. It's lukewarm but I keep sipping anyway, not wanting to risk losing my seat by buying another. I'm waiting for my friend the pianist Martin Watkins, and he's not due for another 10 minutes. So I peruse the street while also trying to guard the spare seat next to me by resting my elbow on it and spreading my legs.

Another minute passes.

Now I'm conscious that my spread legs look a bit too spread, like I'm displaying 'the goods,' and as I try to decide whether to keep them spread or cross them, a guy walks out of the coffee shop and plonks himself down on the spare seat.

Great! Now what?

I glance across at him. He stares straight ahead. I glare at him out of the corner of my eye. (Try it—it's not easy.) Still no response. Hmmm. Maybe I should tell him that the seat is taken and that my friend Martin has just popped to the loo. But then what if Martin doesn't turn up for another 20 minutes? Will I have to explain that he's got bowel trouble and he may be a while?

The more I mull over the consequences (when Martin does arrive, would I have to continue down this route by asking in a loud voice, 'Have you tried eating boiled rice?'), the more the 'You're in my friend's seat' moment passes. So I reach forward and take another sip of my now iced latte. Just then, my mobile rings.

'Clay, I'll be there in five minutes. Just walking through Soho Square. Save me a seat!'

'Er, okay.'

I look to my right. There's only one other spare seat but it's not under the canopy and it looks like it's about to rain. So I move my chair a bit closer to Mr Chair Thief and then I pull the spare chair closer. There. Now the only problem is that I'm so close to Mr Chair Thief I'm practically sitting on his lap, and though a 'daddy' role-play scene is quite appealing, I don't think the nun sitting next to us would quite understand. Fortunately, before my imagination takes this scene any further, Martin arrives.

'Sorry I'm late. Do you want a coffee?'

'Yeah, a mocha, please.'

Two minutes later we're having a good natter, catching up on everything that's happened since we last saw each other. I tell him about the shop, he tells me about the projects he's been working on. Although we haven't known each other long, it feels like years, in a comfortable way, and the conversation flows.

'Clay, I have to tell you this story... You know I was telling you about that "swingers" site I use?'

'Yes.'

'Well, I was on the other night and this straight guy contacted me and he asked me to come round to his place.'

'Did you go?'

'Of course!'

'You weren't scared?'

'Naaahhh,' Martin replies, reaching for his coffee. 'So I got round there and it was on this really rough council estate. He opened the door and then he told me that there was another guy upstairs, and did I want to join them? I thought, Well, in for a penny. So I went upstairs and you'll never guess who was lying on the bed.'

'Who?'

'A really hunky, hairy guy.'

'And the problem was?'

'He was wearing a PVC nurse's outfit, suspenders and pink kitten mules!'

'Oh, no!'

'And he was blindfolded with an old tea towel.'

'Oh, God. So what did you do?'

'Well, the guy whose house it was didn't want to join in. I think he was a bit freaked out.'

'I can imagine.'

'So I tried to get down to business. But it wasn't really working, if you know what I mean.'

I laugh. 'I think I do. Yes.'

'So I said, "Would you mind taking the nurse's outfit off?"'

'And did he?'

'Well, he took it off. But he wasn't happy. And then it got even worse!'

'Why?'

'He had crotchless panties on underneath! So I said, "Look, I'm sorry mate, but it's not going to work unless you take everything off."'

Suddenly, Mr Chair Thief stands up and storms off. Very quickly. And very wide-eyed.

March 24th, 2008: A Mooning Mother

'Clayton! This is Mother!'

It's Simon. Again. Standing in the doorway supporting a very old woman who is bent over with age. They shuffle slowly toward me.

Simon's dressed in the same outfit as yesterday: striped jacket and polyester tracksuit bottoms. His hair's still ruffled and he's grinning, while his companion, her fine silver hair parted to one side, her complexion as silky-smooth as the Queen's, attempts to raise her head and wave. Once at the counter they position themselves. The old woman adjusts her hair and Simon clears his throat. I wait for them to speak. It's like an *X Factor* audition.

'Mother,' Simon says finally, 'this is Clayton.'

'Hello, it's a pleasure to meet you,' I reply, offering her my hand. She smiles back meekly and extends hers.

'Mother knows all about you,' Simon says with a smirk, as if I have a murky past that they're prepared to overlook. 'You used to work just near here, didn't you, Mother?'

'Oh, really?' I ask. 'Whereabouts?'

No response.

'At the Windmill Theatre on Archer Street,' answers Simon as Mother inches even closer in what looks like her bedroom slippers. 'Mother was a singer and a stripper back in the sixties. Do you want a quick performance?'

A vision of Mother stepping seductively out of a pair of M&S knickers appears. As if reading my mind Simon whispers reassuringly, 'Don't worry, she won't take 'em off.'

All of a sudden Mother throws back one hand and starts to sing. *"Moon River, wider than a mile..."* We both turn around and stare at her. Then she stops. Just as suddenly. Simon gives her a little nudge, as you would the arm of a record player. It works. *"Moon River, wider than a mile..."*

'She isn't really my mother,' whispers Simon as Mother

repeats the one line she seems to remember. 'We met in 1993 at one of Roslyn's theatrical parties. Her name's Meryl.'

"Moon River, wider than a mile…"

'Would you like to come to one of Roslyn's parties?' Simon asks.

'That would be, er…lovely.'

"Moon River, wider than a mile…"

'She only invites the crème de la crème of the theatre world.'

'Bunch of has-beens, more like!'

'Mother!' snaps Simon. 'That's not very nice!'

'It's true!' she cries. 'They're loonies, the lot of 'em!'

With that, Simon grits his teeth and, promising to be back soon, carefully ushers the singing mother slowly back out of the shop.

March 25th, 2008: Shutting Up Shop

'Lost a bit of weight, have you, dear?'

Angie swans in. Totally glammed up, as always. Hair pinned back, cheekbones to die for, cherry-black lipstick. Like a Hollywood actress from a bygone age.

'I've been running,' I reply.

'About time too, darlin!' she reprimands, taking the seat I offer her. 'You were startin' to pile on the pounds a bit.'

Ignoring the comment, I decide to ask her something. 'Angie?'

'Yeeeessssss,' she purrs as she settles in.

'I was wondering if… What I mean is, I was thinking—'

'Well, spit it out, then!'

'I wanted to write something about you and wondered if you'd mind.'

She narrows her eyes. 'Hmmm… There'd be my fee to consider, of course.' She says it in such a way that I can't make out if she's joking or not. Then she opens my laptop, logs on to her email account and says offhandedly, 'Oh, write what you want. Don't bovver me.'

While she's reading her emails I reach into the top drawer of the desk and take out my new voice recorder. Angie turns around in a flash, eyebrow rising like a deadly weapon. 'Wot's that?'

'Er…it's a voice recorder. You don't mind, do you?

'Oh, go on, then,' she tuts. 'If you must.'

I stand the recorder on the counter facing in Angie's direction, press Record and pull up a chair next to her. 'So… I thought I'd write about your bad dates.'

'Darlin', where do I begin? My life's bin a history of bad dates. Dysfunctional, the lot of 'em.'

'All of them?'

'All of them, darlin'! Oh, I've met lots of men, but no Romeos. They've all been disasters.' She lists them. 'I've been raped, strangled. I've dated a villain—'

'I remember you telling me about that one.'

'That was the one that burst me tits!' she shrieks, oblivious to the group of Italian tourists who have just descended on the shop. 'An' I've had to deal with all their issues. Oh, yes. Issues. Agendas. To be honest with you, Clay, I'd rather have a dog!'

One of the things I like about Angie is her way of describing really tragic circumstances and then throwing in a comic line at the end. What I'm not so taken with is the way her voice goes up a few decibels when she's on a roll, as it always seems to coincide with the rare moment when we've got a shop full of customers.

'You see, that's why I've always been a hooker,' she informs me at full volume, while the tourists peep nervously through the jeans rack. 'It's so much easier. They pay their money an' it's just business, innit?'

'When was your last relationship?' I whisper, hoping she'll follow my lead.

'Relationship? Me?' she shouts back. 'I don't think so! The last one I 'ad was with a confused actor. He just wanted to see me box. He was *intrigued*. I said to him, "I ain't yer bleedin' therapist, darlin'—get yer own box fitted if yer that interested!"

You see, Clay, most of the time they don't see me. They don't see Angie. They see the fantasy of Angie. I'm a walkin' fetish, darlin'—that's wot I am! Anyway, there'll be no more dates for a while. Not 'til I've gone to court.'

'What're you going to court for?'

'Me tits, darlin'!'

The tourists take a step back.

'Why, what's wrong with them?' I ask, thinking now is a good a time as any to find out.

'The bleedin' surgeon left non-dissolvable stitches in 'em. That's why they bin swellin' up. So I've gotta have 'em taken out.'

'Oh, poor you…'

She grabs my hand and thrusts it underneath her bra so that I'm now cupping her right breast.

'Can you feel 'em?'

'Er…I think so,' I reply nervously, not quite sure what's stitch and what's silicon.

The tourists edge back toward the doorway.

'Sooooo,' Angie sighs, 'I gotta go to court.'

'When are you going?' I ask, wondering what the etiquette is for hand removal.

'Oh, not for another year, darlin'!' I'm takin' on the whole medical profession. Little ol' me. I'm meetin' the nurse in a few minutes, actually. She's gonna be me witness. But I'll have no tits for six months!'

'Really?'

'Well, they can't put 'em back in 'til I've healed, darlin'! So there'll be no more punters for me. I'll have to shut up shop. Oh, yes. Angie'll be closed for repairs. Six months with no tits! Who'd have thought?' she shrieks, her voice now almost stripping the paint off the ceiling.

'That's terrible. How painful,' I say, wincing, as my fingers tiptoe quietly back out.

'Oh, I'm not bothered about the pain, darlin'. Once you've 'ad yer cock chopped off, what's a couple of tits? But I'll miss me girls.' She pats them affectionately. 'Oh, well. Luckily me la-la's all in workin' order.'

I quickly sit on my hands.

'I dyed it this mornin'. Well, I'm at that age,' she says. 'Grey pubes. Well, we all get 'em! But I 'ave to tell you, I'm lovin' that L'Oreal Ten. When I left this morning me fanny was a lovely shade of blue-black.'

Not surprisingly, when I next look up, the shop is completely customer-free.

March 25th, 2008: An Interested Party

Angie safely outside, I'm standing by the doorway, praying for more customers so that I can show Jorge some takings when he gets back from the gym, when a familiar face walks in.

'Hi! You've been in before.'

'Yes. Yes. I have,' says the tall, mixed-race gentleman. 'Er, the lady that just left... Do you know her name?'

'Yes. It's Angela. Angela Pasquale.'

'Angela Pasquale,' he murmurs, looking longingly down Old Compton Street, as if trying to will her back. Then, just about to leave, he says, 'You don't happen to know if she's single, do you?'

I think back to her recent dates. 'Yes, she is... Angie's definitely single.'

'You don't have her number, by any chance?'

'I do. But I couldn't—'

'Oh, yes, of course. Well, ummm, could you give her mine?'

'O. Kay,' I reply cautiously.

We walk to the counter and I write down his number.

'Could you please tell her that Robert was asking after her and, er... Could you tell her I'd like to take her to dinner.'

'Okay, Robert. No problem.'

As he leaves I think, Angie, I may have just found you a Mr Right.

March 26th, 2008: The Return of the Wolf

'Are you still coming to my dinner party?' Wolfy rushes into the shop, looking just as stressed as before. 'It is in June. It is a dinner party. Dinner party.'

Jorge jumps off his seat and rushes downstairs.

'You will come to my dinner party?' Wolfy pleads. 'I will be very upset if you do not come.'

'Er—'

'It is going to be a beautiful dinner party. For my birthday. I will be forty. It is a dinner party. Yes. I am training to be caterer. I hope my boyfriend comes. I will be very upset if he does not come. We are not getting on.'

You don't say.

'But I need black. Black and fitted.'

Oh, no—here we go.

'And it has to be plain. Oh, and black and—'

'It's Wolfy, isn't it?'

'Yes. It is,' he says, jerking his head nervously. 'How did you know?'

'You told me the last time you were here.'

'Oh.' A pause. 'But it has to be black and...'

OK. If I'm going to have to put up with this, the least he can do is buy something.

'...fitted and—'

'Wolfy.'

'—plain and—'

'WOLFY!'

'What?'

'I think we have something over here you're going to love.'

'Is it—'

'Yes! It's all the things you want.'

I lead him over to the rails, to the Costume National section, and I pull out a plain black, fitted shirt, noticing Jorge giggling on the stairway below as we pass.

'What do you think?' I ask, holding it up.

'Is it my size? Is it—'

'YES! IT'S YOUR SIZE' I whip off his T-shirt, push his arms through the sleeves, button it up in 0.1 of a second and drag him toward the dressing room mirror.

'There!'

He stares at himself. Runs his fingers through his black, heavily gelled hair. Frowns. 'But I need plain black—'

'It is plain black!'

'But it is not fitted.'

'It is fitted!' I insist through gritted teeth. 'Any fitter and your head'll pop off!'

More giggling from the stairway.

'But it is for my dinner party. Dinner party. And it needs to be—'

'OKAY!' I say, my hands turning to fists. 'If you want it even more fitted we can take it in for you.'

'Yes, please. Can you—'

'I don't know how to do it but I know someone who does.' The giggling on the stairway suddenly stops. 'Jorge!' I sing. 'You have a customer!'

'Bastard!'

March, 26th 2008: The Mermaid

I dial Sebastian's number.

'*Yeeessssss?*'

'It's Clay.'

'*Oh, hullo, my darling. I'm just receiving a blow job. Could you call me back?*'

'I, er, just wanted to know if you're free for dinner tonight?'

'*Yes. Lovely… Lovely.*'

'That's a deal, then?'

'*Sorry. I was speaking to the lady below. What did you say?*'

'Dinner tonight? On me?'

'*Oh, that's very kind of you. But what with the poverty we're*'

97

both going through, I am reluctant to be treated in any way. You could always post some crisps through my letterbox?'

'What about The Mermaid? That's cheap.'

'Oh, why not. Let us loosen the corsets of life and fondle her breasts. I'll see you there at seven.'

There's a moan and then the line goes dead.

* * *

We're inside the Lorelei Restaurant on Bateman Street (aka The Mermaid). Sebastian's wearing a flamingo-pink silk suit, a silk tie peppered with diamante and one of his famous shirts, The Horsley Shirt, which has a four-button cuff, a five-inch collar point (wide enough to fly), and covered buttons ('Clayton, there is something so rude about a naked button. It's like peeping up an old lady's bottom.').

We place our orders.

I notice Sebastian appears to be down, so I ask him if he's all right after the New York episode.

'Oh, I'm okay, I suppose.'

'It's been all over the press.'

'Yes. Well. The press have been quite supportive. Even *The Guardian*, would you believe? But there have been some that have not been so pleasant.'

'Like who?'

'Oh, that old friend of mine, Will Self, for instance. Mind you, what does he know? Will's life has been one long descent into respectability. He's just jealous because he couldn't get thrown out of a Greenpeace barn dance.'

I laugh. 'Your sales must've gone up, though?'

'The book is out across the States. And I am all over the newspapers. But then a stranger said to me outside the cash point machine this morning, "Now you are rich and famous." The machine didn't seem to agree, though. Not only did it not recognise me but it had the gall to insult me. "You can only withdraw ten pounds!" it said. Clay, I am completely broke.

It's very annoying. I was due to see Sonia, one of my favourite whores, today. She won't give me credit either. It is pay as you enter.'

The Italian waitress brings over our food. We start eating. Then I ask, 'Are you really that poor?'

'Yes, my darling. I shoplifted some sausages for breakfast. Oh, well. I'd rather have fame than riches. I'm all fur coat and no knickers. A cowboy with a five-dollar house and forty-dollar saddle.' He reaches for his drink and takes a sip. 'Fortunately I have credit at The Ivy. I sold them a painting and they are going to pay me in nosh. So I shall go there for breakfast. And lunch. And dinner. Until it's all used up. But then what?' He sounds desperate. 'Oh, Clayton, darling, what am I going to do? Will the book make any money?'

'Oh, I'm sure it will,' I say soothingly, trying to reassure him. 'You're a famous writer now.'

'The problem is, I'm not really a writer at all. Or an artist, for that matter. I am a dandy. And the difficulty of recreating the quality of a dandy is almost insurmountable. They are not interesting for what they write, or for what they make, but for something that they are.' He places his glass back on the table. 'And who could have come up with me? If I had never existed, it is unlikely that anyone would have had the nerve to invent me. Even I, inventing myself, had my doubts.'

'But you have had some good reviews,' I say encouragingly.

He thinks for a few seconds. But looks unconvinced. 'Actually, my darling, they've been quite mixed. It did hurt initially when I read the bad ones. But I try to remember: men are not against you, they are merely for themselves. We are all prejudiced in favour of ourselves. Once I realised that, life became easier.' He takes another sip of his drink. 'Balls, Clayton. Balls. Most people don't raise their head above the parapet lest it get neatly sliced off. Not us, my friend. We need to be warriors.'

'Why, what have people been saying?'

'Oh, nasty stuff. Some people reviewed the book without even reading it! My view was, if you don't like what you think will be in my book, don't fucking read it then, you twat! And if you can't help yourself reading it and you don't like it—write your own! Either way, leave mine alone.' He's momentarily angry. Which is unusual for Sebastian. But then he checks himself and continues calmly, 'But getting upset is really just a personal choice. You can't control what other people do, only the way you react to what they do. If other people annoy you, it is not they who are being annoying, it is you who are being annoyed. Remember, Clayton, some praise from politeness; others criticise from vanity.' He reaches for his napkin and lightly dabs at the corners of his mouth. I wait for him to continue. 'But who cares? Popularity is the one insult I have never suffered. And what is fame anyway? It is but a vapour. An illusion. The only earthly certainty is oblivion.' He taps me on the arm and smirks. 'By the way, I met your voluptuous friend Juliette the other day at a book signing. She ordered me to spend the money she paid me for my book on whores. Do you think she will come over for eight pound ninety-nine pence?'

I laugh.

'Anyway, enough of me, I have news for you.' He suddenly seems genuinely pleased. 'I have reviewed your book and I sent the review off to the *New Statesman* and they are going to publish it.'

'Really?' I gasp.

'Yes! Although they have rather cut it, unfortunately. And when I asked for a fee I was told by the editor, "The glory of merely being solicited for your opinion in the company of Peter Mandelson and Will Self is meant to be repayment enough." In my book that is punishment not payment.'

'Ah, well, that was very nice of you.'

'Darling, as I've said before—us minorities need to stick together. This is only fun if we both enjoy it. All we need is a little powder and a sparkle or two to explode most gloriously.

We must keep on being inspired. The mind learning. The heart burning. The wallet earning.'

When I met Quentin Crisp he was in his 80s and the persona he'd created had become so impenetrable he would converse in quotes, quotes I'd heard many times before. No matter how much I tried, no matter what question I threw his way, he batted back answers like a shuttlecock over a net. Sebastian's not yet at that stage. His persona is still under construction. You can still delve beneath the surface. He does quote. A lot. And his aphorisms regularly make their way into newspapers and will, no doubt, be handed down in the years to come. So it's an interesting stage in which we've met. In fact, meeting Sebastian is one of the highlights of my life.

Once outside on the street we say our goodbyes.

'Bye, Sebastian. I'll see you soon.'

Towering above me in his Paul Stanley-style platforms, with their seven-inch heels, he is at least six foot nine. 'Remember, Clayton,' he says gently, stroking my cheek, 'Armageddon is coming for us all. Which is all very well, but one must always be dressed for it.' Then he bends down and plants a kiss on my lips. 'Until the lights go out for us all and the waters wash over us. Goodbye, my darling.'

March 27th, 2008: Protection

I'm leaning against the shop window, having a few minutes' break, watching the world go by.

Outside The Groucho a guy sits and begs. Homeless, friendless, toothless, he's a Soho regular. He's cheerful and upbeat. Until the next hit of crack, that is. I look down Dean Street toward the French House. A few customers are drinking outside; the tall guy who dresses in 50s suits, The Rubbishmen, Nervous Stephen, Hilary Penn the manageress, everyone making the most of the sun's rays, which creep down the street, lighting it up like a yellow brick road all the way down to theatre-land.

And then, walking past Paradiso Boudoir, I spot Pam. Her face scrunched up like a newborn puppy, eyes whizzing from side to side, on the lookout for a generous local.

Then, just as I'm about to head back inside, a vision stomps toward me. Bottle-blonde mane swishing from side to side, hips and breasts a-go-go, trackie bottoms and a face of thunder. It's Sue. The Soho madam.

'Hi, Sue!'

Her mouth morphs from grimace to grin. 'Hi, Clay, wot's going on?'

'Not much really,' I reply cheerfully.

I have a deep respect for Sue. Running a brothel for 12 years in the heart of Soho, dealing with violent drunks, an ineffective police force, drug dealing in her doorway, all the usual problems associated with trying to run a Soho business, Sue's a shining example of how to survive, and she does it by the sheer force of her personality and the respect she's built up from police and criminals alike. No one messes with Sue. No one. I've seen a few try, but they only ever try once. Sue rules this corner like Margaret Thatcher guarding the Falklands. Step out of line and she'll sink you. She has the same peroxide mane, the same steely stare, ready to wallop you with her (Tesco's) handbag if you disagree. But as well as being an assertive ruler, just like Mrs T, Sue also has a good business head. She watches the pennies. And though she has fewer customers at the moment (people even cut back on blow jobs when the going gets tough) Sue's not gone yet and I'm sure she'll still be here when the majority of the businesses have shut up shop. Sue created this empire and she intends to keep it.

'You 'ad any trouble 'ere recently?' she asks.

I clear my throat. 'Just the usual.'

'Wot's that, then?'

Why's Sue asking me this? Is she about to offer me protection? I catch my breath. Protection from Sue would be like UN backing.

'Well, we've had twelve gang attacks since we've been here,' I explain.

'Twelve?' she says, 'Bleedin' hell! Wot 'ave the police done?'

'What do they ever do? They turn up half an hour later and ask, "Where are they?"'

'Typical. Never 'ere when ya need 'em.'

'We've even had a panic button fitted that we pay five hundred pounds a year for.'

'An' it don't work?'

'Nah... They turn up twenty-five minutes later instead of thirty. And then they had the cheek to say they're going to withdraw the service because the gang wasn't here when they arrived!'

'Like they're gonna 'ang around!'

'Exactly!'

'Listen,' she says with a knowing wink. 'You get any more trouble, you just let me know.'

'Er...thank you, Sue... We will.'

With a flick of her highlights she stomps off. So I skip back inside the shop and tell Jorge we need never worry again—Sue is finally on our side.

March 27th, 2008: 1982

The phone rings. Jorge reaches for the handset.

'Hello, Dirty White Boy.'

'Jorge?'

'Yes.'

'It's Chico.'

'Hi, Chico! How're you?'

I stand up quickly, eavesdropping.

'Not good.'

'Why?'

'I'm...' The line goes quiet as if he's choosing his words. *'I'm...positive.'*

I catch Jorge's eye. He's calm and carries on talking. 'When did you find out?'

'Today.'

'Chico, it's okay. You're going to be all right.'

'You sure?' Chico sounds distraught. *'I didn't know who to speak to. An'—'*

'All my friends are positive,' Jorge says.

There's a pause.

'Really?'

'One of them has been positive for twenty-six years. He was diagnosed in 1982.'

Another pause.

'Jorge, I... I never—'

'And look, he's still here! So, take it from me—you're going to be all right.'

And as Jorge reassures him, telling him who he should speak to, what medications are available, what to read up on, I think about how much Jorge's been through: losing a whole address book full of friends and lovers back in the 80s, living through the plague years long before AZT (let alone combination therapy), seeing friends being experimented on by baffled doctors (who injected the fluid from the thyroid gland of a cow into one friend, who removed a lymph node from the back of the neck of another while he was still awake), caring for them, attending funerals and remembrances, comforting their families—having to go through all those things while a whole generation fell around him. I think how lucky I am to have met him, to have fallen in love with him, to have someone like him enriching my life.

'Look, call me whenever you want. Okay?' he says.

'Thank you, honey,' says Chico. *'I feel better now. Give my love to Clay.'*

Jorge throws me a smile. 'I will. Bye, Chico.'

And as he puts the handset back down, I kiss him tenderly

on the forehead. Then we open up the shop, ready to face another day.

March 29th, 2008: Leslie Owns Up

I'm not sure what its name is. This coffee shop. The blue one on the corner of Old Compton Street and Frith Street. But there's something about it that I like. It feels like the real deal, as if it's been here for years. Plus, you can always get a seat. And this is where I sit when I want to get away from the shop, tucked away in the corner, by the window, watching Soho life drift by.

'Your change!'

I turn to face the Italian assistant. She smiles politely. Brushes a lock of auburn hair from her face and pushes a plate toward me.

'Thank you.'

I swivel back in my seat. Stir my coffee and watch a couple of fashion queens mince by.

It's busy for a Monday. The drift from 'media crowd' to 'party crowd' is a couple of hours away. I take a sip of my drink. Then the door opens and a blast of icy air sweeps inside. And that's when I spot him, through the open door, the crowds around him parting like stage sets as he sails through. A beige, mid-length coat, a paisley silk scarf, a tan leather shoulder bag and of course the hair, parted perfectly. Faded glamour. Faded Soho. Soho, so long ago.

He reaches the crossroads. Checks his watch. And I mine. Three o'clock, dead-on. He tilts back his head, surveys the coffee shop, then that wry smile as he spots me. I quickly pull up a chair, order another coffee and seconds later we're chatting away and the time apart departs.

We chat for half an hour or so. The shop. His friend Dolly. General stuff, nothing important. Although there is something important that I want to talk about.

'I meant to ask… How's Charlie?'

There's a pause. Then Leslie says, 'Good,' though he's slightly defensive, not quite as talkative as he was just minutes before.

'Have you seen him recently?'

'Not for a couple of days, ducky.' His voice is brisk. 'You know our Charlie. Keeps 'imself busy.'

'But it's going okay between the two of you?'

He glances in my direction, eyes narrowing suspiciously. 'Oh, fine, dear. Fine… Now, did I tell you about Dolly—'

'He came into the shop.'

Silence.

Leslie takes a sip of coffee. Then it's as if all the background noise, the hum from the coffee machine, the shouting from the street, people chatting on stools nearby, it's as if someone's pressed the Mute button and it all fades away until it's just our voices left.

'So, anyway,' Leslie continues, completely ignoring me, 'Dolly's not sure what—'

'I asked him about your holiday.'

Leslie freezes, coffee cup poised at his lips. I decide to tread with caution. 'Leslie?'

'What?' he snaps, without looking at me.

'You haven't seen Charlie, have you.'

He places his cup carefully back down on the counter. Purses his lips and looks out the window. I'm about to prompt him again when he says, 'No. No, I haven't seen Charlie.'

'I don't understand.'

He licks a forefinger and runs it along his eyebrow, up and down his eyebrow, they way he does when he's deep in thought. The waitress walks over, wipes the counter in front of us. Once she's gone Leslie says, 'Not everything is what it appears to be.'

'What do you mean?'

'Just that.'

I decide not to interrupt. To let him open up. Which, gradually, he does.

'I thought it was everything.' His voice is quieter now, as though he's not really speaking to me at all. 'I thought I'd never be alone again. No hassles. No one pointing. I thought together none of that would matter. That nothing would ever harm us... But I was wrong. Something did harm us. Charlie harmed us.'

'But that was over forty years ago. It was so long ago.'

His head turns sharply. 'To you, maybe!'

'So why did you go and see him in hospital, then?'

'To see if he was real... To lay him to rest.'

'But you could still have a future.'

'Could we?' He arches an eyebrow. 'Ducky, look at me. I'm an old queen. Oh, I know the person I've become,' he adds guardedly. 'But it's who I am now and I've learned to live with it. But to be gallivanting off on some crazy love affair. No, ducky. Not at my age. One broken heart is quite enough, thank you very much.'

'But you just don't know—'

'I don't want to know!' he snaps back. 'This is who I am now. And quite frankly I'm happy with it!'

I leave it a few seconds before continuing. 'But what if this was the way it was meant to be?'

'Oh, I don't believe in all that mumbo jumbo! All that stars colliding rubbish. No, ducky. I may be a washed-up old queen. But I'm a contented washed-up old queen. An' I don't want nothin' upsettin' the apple cart. Not at my age.'

Now we're both looking out the window.

'It's such a shame... Because I know Charlie would have you back in an instant.'

'Perhaps,' Leslie replies archly. 'But Charlie wants what Charlie has always wanted. He wants a rock to cling to. I wasn't a strong enough rock back then, so he found another one. And now... Well, I've no feelings left. For him or anyone else, for that matter. I shut all that business out a long time ago.'

'Couldn't you at least be friends?'

'Ducky, I've got all the friends I need! There's Dolly. There's the girls from the Bloomsbury Association. There's the Opera Club—'

'I think you're making a mistake.'

'Well,' he sniffs. 'You're entitled to your opinion but it won't change mine. And now, *if* you don't mind, I'd like to change the subject.'

So we do. And we carry on talking, just general chitchat again. But it's strained. We finish, say our goodbyes and I step outside, leaving him to finish his coffee. Then, for some reason, I look back. And I see Leslie reaching into his coat pocket, pulling out an embroidered hanky and dabbing at his eyes, staring straight ahead, thinking back to what might have been.

April 2008

April 2nd, 2008: An Invitation

The phone rings.

'Hello, Dirty White Boy. Clayton speaking.'

'Oh, you're still alive, then.'

'Sorry?'

'I said, You're still alive, then.'

'Who is this?'

'Simon.'

'Simon?'

'Don't tell me you've forgotten me already.'

'I, er—'

'I came into your shop with Roslyn.'

I pause for a second. 'Oh, Simon! Sorry. How are you?'

'Did you know a bomb landed just outside your shop during the war?'

'Er... No, I—'

'Four people were killed. Legs everywhere! And Saint Anne's. That got hit too. Took them forty years to repair the damage. Not that I remember it, of course. I'm still in my prime! Ha-ha! Anyway, Roslyn's having one of her parties on Saturday nineteenth and we wondered if you were free.'

'Er...'

'At eight o'clock.'

'Well, I—'

'Oh, good. That's settled, then. It's not far from you, either.

It's on Frith Street.' He tells me the address. *'Roslyn's so excited. She's told all her friends that you're coming.'*

'That's—'

'So we'll see you on Saturday! Don't be late!'

Click.

April 8th, 2008: St Anne's

Tuesday morning. We're walking up Dean Street. The sky is charcoal grey, a fine aerosol-like mist in the air, which, by the time we reach The French House, quickly turns to rain.

'Come on!' I shout to Jorge, who is tagging along behind. I run toward St Anne's, the church sandwiched between an old Victorian building and Denny's Uniforms, the catering clothing company. I push open the metal gates and we walk in, standing in the entrance by the stone plaque commemorating the church's opening by Lord Henry Compton in 1677.

As it looks like we'll be here for a while, I walk down the narrow passageway, through the double doors, beckoning Jorge to follow me until we're inside the church. For a few seconds we stand at the back watching a service. There're a handful of people scattered amongst the pews, some sitting, some standing. The light filtering through the stained glass window and the solemnity of the place, the austere grandeur, make me feel like a trespasser. Just as I'm about to turn back, Jorge whispers, 'Look who it is!'

I follow his line of vision, scanning the seats, the local residents—different ages, nationalities, backgrounds, sexualities, a microcosm of Soho life, all reading from a prayer book.

'Whereabouts?' I whisper back.

'At the front!'

I look toward the altar, at a tall podium on the right, behind which an elderly man addresses the audience. He's wearing a long white robe, glasses, with wispy black/grey hair. It's Charlie!

'What's he doing here?' I whisper again.

'Don't know.'

As the service draws to an end we position ourselves at the back, allowing the congregation to pass down the aisle while we wait for him to finish. Moments later he comes rushing toward us.

'Well, if it isn't my Dirty White Boys,' he says, smiling, with a raise of his bushy black eyebrows. 'Have you come to ask for God's forgiveness?'

'No, we—'

'And what a coincidence. Today, of all days.'

'Why's that?'

He steps closer, points toward his crotch and whispers, 'I'm wearing one of your L'Homme Invisible thongs under here. The gold lamé.'

'No!'

He steps back and grins. 'Oh, yes, my child.'

'You're wearing a thong under there?'

'Shhhhhh!'

I lower my voice. 'But isn't that sacrilegious?'

'Of course not!' he laughs. 'I'm sure our Lord would want me to be cradled comfortably while I address His flock, don't you?'

'I suppose.'

'And the reading was perfect, was it not?'

'Yes,—'

'You see, when Rodney's in the right position everything just flows. And I must say, the feel of the cloth against the bare bottom certainly adds a touch of je ne sais quoi to the proceedings.'

I bite my lip, trying not to laugh. Then I have a thought. 'Charlie, we've been invited to a party on Frith Street next week. Would you like to come with us?'

He beams. 'It'd be a pleasure, my dear. Oh, and I can wear my new dragon-patterned thong! Now—how about a glass of church wine?'

April 8th, 2008: Howard Hughes

A man's just walked in, sweating profusely, disheveled hair, wearing a mud-spattered T-shirt, a whiff of body odour following him around the shop.

He stops by the swimwear section. Pulls out a navy-blue pair by Iceberg. Then he walks over to the counter and drapes them across the glass. 'I'll take these,' he says, gazing down at them approvingly. 'But can I have a pair that's still in the packaging? I'm paranoid about germs.'

April 8th, 2008: The Absence of God

We're at Raqib's studio and I'm staring at a painting titled *The Absence of God*.

There're other people milling about, champagne being poured into long-stemmed glasses, hash brownies on a silver tiered cake stand, conversation, laughter. But I'm not with them. I'm somewhere else. Engrossed. The hallucinogenic effect of the cake coupled with the drink is making my head swim. I look across at Raqib, who's staring at his work.

'What does it mean?' I ask.

He raises an eyebrow and smirks mischievously. 'Claytee, sweets... You wrote about what you went through in your book. Well...this is what I've been through.'

We stare at the painting in silence. Behind us, more people, more conversation, more laughter. And then Raqib drifts off. Or at least I think he does—I'm not really aware anymore. I'm on my own. Glass in hand, staring. My head spinning, slowly but pleasurably, like that heady feeling you get just after you've taken a sleeping tablet, just before you drift away. Which I'm doing now—drifting away while the painting draws me slowly in.

The first thing I see is the naked babies. Three of them. Skewered. Screaming babies with erect cocks, pliers attached to the veined shafts, cutting into the skin. It's shocking but fascinating. My eyes follow the skewer. Humans with animal heads wearing bejeweled S/M harnesses. Monkeys being stabbed, holding up their entrails on meat hooks. Blood and guts spilling down the canvas. An orgy of mystical creatures in an enchanted forest. It's a real head-fuck. And in the middle, bursting out of one of the animals, a huge erect cock, like Cleopatra's Needle. Tall, straight. Dripping diamond-encrusted blood from cuts that circle the shaft. Shooting a stream of white cum. Like a billowing cum cloud orgasm that's about to shower the mayhem below. And all this set on an orange background, on a round canvas. The overall effect, concave, pulling you in, deeper and deeper.

I take another sip of champagne, feeling dizzy but transfixed, vaguely aware of music somewhere behind me.

'Come on, Claytee! Let's go downstairs and see the flowers. Come on!'

I turn my head. Raqib's by my side, Jorge next to him. I try to focus. 'Sorry, I was…somewhere…' Then I take Raqib's hand, walk slowly down the stairway and sink into his velvet settee, surrounded by a roomful of red and white roses, a sea of roses that stretches as far as the eye can see.

April 9th, 2008: A Pistol in Your Pocket

It's 8 pm.

Jorge's cashing up, his nose nestled in the accounts book. I'm staring aimlessly out the window, counting QX hookers outside Costa. Everything's quiet and peaceful. The day almost at an end.

Then, out the corner of my eye, I glimpse an enormous white shape tearing across the street, blonde tresses flying, bawling something undecipherable into a mobile. It's Sue! I watch, wide-eyed, as she storms through the brothel doorway and up the stairway like a stampeding elephant, the clomp! clomp! clomp! of her Nike trainers echoing around the shop.

I catch Jorge's eye. We both shrug. What was that all about?

Suddenly there's an almighty CRASH!

'What the fuck was that?'

'God knows!'

Our eyes travel up to the ceiling, expecting the brothel to come crashing down at any second, a sea of naked bodies, women in suspenders, men in nurse's outfits, sprawled at our feet.

CRASH!

'What's going on?' says Jorge.

'I'm going up there!' I say, jumping out of my seat.

'Wait for me!'

We lock the shop door, rush past the bemused passersby, through the brothel doorway, racing up the dimly-lit stairway, holding on to the rickety wooden banister, running up the stairs two at a time, until we're outside the first-floor flat.

I turn to face Jorge, panting. 'Now what?'

'Well, knock and see if everything's okay!'

Knock! Knock! Knock!

'GET THE FUCK OFF ME!' screams a woman's voice.

'I'VE GOT 'IM!' screams another.

The door flies open.

For a second I'm rooted to the spot, staring at arms and legs flailing, hair being pulled, a T-shirt being ripped, a man's back, bleached-blonde hair, bountiful breasts, girls screaming and swearing, ripping and riding, like grappling sumo wrestlers—and somewhere underneath, a bald man with his arm bent behind his back crying out in pain.

''E'S GOTTA GUN!' screams Sue.

'CLAY, THE GUN!' bawls Maggie.

Oh my God! Is this really happening? Jorge pushes me aside, dives onto the floor and grabs it. Then he pulls a face. 'It's a water pistol!'

'A WATER PISTOL?' yells Sue, and she pushes the man out the door. 'GET THE FUCK OUTTA HERE!'

Maggie kicks him in the bum. 'AN' DON'T FUCKIN' COME BACK!'

The man, who appears to be drunk, falls outside in a heap, attempts to get up again, then staggers down the stairway, holding onto the walls for support, mumbling obscenities as he leaves. 'Fuckin' bunch o' lezzies!'

Maggie slams the door. Leans against it. 'Sorry 'bout that, boys,' she says, seemingly unconcerned. 'There's always one tryin' to get away without payin'.'

'Yeah, fanks for that!' adds Sue, patting Jorge on the back. 'We owe yer one.'

While we're deciding whether we should call the police, a bedroom door creaks open. We stop talking, look around. Out steps a tall pale man in a stovepipe top hat and a red sequined suit.

'Sebastian!'

'Is there a problem?' he drawls as he elegantly zips up his flies.

April 10th, 2008: Back to Black (and Fitted)

11 am. I open the doors to the shop, letting out the musky smell that's drifted up from our damp underground flat, allowing the fresh breeze to flood in. Jorge's turning on the lights, the alarm, about to start polishing the glass display cases. Both of us getting ready for what we hope will be a profitable day. Then we take our seats, Jorge behind the counter, me on my little red chair. The stage is set. And the first customer of the day is...

'Oh, hi, Wolfy.'

'I had to see you both. I had to. Yes. So many things have happened. I am caterer. You know that. Yes? I told you I am caterer. From Denmark. My boyfriend. It is my fortieth birthday. Dinner party. Yes. Dinner party. In June.'

He rushes up to the counter, running his fingers through his hair, looking fraught. Jorge leans back in his seat. 'Wolfy, are you okay?'

Wolfy's eyes are wide and he's sweating, words spilling out of his mouth like an erupting volcano. 'I am having dinner party. Dinner party. And I need clothes. Fitted. Black. Has to be black. Has to be—'

'Wolfy, we have all the clothes you need. Whatever you want. But you need to calm—'

'But, but, but—it is for my dinner party. Dinner party.'

'Yes, we know. It's for your dinner party,' Jorge replies soothingly, trying to slow the pace of the conversation. Wolfy looks from me to Jorge and back to me again. 'Will you come to my dinner party? It is in June. I tell you the date now. Eleventh June. Please write it down. It is my dinner party. Eleventh June.'

Jorge walks from behind the counter and puts an arm around Wolfy's shoulder. 'We'll be there. Now, just—'

Wolfy throws off his arm. 'IT'S FINISHED!'

Jorge takes a step back.

'Me and my boyfriend!'

Jorge glances in my direction, then back at Wolfy, who's started to cry.

'He, he, he...' he stutters, overcome by sobs. 'He said, he said... He, he, he does not care about the dinner party. And he, he...' Reaching into his pocket, he pulls out a grubby handkerchief and blows his nose at full velocity. 'He said I talk too much.'

Surely not.

Wolfy reaches for Jorge's hand. 'You do not think I talk too much, do you?'

'Who, me? I, er—no, I, er...I just think you're a very, er, what's the word?' Jorge flashes me a look of panic. I mouth the word *sociable*.

'Sociable! That's what you are, Wolfy. You're a very sociable person.'

He looks into Jorge's eyes, beseechingly. 'But it is my fortieth birthday. And it was going to be such a beautiful dinner party. Dinner party. And now... He, he...'

'Come on, Wolfy,' I add carefully. 'It's going to be all right.'

'Yeah. Come on. Everything will be okay,' Jorge confirms. 'You can still have a fabulous dinner party. Just because you and your boyfriend have split up doesn't mean you can't have a great night.'

He blows his nose again. 'You really think so?'

'Really! How many friends have you invited?'

'Just you two.'

Well, I suppose it'll make a change from The Stockpot.

April 10th, 2008: Thames Water

It's 9 pm. We've just closed. The stress of the day finally at an end. So I sit down to finish my Thames Water Compensation Form, targeted at local shop owners affected by the ongoing building work.

Please use the space below to add any further comments.

Oh, goody. I start writing.

Dear Thames Water,

1. Your green wire fences have become a real eyesore and Old Compton Street now resembles a gigantic pig-pen. I know that there are a few on this street that would benefit from being caged, but please remember that Soho is the centre for all things creative. So how about decorating the fences? I would suggest a few velvet drapes, some sparkly bits, or, failing that, a row of hand-cuffed drag queens.

2. I often sit by my window gazing outside. Unfortunately, for the past seven months this view has been completely obstructed by builders. Now, I like a man in a uniform as much as the next queen, but enough is enough. I'm ODing on bum crack. So, by

way of a contrast, could you perhaps provide the odd toned and freshly washed buttock instead?

3. While we're on the subject of builders, let's talk about their working hours, i.e., start time 8 am, finish time 1 pm. Now, maths was never my strong point at school (I excelled at cookery) but even I can see that there's a correlation between hours worked and the length of time you've been here. (By the way, could you remove your 'We Won't Be Here For Long' sign? The paint's faded.)

4. Moving on now to the difficult matter of compensation...

You are no doubt aware of the credit crunch. Shops in Soho are closing on a daily basis. And on top of this we have your building work affecting sales. It'll be a miracle if this street survives. So unless you'd like to see Soho transformed into Bluewater, can I suggest that you take our compensation claims more seriously—as having to wait six months to receive the equivalent of an Oyster Card 'top-up' doesn't really help.

Finally, I do appreciate that the water pipes have been here since God was a lad and need to be replaced. My only concern is that I might not live long enough to appreciate the result.

Yours, in desperation,
Clayton Littlewood

April 11th, 2008: A Phone Call
'Is that Clayton?'

'Yes.'

'This is the Chaplain from HMP Littlehey... Chico asked me to call you. There's no easy way to say this... Chico was admitted to hospital today. He has three tumours on his lungs...

It's terminal, I'm afraid. The initial prognosis was that he had another two years, although, after further tests, realistically, it's probably more like two months.'

Silence.

'I... I can't believe it.'

'I know. It's very sad. Everyone loves Chico here, you know. He's very popular with the staff and the inmates. We're really going to miss him.'

I'm still holding the phone five minutes after the call has ended.

April 11th, 2008: Ben

There's a young boy leaning against the shop window as I type this. I haven't seen him for well over a year. Ben is his name and he's barely in his twenties.

Rent boy, dealer, pimp, thief—Ben's seen it all, done it all, had it all. And to prove it he adopts an all-knowing street hustler pose, which, in the age of the *QX* hookers, with their chiseled bodies and their glossy ads, is unusual. But the other thing that's unusual about Ben is that he's strictly 'gay for pay'. He views himself as 'straight'.

I watch him watching the crowds, his eyes flitting from side to side (punter or police? friend or foe?), smiling broadly each time a well-dressed businessman walks past ('Step right up! Everyone a winner!'). It's an elaborate game and he plays it to perfection. As I watch, waiting for someone to bite, I start to wonder where he's been. So, intrigued, I close my laptop and step outside to find out.

'Hi, Ben!'

He looks around, sizes me up. Throws me a look that is half grin, half snarl. As cocky and confident as I remember, with the same grubby sky-blue track jacket, the same patchy, youthful stubble, the same inquisitive, fox-like face.

'Whatta ya lookin' for?' he says, and he puffs out his chest, making the most of his small frame.

'Nothing. It's just that I haven't seen you for a while.'

I step closer. His eyes follow a guy crossing the street. Then he drops his guard and says, 'Bin in prison, innit.'

'Oh, okay. That explains it.'

Now he's watching two men outside Soho Books. I'm about to ask what he was in prison for when he adds, 'Got done for robbery.'

'Did you do it?'

'Yeah,' he brags. ''Course.'

It seems silly to ask why. Patronising, in a way. After all, as hard as it is at the shop, we have a roof over our head, food, each other.

He digs into his pocket. Pulls out a half-smoked cigarette, lights it, holding the cigarette between thumb and forefinger, smoking it in an exaggeratedly masculine manner. He reminds me of myself at his age: in Soho, around Brewer Street, or outside Marc Almond's recording studio in St Anne's Court, hanging out with all the other waifs and strays, clubbing at the Asylum or The Bat Cave and then, still high on speed, at The Pink Panther on Wardour Street, an after-hours club frequented by trannies, criminals and rent boys.

Ben takes another drag and looks in my direction. 'I learnt a lot inside.'

'Did you?' I reply offhandedly, still thinking back to my own past and the boyfriend I had at the time. Then I snap back to the present. 'Sorry, er... What about friends? Did you make any friends?'

He screws up his face. 'Nah—don't need 'em.'

I don't respond. And we stand there for a further minute without speaking. Then, without saying goodbye, I step back inside and watch him by the window for a few more seconds. Watching him, watching the crowds. Then, strangely subdued, I head downstairs to bed.

April 14th, 2008: Handcuffs

It's a shock at first, seeing him in there. An ex-drag queen, thin, fragile, riddled with cancer, in his lungs, his spine, lying on a hospital bed.

There's a cannula strapped to his wrist and my eyes follow the tube as it snakes its way up his arm to a bag of clear liquid hanging from a tall stand. Then I notice the other wrist. It's handcuffed. A large, gleaming, metal handcuff is attached to a prison officer seated nearby. It catches me off guard, the whole scene. I mean, I knew it wasn't going to be easy, but I wasn't expecting this. So I take a deep breath, try not to look surprised and step into the room.

As if sensing my presence Chico turns his head. His eyes widen. His expression changes. He looks happy.

'Honey!' he says excitedly, arms outstretched, jolting the seated prison officer awake. 'You're here!'

Then I notice that there's someone else in the room. Another prison officer, a woman. Two prison officers guarding a dying man? I feel myself tensing up again. I want to tell them to fuck off but instead I force a thin smile, edge around the room and take a seat on the bed.

'Do you want a chair?' asks the female officer politely from somewhere behind me.

'No, thanks,' I grunt back without turning.

It's an unreal situation. I want to hug Chico, tell him everything will be all right. But of course it won't. I'm speechless. I'm conscious, too, of the officers listening to our every word. I try to blank them out, focus on Chico's face: his cheeks, slightly sunken now, indentations just below the eyes large enough to put a finger in, his parched lips, crisscross cracked. A black bandana is tied around his shaven head. His silver earrings match his handcuffs.

Looking at him, being this close, I can't believe he won't be here in just a few months. He's become such a part of my life.

I try to look cheerful, try to disguise what I'm thinking. I've been through this before with friends, lovers. You'd think it'd get easier. I reach over, stroke his arm. 'Chico. I, I don't know what to say.'

The whites of his eyes are really white, lined with tears, welling up, but not quite heavy enough to fall. He reaches for a box of tissues on the bedside table and wipes them away anyway.

'You don't have to say anythin',' he sniffs. 'I'm just glad you're here.'

He tells me about the chemo that starts next week, the antibiotics that he's on to alleviate the AIDS-related pneumonia, the radiotherapy treatment, and how he just wants to get out of hospital, out of prison, back with his sisters in the States. As he's talking I suddenly remember what he'd asked me to bring: 20 Marlboro and a lighter. (Are you sure? I'd asked, hoping he'd change his mind. Yes, he said. And could you get me the red ones? He giggled, which I read as, Clay, I'm dying. It's too late to be worrying about smoking now.)

I reach inside my pocket. 'Chico, I've got the, er—'

'Okay,' he whispers, and he stares at me intently. 'Under the blanket.'

I feel for the cigarette box. It feels huge, like a book. Where's the lighter? I dig deeper. Oh, here it is. I glance over my shoulder. The female prison officer looks up from her newspaper. I look over at the other officer. He's watching TV. But the TV's just above Chico's head, directly in his line of vision. Shit. Now what? I grip the cigarettes and the lighter tightly, remembering the signs in the prison about smuggling in drugs. Are cigarettes classed as drugs in here?

I'm tense again, listening to Chico but not listening, if you know what I mean. Oh, for God's sake, Clay, it's only a pack of cigarettes! What are they going to do? Lock you up? But it's not just the cigarettes. It's more than that. Something's just flashed into my mind, a memory of a young boy. In a car, my dad's car. Forty years ago...

* * *

We're driving home. I'm in the back seat. I've got one hand dug deeply inside my coat pocket. Really deeply. And I'm sitting bolt upright. Frightened. We've just been to visit one of my dad's friends, and while they were having coffee I was in one of the bedrooms, jumping on the bed. Singing. Jumping. Higher and higher. Then I spotted something: a jewelry box on a side table. I stopped jumping. Reaching forward, eyes wide, I lifted the lid. And then the sound of tinkling music, like the ice cream van. And inside, twirling round and round, a little ballerina. Now, in the car, I'm holding that little ballerina in my pocket, tightly. I know I shouldn't have taken it, but she was just so beautiful. Her pink dress, her pointed toes, her tiara—I had to have her. And I couldn't ask for her, I just couldn't, I'm not quite sure why. But what am I going to do now? My eyes are starting to water now. We're nearly home. I know I shouldn't have taken it. I'm panicking. Then my dad's voice, Clay, what have you got in your pocket? I dig deeper. Crying. Clay! Take it out of your pocket!

* * *

'Honey, take it out of your pocket!'

'What?'

'The cigarettes!' whispers Chico, folding back the blanket. Then he says to the prison officer, 'Can I have a glass of water, please?'

The officer reaches toward the table behind, and as he does I quickly pull the cigarettes and lighter out my pocket and stuff them under the blanket, then carry on talking, quickly, meaningless rubbish, pushing the mound forward, inch by inch, too nervous to look around at the other officer to see if she's noticed.

There. It's done. We look at each other, grinning.

A few minutes later one of the officers says, 'This is the happiest he's been all day.'

'All week!' chips in the other.

124

Then I have a thought. 'Can I take Chico downstairs to buy some drinks and magazines?'

The male officer nods at the female officer. 'I don't have a problem with it. Do you?'

'Not if we come too.'

A few minutes later we're in the corridor: me pulling the drip, two officers, Chico in a wheelchair, still handcuffed. People are staring—openly staring. I glare at them, feeling really protective, getting angry. Then Chico reaches for my hand. 'Honey, don't worry. Do you really think I care what strangers think of me now?'

I look down at him and smile.

Now we're in the newsagent, trying to navigate the aisles. I'm pulling drinks down from the shelves, sweets, filling up his basket. We get to the magazine section. I reach forward. 'I suppose *Homes and Gardens* is out of the question?'

Then Chico laughs. And I laugh. And we both laugh, and laugh, and laugh. Because that's all that we can do.

April 15th, 2008: The Photograph

A little old woman shuffles across Dean Street, slowly, bent over, wearing battered shoes, half on, half off.

As she nears the shop she reaches out her hands, holds on to the window frame for support, stopping to catch her breath inches from where I sit.

Her skin's relatively unlined but white, whiter still against the green of her jacket, the whiteness in contrast to her once deep-blue eyes that are now watery with age.

I watch as she brushes a loose strand of grey hair from her face and tucks it behind her ear, staring at the floor, deep in thought. What is she thinking? Then she turns, still unaware that I'm so close, and pulls something from her inside jacket pocket: a black-and-white photograph of a man in uniform. She holds it with both hands, gazing at it. Her face lights up, as if remembering. Then, gradually, her expression changes, as if remembering again. Now she looks sad, very sad, her blue eyes even more watery now.

It's one of the most touching scenes I've witnessed on this street.

April 19th, 2008: They Meet Again

'Clayton! You made it!' shouts Simon excitedly from the back of a crowded hallway. 'There're so many people here dying to meet you!' He nods toward a haughty-looking woman with the look of Queen Mary, who scrutinises me as if I am something her dog left on the lawn. I make my way toward them. It's like walking through a theatrical nursing home. People are laughing, singing, operatic music sweeping from room to room, glasses being clinked. I brush past a sea of wizened faces until I'm by their side.

'Clayton! Meet Katherine. Katherine, Clayton.'

My eyes are immediately drawn to Katherine's hair (cobalt blue) and her eye shadow (black). The overall effect is that of an aging Liquorice Allsort. She catches me staring and with a huff flicks what appears to be roadkill over her shoulder, revealing a pale hand previously hidden behind the animal's bottom, which she offers to me (the hand not the bottom).

'I'm Katherine—with a *K*,' she announces, through pursed lips.

I'm tempted to reply, 'I'm Liza, with a *Z*,' but instead what comes out is 'Pleased to meet you.' But as I reach to shake her hand, it recedes from whence it came, so that I end up grabbing her forefinger instead.

'Do you like opera?' she asks, looking down, slightly alarmed.

'I'm not really a fan.'

'Oh,' she replies, and pulls her finger back sharply. Even the roadkill glares back.

The next on the list of people dying to meet me is an actor

by the name of Gerald. Gerald looks to be in his eighties, distinguished, with a campy Matthew Kelly air about him. We chat for a while and he reminisces, talking about Soho in the 40s and 50s and his first big break into show business as a stagehand in Drury Lane. He's interesting, charming, but slightly deaf, so having a conversation proves quite difficult.

'So, my dear boy, how do you know Simon?'

'He came into my shop.'

'Shop? What shop?'

'My partner and I have a shop in Soho called Dirty White Boy.'

'Dirty boys? Oh, yes, I've had a few.'

'No, our shop's called Dirty White Boy! It was named after a song by Foreigner.'

'Yes! Too many foreigners!'

Fortunately, Simon comes to the rescue. 'Clayton, look who's here.'

Over his shoulder I spot a slightly tipsy Roslyn easing herself along the hallway with one hand, holding a large bottle of sherry above her head with the other. As she nears I glance at her low-cut evening dress. It's cobalt blue (did I miss something on the invite?). But it's not the colour that my eyes are drawn to. It's her breasts.

Now, breasts, as you're probably aware, are not my thing. Don't get me wrong, I can quite happily stare at a pair, but my gaze is more like your local vicar studying his prize begonias than anything approaching a leer. But Roslyn's are distracting in a particular way: every time she talks, the left one pops out of her dress. This, again, makes for a difficult conversation.

'Thank you for inviting me.' I say.

'Did you say you liked opera?' she asks. (Out it pops.)

'Ummm...' (In it goes.)

'It matters not.' (Out it pops.) 'You are here—that is music enough' (In it goes.)

Strangely, neither Gerald nor Simon appears to notice Roslyn's bopping boob, though the longer it bops, the more hypnotised I become. Tearing my eyes away, I excuse myself and make my way to the kitchen to look for Jorge and Charlie.

The kitchen is empty, so I decide to help myself to a drink. I check the cupboards. Find a glass and turn the tap on to wash it. In the background Roslyn's voice greets someone at the door. Then, just as I'm about to pour myself a vodka—

'Ducky?'

I spin around. 'Leslie?'

'Well, it ain't the bleedin' cat's mother!'

'What're you doing here?'

'Ducky, I've been coming to Roslyn's parties since—'

'Charlie's here!'

Leslie's face drops.

'He came with me and Jorge.'

Then a voice at the doorway. 'Leslie?

This time it's Leslie's turn to turn around. Charlie's standing there.

All eyes fall back on me. Then suddenly there's a huge BANG! as Roslyn falls into the room, landing in a heap on the floor.

'Hello, darlings!' she giggles, still waving her bottle above her head. 'Anyone for sherry?'

April 20th, 2008: The New Bond Girl

I'm leaning against the shop window, watching the morning crowds. Someone walks toward me, waving. I can't quite make out who it is, but wave back anyway. Then Maggie walks into my line of vision.

''Ello, luv!' she says with a smile, leaning against the window beside me.

'Hi, Maggie!'

She rummages inside her tan fake-leather handbag and pulls out a pack of 10 Marlboro Lights and a yellow lighter. She lights a cigarette, takes a drag and throws her bag back over her shoulder. 'We keep seein' each other but we never get a chance to chat, do we, luv?'

'No, we don't, do we.'

''Ow's business?'

'Oh, you know. Up and down. One minute I think we're doing okay. Then it drops again. It's so unpredictable. Although we did have Graham Norton in last week. He spent a fortune. That's what we need—more celebrity customers.'

Maggie takes another drag, this one longer, blowing the smoke upwards. 'We get our share upstairs,' she winks.

'Really?'

'Yeah!'

'Like who? Can you tell me?'

She reels off the names, a well-known tennis player, a drugged-up rock star, a world-famous teenage actor, but I'm already somewhere else, not really listening, my mind drifting, imagining what it must be like to be lying there, selling yourself, giving yourself up, to a famous...

* * *

There's a knock on the door. It opens, revealing the silhouette of a broad-shouldered man, the light from the hallway streaming around him, like a scene from a film I can't quite place. I catch my breath in anticipation as he swaggers slowly, ever so slowly, toward me. Stepping closer. And closer.

Hold on. I know him! That sandy-blond hair. Those piercing blue eyes. No! It can't be! Oh my God, it is! It's Daniel Craig! I smile. But I'm nervous, as he looks me up and down. Feasting. Leering. I'm trying to look seductive, but at the same time I'm hesitant, watching as he unbuttons his shirt, moving closer and closer.

He throws his shirt on the floor and starts unbuttoning his jeans. Letting them fall. All the time staring, staring. Now I'm looking him up and down. At his big, pumped-up pecs. His bronzed six-pack. The sky-blue trunks that he wore in the Bond film. And... God! Look at the size of that package!

Now he's climbing on the bed next to me. I'm shaking. I'm the one who's meant to be in control here. But those deep-blue eyes. I just want to fall into them.

He reaches for my panties. Pulls them down in one quick movement, nuzzling my earlobe as he kicks off his trunks, his stiff cock pressing into me. Rubbing. Sliding.

Now he's turning me over. Whispering in my ear, 'You're about to become a Bond Girl.' Feeling my ass, fingering my hole. I open my legs. Just a bit. He reaches for a rubber on the side table. Spitting on his hand. Pushing his way in. 'I'm not sure I can take it,' I squeal. 'You'll be fine,' he laughs. 'You're the new Pussy Galore!' Then he starts, slowly. The rhythm building, faster and faster. His stubble on the back of my neck. His hot breath. His sweat. Pushing, faster, and faster.

* * *

'I said, 'ow's that for a celebrity story?'

'Yes... Yes,' I reply dreamily.

Maggie's looking at me strangely. 'Well, I gotta dash—you never know who might be waitin'.'

'Oh. Er... Yes. Er... Bye, Maggie.' (Did he come already?) 'Let me know if you ever want to do a celebrity job swap!'

'I'll hold you to that!' she laughs, and off she goes. And after readjusting my panties, so do I.

April 20th, 2008: Bury My Bosoms

We've folded rows of jeans (Cavalli and Versace) and stacked them with military precision. We've pressed boxes of shirts (Lacroix and Mugler) and covered them in plastic sheets. All the new shoes (Basi and Rykiel) have been polished and displayed. We're all set. There's only one thing missing—customers.

Across the road, Pat from Paradiso is standing outside

her doorway, looking from right to left, biting her nails. Outside Pulcinella the boys are doing the same. It's the same outside Soho Books. And American Retro. Everyone praying for business. Everyone waiting for that one big-spending customer who could transform the day. Even Sue's outside! Leaning against the neon 'Model' sign. Scouring the street, like a maître d' outside a restaurant trying to entice people in. 'And the specials today are the Lithuanian blow job, followed by the lezzie two-way. We also have a rather succulent finger buffet—'

'Clay!'

Crossing the street is Angie. Everything about her is cut and styled to perfection. The clothes. The hair. The cheekbones.

'Wot's going on?' she asks as she nears, her eyes hidden behind her huge sunglasses.

'Nothing. It's dead.'

'Where's the 'usband?'

'Inside.'

She swishes in.

'Wot's goin' on?'

Jorge shrugs, looking glum.

'It's terrible, innit?' she says, settling by the window. 'Everyone's talkin' about it. No one's got any bleedin' money!'

I can tell Jorge's not in the mood to discuss it, so I quickly change the subject. 'Have you been to the gym?'

'Yeah,' Angie replies. 'Workin' me legs.' She extends a toned limb and lets her fingers travel lightly up it.

'Were you training with Paul?'

'That old queen,' she sniffs, withdrawing her leg again.

'I thought Paul was your friend.'

'Not anymore. We ain't speakin'.'

'Why's that?'

'She turned on me, din't she. I think she had the you-know-whats.'

'What?'

'The hots!'

'No!'

'Honestly! I couldn't believe it! I'm being stalked by a sixty-year-old queen who likes being fisted—that's how bleedin' hot I am!'

'Why, what did he do?' Jorge asks.

'Came round me house 'n tried it on!'

'But I thought he was your sister.'

'So did I, darlin'! I said to 'im, I said, "Whaddya think you doin'?" You wanna talk bad dates? Hello!'

I pull open the desk drawer. Rummage through the paperwork and remove a slip of paper with a phone number written on it. 'Well, maybe this one'll be different.'

Angie arches an eyebrow.

'Someone's been asking after you. And he left his number.' I wave the note in her direction. 'He's very nice-looking.'

She snatches the paper from me and squints at the number. 'Oh, posh writin', innit?'

'You've already met him.'

She looks up. 'Oh, don't tell me it's a punter! I couldn't date a punter. How can you act all coy when they've already had their mouth round yer minge?'

'Er... No. You met him in the shop. A while back. He was coming in just as you were going out. He's tall and distinguished—'

'Darlin', I've met a lot of tall and distinguished men in my time.'

'Well, he thinks very highly of you. He wants to take you to dinner.'

'Why don't you call him?' asks Jorge.

Angie stares at the piece of paper. 'I dunno...' She sounds uncharacteristically hesitant. 'I dunno if I'm ready.'

'Angie. He's perfect! He's romantic. Good-looking. What more do you want?'

'I'm not sure...'

'Come on, Angie!' I say, joining in. 'It's about time you had a boyfriend.'

She turns to face me. 'Darlin', there's no point. They all die on me. I can't even keep a pot plant!'

'You could at least call him.'

She folds the paper in half and drops it into her handbag. 'There's a lot to think about.'

'What's to think about?'

'Yeah, just call him!' adds Jorge.

'I can't,' she fires back.

'Why not?'

She removes her glasses and positions them in her hair. Takes a deep breath. 'I'm havin' my tits taken off.'

The lighthearted mood instantly dissolves. I glance in Jorge's direction, then back to Angie. No one speaks. Then Jorge says gently, 'But Ange... They're not real tits.'

'They're real to me!' Angie says. 'They're my baby girls. They're part of me.'

'When are you having them taken off?' I ask, carefully.

She watches a mother and her young daughter cross the street. 'Next Wednesday,' she replies quietly. Then she turns to face us, her eyes glistening as if she's about to cry. 'Would you... Would you come with me?'

Jorge nods at me. 'Of course. We'll be there, won't we, Clay?'

'Yeah, of course. We can get Elton to cover.'

Angie reaches inside her handbag, pulls out a tissue and blows her nose. It's a real tear-jerker moment. I've never seen her like this and it's heartbreaking to watch.

'Thank you, boys,' she sniffs.

Another awkward few seconds pass by while she composes herself. Finally: 'Would you mind if I asked you one more favour?'

'No, of course not,' Jorge says, almost in a whisper. 'What is it?'

She shakes her head. 'No, no, it doesn't matter...'

'Come on, Ange. What is it?'

She scrunches the tissue up in her hand and hangs her head. 'I wondered if...if you'd come with me to Regent's Park after the operation. To the Rose Garden. There's a little spot there where I want to bury them. I just wanna give 'em a proper send-off.'

Jorge glances at me, nods understandingly, then turns to face Angie. 'If that's what you want.'

'Thank you. It would mean a lot.' Then she stands, slowly, reaching for her handbag and her walking stick and putting her sunglasses back on, already the glamorous widow. It's all very "Back to Black" (R.I.P.). She walks elegantly toward Jorge, kisses him on each cheek, and does the same to me.

'I love you guys,' she whispers.

And we watch as she walks calmly toward the doorway, head held high. Serene and beautiful. Suddenly she stops. What's the matter? Is she about to collapse? Has the emotion got too much? Then she turns, perfectly poised.

'Suckers!'

And she swishes out the door, laughing all the way down the street.

April 21st, 2008: A Helping Hand

The postman's just walked in. He pulls a pen from behind his ear and points to his notebook. I sign my name. He hands me a package and a bundle of letters bound with an elastic band. But it's only once he's left that I realise one of the letters is for the girls. I rush to the doorway: too late, he's gone. I tell Jorge I have to pop upstairs.

Seconds later I'm outside the first floor flat, knocking on the door. Almost at once it opens and I'm greeted by Maggie. She's wearing a tight black sweater, and with her newly straightened hair, cherry-red lipstick and radiant face, she looks really attractive. I hand her the letter and tell her so.

'Ahhh, fanks, luv. You say the nicest fings.'

I'm just about to head back downstairs when she calls me back. ''Ere, Clay, you wouldn't do me a favour, would ya?'

'Sure!'

'Would ya look after the place 'til Sue gets back? She'll be 'ere any minute. I jus' gotta go an' pay some bills.'

'Er… What do I have to do?'

'Just make sure there's no trouble. It'll be fine, though. We've only got one punter.' She cups her hand to her mouth and whispers, ''E'll be a while. 'E's gettin' on a bit.'

Maggie grabs her keys and handbag, and I take a seat on the flowery-patterned settee, pick up a copy of *Heat* magazine from the glass coffee table. Maggie blows me a kiss and closes the door behind her with a click.

I take in my surroundings. Apart from the single red bulb hanging above the main window, it could be a doctor's waiting room. There're a couple of paintings of shipwrecks in fake gilt frames, drooping daffodils in a Chinese vase, a drop-leaf wooden table in the corner on which sits a bowl of not yet ripe bananas.

A minute passes. I'm surprised at how quiet it is. Not quite what I was expecting. Then a bedroom door creaks open, the sound of two people stepping out. I hear the front door open. Someone leaves. The door closes again and a blonde Eastern European girl enters the room.

'Hi!' she says.

'Hi!'

'Are you waiting?'

'Er…no. I'm just covering for Maggie. She's just popped out.'

The blonde girl pins back a lock of hair behind her ear and frowns. 'Are you from downstairs?'

'Yep.'

She walks across the room to the line of cupboards, a sink and small Formica-covered work surface that make up the kitchen.

She opens the cupboards and says over her shoulder, 'You're always writing late at night.'

'I'm writing a book.'

'What about?'

'Soho.'

She nods and without questioning me further turns on the tap and fills a red kettle. 'Coffee?' she shouts above the noise of the running water.

'Yes, please!'

'Are you gay?'

Her directness takes me back. 'Er... Yeah. Yeah, I am.'

She turns to face me, kettle in her hand. 'Have you ever been with a girl?'

'I, er, came close, once or twice...'

* * *

Picture the scene.

A school playing field. I'm 15. I'm lying on top of a girl called Caroline, also 15. We've been kissing for ages and I've been rubbing up and down on her so frantically I've practically worn her down to the bone (no mean feat, given her size).

Caroline, I should explain, though not the prettiest girl on the block, is definitely one of the easiest. Unfortunately this isn't helping. Whereas at 15 I'd normally get an erection on the hour, on top of Caroline, squirming and moaning beneath me, it's just not happening. If anything, it's retracting. Forceps will be required to bring it back to life.

Thirty minutes into this love tussle and I've already given up on the idea of trying to prove my manhood; now I'm thinking about anything just to try to get it hard. This alternates between imagining that I'm snogging the face off the Six Million Dollar Man to participating in an orgy with the entire cast of *Bonanza*. But still nothing! Caroline, however, has not given up on the idea and has now 'accidentally' opened her blouse, revealing a pair of gigantic breasts. These I play with, as a potter would a wet clay vase, while intermittently checking my watch to make sure I haven't missed the six o'clock *Charlie's Angels* cliffhanger.

If the breasts of a woman lying on her back can be said to have a 'fried egg' appearance, then Caroline's are 'ostrich.' This is making it near impossible to get one in my mouth. I'm also slightly put off by the angry red spot on the edge of her left nipple, which looks about to burst. You could say things aren't going well. Nevertheless Caroline, oblivious to my lack of prowess, has her legs, which at the start of this meeting were just inches apart, now spread so wide that her toes appear to be directing aircraft. On two occasions so far, she's grabbed my hand and shoved it up her skirt. And, like Pavlov's dog, I've immediately pulled it back out—the first time on the pretext of wiping my nose on my sleeve, and the second to recheck my watch. (Farrah was in mortal danger.)

'Caroline?'

'Yes! Yes! Yes!' she cries ecstatically, thrashing about like a landlocked fish.

'I have to go.'

Her legs immediately clamp themselves around my back in a vice grip.

'Caroline, I really have to go.' (It won't be long now, Farrah, I promise.)

I prise her legs apart and jump safely out of reach. And my last image of Caroline is her lying on the grass, in starfish position, giant white breasts exposed to the hot baking sun.

* * *

'Sugar?' asks the blonde girl.

'Er, one, please.'

She hands me a large mug with the words 'I' and 'Soho' emblazoned across it, a heart nestled between the two. Then she takes a seat on a battered armchair and watches me—only for a second, but it's slightly unnerving. 'I've been in your shop,' she says. Again her tone is flat and direct.

'I thought I'd seen you.'

'My boyfriend—he lives in Lithuania. He's been in too.'

I nod.

'He said, "Do you know the shop called Dirty White Boy? They do cool T-shirts. Will you get me one?" So I did.'

'Did he like it?'

'Yes, but I panicked.'

'Why?'

'Because he thinks I'm a waitress.' She takes a sip of her drink and looks up sheepishly from above the mug. 'That was a big coincidence him coming into your shop.'

'So he doesn't—'

'No. He wouldn't like it.' She takes another sip. 'He must have been in your shop while I was up here.'

I'm about to say, 'One buying, one selling' but keep my mouth shut.

'I need this money. It's more than I can earn as a waitress. And it's less hours.'

I take a large gulp of coffee, trying to think of something to say. 'Is it, er...hard work?'

'No.' She stares at me blankly (not surprisingly, given my stupid question). 'What's your name?'

'Clayton.'

'I'm Valda.'

'Hi, Valda.'

'Hi, Clayton.'

She places her mug on the floor, kicks off her shoes and tucks her legs up on the armchair, more relaxed. 'I work two weeks on and two weeks off. Where else could I do that?'

Her face is lightly made up, her complexion creamy white, and with her petite frame and golden-blonde hair it's like having Kylie sitting opposite me. I must be staring too much because she says, 'You don't approve...'

'Oh, no! Not at all,' I assure her. 'I mean, I don't disapprove.

I think you provide a great service. And there's been sex in Soho for hundreds of years. Soho without sex would be like the Queen with no knickers.'

She laughs. Then stops, a flicker of doubt appearing. 'I'm worried about my boyfriend. That he will find out...'

The sentence hangs in the air ominously. Then there's a sound of a key turning in the lock. Valda looks over her shoulder. The door opens. It's Sue. She takes off her track jacket and hangs it behind the door. Then she sees me.

She grins craftily. 'Got fed up with cock, then, 'ave ya?'

'No, I'm—'

'Lookin' for summat to spice up yer love life?'

I shake my head and half laugh. 'No, Maggie asked me to cover.' I stand and take my mug to the sink. 'I'd better be going. Jorge's on his own.'

'Sure we can't tempt ya?' Sue jokes, shimmying her ample bosom in my direction.

'No, thank you,' I laugh. A vision of Caroline's angry red spot reappears. 'But thank you anyway... Bye, girls.'

And I troop back downstairs, ready to start the day.

April 22nd, 2008: Dolly

2 pm. Jorge's at the gym. I'm behind the counter pricing the Dirty White Boy T-shirts. An old man steps in. He stands in the doorway, his eyes travelling around the shop. He nods as if confirming that he's in the right place. Then he makes his way slowly toward me.

'Soooo,' he says wryly, resting a trembling liver-spotted hand on the counter. 'You're the legendary Clayton.'

'I don't know about that.'

'Well, I've being hearin' a lot about you.'

'Really? Who from?'

'Leslie.'

'Oh! So you must be his friend Dolly!'

He smirks. 'The one and only.'

'Pleased to meet you, Dolly. I've heard a lot about you, too. Please take a seat!' I gesture toward the little red chair.

'Not just at the moment, thank you, dear. I've got a little problem down below, so I'll stand if you don't mind.'

As we've only just opened and the shop's empty, I'm able to give him my full attention.

'Of course I 'ad to see you for meself,' he says, his inquisitive eyes wandering around the shop again.

As he's looking around I study him. He's a small, pudgy gentleman, like a wrinkled chestnut, as round as Leslie is angular, as squat as Leslie is erect. And, just like Leslie, he's well dressed, with a herringbone suit, a crisp white shirt, a mauve woolen tie and, adding a touch of eccentricity, a black beret perched on the side of his head, curly gray hair springing out from the sides, the beret fighting to keep it in place. He catches me staring.

'Oh, it's a habit I've never dropped.'

'I'm sorry?'

'The drag, dear! You see, clothes were rationed in my day. So whenever we came to Soho we always tried to give the impression that we had money. Suits, ties, hats—that sort of thing. Oh, yessss. A lady could never be seen without her hat.'

'So you know Soho quite well, then?'

'Quite well? I practically lived here!' He eyes the chair. 'Actually, I will take that seat if you don't mind.'

I pull it out for him, watching as he carefully lowers himself. He winces as he sits. 'Oh, that's better,' he says, once he's settled. He taps the chair for effect. 'Soooo, this is the spot.'

'Where Leslie met Charlie, you mean?'

'Yessss… Now, I suppose you know the history of the place?'

'It used to be a café called Torino's. Quite a glamorous—'

'Glamorous? Is that what Leslie told you?'

'Yes, he said it—'

'Oh, it weren't glamorous, dear. Oh, no. It was a rough old caff. Rough as ninepence. Full of poets and writers, it was. Francis Bacon, Henrietta Moraes, all that crowd. An' it used to have a ten-foot-tall marionette outside, just above the doorway.' His eyes travel the room. 'Still, it was a pleasant enough spot to sit and watch the world go by.' He looks out the window, doing just that.

'You don't come to Soho very much now, then?'

'No, dear,' he says, his voice barely above a whisper, as he gazes outside. 'I've been livin' in Brighton.'

'And you live here now?'

'Yes… Gary, that's my…was my partner. Gary died last year.' He pauses momentarily. 'Forty-two years we were together.'

'Oh. I am sorry.'

He waves his hand, which I take to mean the subject's off-limits. A few comfortable but quiet seconds pass as his eyes follow a couple walking down Dean Street. Then he sighs and continues. 'Anyway… Brighton's gone now. All sold. It's time to start afresh. An' I thought, well, what better place than me old haunt.' His voice is more animated now. 'Cos I used to work round here, you know.'

'Really?'

'Oh, yesssss! I worked here for years, dear. British Telecom on Shaftesbury Avenue. Started off as an operator.' He turns in his seat, looking at the neon 'Model' sign next door. 'An' we used to have a brothel next to us too. I remember an old queen who used to work there. What was her name? Rosie. That was it, Rosie. Plastic flowers in her hair. Always singin', she was. Always drunk. Worked on the market but doubled up as a maid. There was a *huge* procession when she died.' He pauses. 'An' you see that pub down there?' He points toward Shaftesbury Avenue.

'The Golden Lion?'

'That's where I met Dennis Nielsen.'

'You knew Dennis Nielsen?'

'Oh, yes! Dennis was a friend of mine. He used to work at the Job Centre round the corner, an' what with us both being Scottish 'n all, we used to meet for tea. Very sweet and gentle, he was. So, o' course, when it all came out in the papers about him murderin' all those boys... Now, that was back in...let me see... Eighty-two? Then Gary bought a place in Brighton an' we moved down there. Quite a treat at the time. Being by the sea 'n all. Not now, though. Oh, no. Now he's gone it's time to get back to my roots. An' you know what?' He smiles broadly. 'It feels like I've come home.'

I don't reply. Quite happy to let Dolly take control, fascinated by his stories.

As he talks, Big Jim the policeman strides past the window. Then Sebastian, passing Soho Books, in an off-white floor-length coat, a little wave as he passes by.

'You know him?' asks Dolly.

'Yes. That's Sebastian.'

'She looks a queer old thing.'

'Oh, Sebastian's adorable.'

'Mind you,' Dolly says, 'Soho's always attracted the fruits.'

'So is this where you socialised? Oh, sorry, I didn't mean—'

'Oh, don't worry, dear—we were the biggest fruits of 'em all! 'Ere all the time, we were. The A & B. The Rockingham. Only they weren't called gay clubs back then. They were called "drinking clubs". All very furtive. An' then if we wanted a posh night out we'd go to the Tower.' He notices I look confused and adds: 'The Post Office Tower. That big tall thing back there! This was back in the days when it 'ad the revolvin' restaurant. Oh, it was all very high camp. I saw Liberace in there one night. She was wearin' a sapphire bugle bead jacket. I'll never forget. An' she had a lovely blond Californian surfer boy with her.' He pauses. 'Who else did I see there? Grace Kelly. Liz Taylor. You even got royalty! Then o' course the IRA blew it up an' that was it. Run by a lovely old queen, it was...'

'Were you and Leslie friends back then?'

'Since the fifties. It was me that brought her out! Although a queen like that, well, love her to death, but she's never really been "in", has she? Unlike me butch self.' He giggles. 'I remember one night I took her cottagin'. Just behind the Astoria. Falconberg Court. One of those Victorian things, The Iron Lung it were called. Anyway, there was a power cut going on so o' course the place was heavin'. Packed in like sardines, we were. Then someone said, "'Ere! Have a feel of this!" An' it was the biggest cock I'd ever felt in all my life. Oh, a monster, it was. Everyone was queuin' up for a feel! So eventually we all trooped out an' the last one out was this old homeless tramp. Pullin' up his dirty trousers with a big leer on his face, he was. Well, o' course the girls all screamed when they realised what they'd been gobblin'.'

I laugh. 'I can't imagine Leslie getting involved with that.'

'Oh, she never got involved with that, dear. Oh, no. She was always too prim and proper. She kept lookout. 'Cos the police were vicious back then, see. They'd try an' trap you.' He nods. 'They'd entice you into a cottage, battin' their eyelashes. Pretty policemen they were called. An' then they'd arrest you. Oh, the scene were very dangerous back then. Which o' course made it very excitin'.'

'Exciting?'

'Yessss! 'Cos it was illegal. Though now you pick up yer trade on computers. I said to Leslie, I said, "What happened to good old-fashioned cottagin' an' a troll up the Heath?"'

I bite my lip to stop myself from laughing again. Then I say, 'How is Leslie, by the way? The last time I saw him it was at—'

'Roslyn's party. Oh, she's a mad one, that one. She came to one of our parties once. Got through a whole bottle of sherry, she did.'

'So what happened with Leslie and Charlie that night? We left soon after—'

'What do you mean, what happened?'

'Did they make up?'

'Oh, I doubt it, dear.' He adjusts his beret, examining himself in the reflection in the window. Satisfied, he turns back around. 'You see, Leslie never really got over what happened with Charlie. Of course I've tried to set her up over the years. But she's very fussy, is our Leslie. They were either too old, or too young, or didn't work hard enough. She was always lookin' for an excuse. When really o' course she was just afraid of gettin' hurt. 'Cos what happened with Charlie, well... I like Charlie—always have—but Charlie was confused back then and, well, what he doesn't know is... Leslie had a breakdown when he left.'

'Leslie? He always seems so—I don't know—strong.'

'Oh, no! That's all a front. She's quite a delicate creature underneath it all. Yes, she had a breakdown. In a psychiatric hospital for a few months, she was. It were all very hush-hush. Hit her very badly, it did. You see, 'er dad kicked 'er out when she was young, so I suppose it was a reminder. An' after that she closed the door on meetin' anyone again. If anyone got close, she just froze. I've tried to talk to her about it but she doesn't want to know. Which brings me to my point...' Dolly stands, slowly, using the counter as support, his tone suddenly more serious. 'You see, I know you mean well, dear, but I'm not sure if all this matchmaking business is doin' 'er any good. In fact, I think it might be pushin' 'er over the edge again.' He smiles, but this time it's a curt smile.

'But when we were at Roslyn's party I had no idea—'

'I know, dear. I know. But I think it would be best if you just didn't mention Charlie's name from now on. You see, I remember what she was like before, an'... Well, it ruined our holiday.'

'Oh, so it was you who went on holiday with Leslie!'

'Well, who else would it be? Not that it did 'er any good. A limp lettuce all week, she was. Anyway...' He extends his hand, more formally this time. 'It's been a pleasure meetin' you at last. An' I hope we see each other again. But I hope you'll have a little think about what I've just said... For Leslie's sake.'

The conversation over, we say our goodbyes and Dolly totters off, getting as far as the door before he looks around one more time. Then he steps carefully down onto the street, turns to the right outside the shop, passes the Old Compton Street window, and heads toward Wardour Street like a ghost from Soho's past.

May 2008

May 2nd, 2008: The Horsley Riposte

The last time I recall seeing a black silk negligee with a marabou feather–lined neck, it was on Bet Lynch, or was it Joan Collins? Either way, seeing Sebastian Horsley leaning out of a first floor window nestled inside one, his face coated in a fine white powder, his eyes caked in last night's mascara, is a reminder of all those campy days gone by.

'Hello Romeo, Juliet here. Welcome to Horsley Towers,' he purrs sleepily, clasping his negligee at the neck, just as my mum used to do when she bent down to collect the milk from the doorstep each morning.

'I'm sorry, I'm a bit early.'

'Oh, not at all, my darling. Not at all. Hold on, I shall buzz you in.'

Seconds later he's greeting me at his door. 'Come in, my dear. Come in. Make yourself at home while I make some tea.' And then he sweeps out the room, yards of see-though negligee floating in the air behind.

While he's getting ready, it's a perfect opportunity to have a good nose around his front room.

Sebastian's flat is fascinating. It has a Victorian feel to it, with wooden floors, a built-in red velvet seat by the window, an original fireplace. Just above the fireplace is a display case lined with human skulls. I count 24. And on the mantelpiece a row of antique syringes. I count seven. The walls are covered with press cuttings, quotes, photos of himself, his crucifixion, photos of great white sharks; and leaning against an easel is a huge, half-completed painting of a sunflower, with similar, much smaller paintings on the floor below.

There's a cardboard box on the floor. I pick it up and peer inside. It contains a rubber vagina. I quickly put the box down just as Sebastian walks back in with a tray of drinks.

'The *Daily Mail* sent me that. They want me to try it out and write a review,' he says nonchalantly as he places the tray on his writing desk. 'The only problem I've found so far is that you have to keep washing the thing out. Which, of course, you don't have to do with a woman. At least not the ones I've been with lately. Milk and sugar?'

'Er... Yes, please. Both.'

'Here you go, my darling.'

'Thank you.' I take a seat by the window and take a sip. 'So how've you been? I haven't seen you for ages.'

'Oh, I have been miserable of late,' he says, pulling a face. 'More than usual. Sleep is good. Death is better. But the best thing would be never to have been born at all.'

'That bad?'

'Life is travelling downhill in a car with no lights at terrific speed, driven by a four-year-old child. Oh, well, if you can't repair your brakes, make your horn louder, I say.'

'Maybe this will cheer you up—'

'They do say that laughter is the best medicine.'

'It's true.'

'Well, if that's the case, why is everyone dying of cancer?'

'I've been asked to write an article about you, for a private members' club magazine.'

'Which one?'

'The Hospital Club in Covent Garden.'

'That bunch of cunts!'

'You know the—'

'Oh, yes, I know The Hospital Club. They are the stench billowing out from a pile of shit, the worm from a gorilla's anus. I detest them!'

'Why?

'Look at this.' He beckons me over to his laptop and shows me the comments on his website. 'Look what they wrote about my book.'

I read the first comment: *I'm sitting here in the book club at The Hospital where we have been discussing* Dandy in the Underworld. *Our verdict: Nobody has finished the book. All of us are leaving our copies here so we don't have to bother carrying them home. Except me—I left it at home because I couldn't be bothered bringing it in. It's also the only book that has prompted us to get online, seek out the author and sledge him.*

He points at the comment below. 'Here's what I wrote back.'

Dear The Hospital Book Club Group.
I am delighted you got as much misery reading my book as I got pleasure spending the money you paid me for it.
Suck My Nazi Cock.
Sebastian Horsley

Then he shuts the laptop and takes a seat on the red velvet throne. 'Did they not realise? Most writers' works are water. I know everybody drinks water. But *Dandy* is not for reading. It is for injecting.'

'It's true. Your book is the most honest autobiography I've ever read.'

He looks pleased. 'Darling, if they ever let me in, we should move to America. We shall never be respected here. As I've said before, success in England inspires only envy; in America, hope. It is because life for the Americans is always becoming, never being. It is because they are unafraid of being positive. Poor old England. Sometimes negativity doesn't pull you through.'

'But you have had some good press over here,' I remind him.

'Yes. Well. I'll soon be tumbling back into that arctic abyss from whence I came. Tossed aside like a used condom. Oh, well, it is better to live one day as a tiger than a hundred years as a sheep. Hmmm... What about one day as a sheep?' He brushes his negligee with a camp flick of the wrist. 'Actually, my darling, I was thinking about committing suicide. Take a look at this. It's my suicide note.' He reaches toward his desk and hands me a piece of paper.

I read it out: *'I am committing suicide today, on my ninetieth birthday. You see, my darlings, I am rather worried about my future.'*

I laugh and hand it back. 'Oh, don't go, Sebastian! I'll miss you.' I walk to the window and look down onto Meard Street, the little cobbled thoroughfare where the famous Soho clubs The Mandrake and The Gargoyle once stood; where Jean-Paul Sartre got pissed, where Tallulah Bankhead danced, where Francis Bacon was entranced, where Daniel Farson took Josh Avery in the book *Dog Days of Soho*. One of the most magical streets in the village. 'I'll miss Soho too if we have to leave,' I add quietly.

'But, my darling, you haven't left yet,' Sebastian says reassuringly. 'But, if you do, remember: Soho will always be a part of you. You would not have sought it unless you had already found it.'

I turn around. 'What do you mean?'

'Your book, my dear. You looked into all of Soho's mirrors and you saw yourself reflected there. You drew nothing from them that was not already within yourself. And it all helped explain you to Clayton.'

I look at him intently, concentrating on what he's saying.

'You see, my dear, the artist tries to make himself whole

through his work. Beethoven was deaf, Byron lame, Keats consumptive and the Guns 'N' Roses singer is mad. It is a fair exchange. New roses for neuroses.' He stands up and reaches for a cigarette from the mantelpiece. 'I always think of art as being for the few. And the higher the art, the fewer the few. And the highest art of all is, of course, for one.'

'I'm not sure I understand.'

He pauses to light the cigarette and takes a drag. 'What I mean is, the real artist creates for no other purpose than to please himself. Those who create because they want to please others and have audiences in mind are not artists.' He taps the ash onto the plate on the desk. 'There are many people who write but have no real need to. Cocteau says, "The muse ushers the artist into the empty room and points silently at the tightrope." Wilde says, "The way of paradox is the way of truth. To test reality we must see it on the tightrope."'

My head's swimming now, but delightfully so, Sebastian being one of the few people who have this effect on me. He sits down again gracefully and continues.

'There is a line in my book, *Perhaps friendship should be limited to a very few—the fountain plays higher by the aperture being diminished.* And indeed, the same is true of art. There are only a few of us, are there not? But this is as it should be. We should not, I feel, feed back to the public its own ignorance and cheap tastes. If one has a heart, one cannot write or paint for the masses. The masses are asses.' He takes another quick drag of his cigarette and stubs it out in a quick defiant gesture. 'The Hospital Club indeed! Bunch of cunts!'

May 6th, 2008: June?

Today we received a letter from the Inland Revenue about our VAT bill. *If you're late with one more payment we will take legal proceedings to confiscate your goods.* And then another from Westminster Council: *If you're late with your next monthly business rates payment, we have the right to demand the full year's rates, £26k immediately!*

So tonight we sat down and had a frank discussion about what we should do. And we decided to try to hang on. Until June. To give it everything we've got in the hope that things will turn around. Although considering what we're taking at the moment, even getting that far is starting to look increasingly unlikely.

May 7th, 2008: A Night Away

The stress has been building at the shop and Jorge suggested I take a night off. So here I am, in The Lowry in Salford, sitting in the second row with my friend Martin and we're here to see Gerry Potter's play, *Miracle*.

Although I've known Gerry for about two years now, being long-distance MySpace friends, we've never actually met, so I'm really excited about meeting him. You see, Gerry is none other than Chloe Poems, the transvestite socialist poet, gingham diva and radical agenda bender, and his poems have been a real inspiration to me.

I flick through the program, taking note of the actors, Martin's music flooding the theatre: church bells, Gregorian monks, an Army of Lovers "I'm Crucified" sample here, a Madonna confession sample there. Then the lights dim, the audience stop talking and within minutes I'm spellbound. The power of the script is extraordinary and we're so close to the actors we can see every bead of sweat. And Gerry—I knew he could write. But act? Wow. I follow his every movement. Watch his fingers, his eyes. Soaking it all up. Watching. Learning. It's the most thought-provoking piece of theatre I've seen in a while. The type of play you're still thinking about days later. Afterwards in the bar we're all sitting around a table, Gerry, his friend John Aggy, Martin and David Hoyle.

David Hoyle is a huge phenomenon on the gay London

underground scene, drawing large audiences and critical acclaim. I've followed his career for many years, from his early live performances, to his Channel 4 series, to the night he killed off his alter ego The Divine David on Streatham Ice Rink in 2000, right up to his recent sellout shows at the Vauxhall Tavern. Now here I am sitting opposite him. It's all very daunting, sitting around a table full of artists whose work I so admire. And, as usual at times like this, I withdraw, stumbling over my words like a virgin at an orgy, reaching for another vodka and coke to help calm my nerves. Fortunately, everyone is very charming and after a few more drinks we decide to hit Manchester's nightlife, starting off at the polysexual Disco Asbo.

In the car on the way there, David offers me his bag of crisps.

'What flavour are they?' I ask.

'Well...' David drawls, in his distinctive, deadpan northern accent, 'My lips taste like I've been rimming a teenage boy, but I believe they're Barbeque Beef.'

'Er...okay. Ummm, do you live in Manchester—I assumed you lived in London?'

'Oh, no, darling,' he says, grinning, offering me some more crisps. 'I live 'ere. If I'm going to be a victim of a serious homophobic assault I'd rather receive it down 'ere from my own kind.'

Disco Asbo is a pleasant relief from the London club scene. David ushers us past the door check before meeting and greeting what seems like the entire club, leaving Gerry, Martin and me to bop away to a mixture of 80s and present-day remixes. During the evening Martin introduces me to two trannies, Amber Swallows (she does) and Linda.

Amber is a stunning blonde, very friendly (none of your London attitude up here), and within seconds she's recounting a tale of paying £15 to visit a tranny sex club in Huddersfield, next door to a bookies, where, unfortunately, all she found for her hard-earned cash was three old men wanking in a dirty old cinema.

Linda, too, has stories to tell. Married for 30 years with two grown-up kids and living in Bradford, she tells me how she was first caught wearing her wife's knickers and how this progressed to full-blown (though, it has to be said, quite frumpy) dresses.

'What's yer name, chuck?'

'Clayton.'

'I've got a nephew called Clayton. Although, of course, he's a lot younger than you,' she replies, quite innocently.

As the club's about to close, we head off to an after-hours called The Company Bar, which, Martin warns me, is where all the dregs end up. Feeling suitably 'dreggy', we make our way down a set of steps and find ourselves in a small underground room full of hard, bearlike tattooed northern men. Gay heaven. As we're all flagging by this stage, Gerry and I order more drinks, and while we're chatting away, about play structure, how Gerry feels about ditching the Chloe persona, my writing about Chico, and striving for honesty in our respective works, I pick up what I think is my drink and polish it off.

Suddenly everything starts to cave in. My words slow down. Gerry's face takes on Celine Dion proportions, and though I'm sitting down, I feel as if sitting is not enough: I need to be lying. I stop Gerry mid-sentence.

'Gerry, I love your play, but I think there was something in that drink.' I plod up the stairway, feeling as if I'm wearing frying pans for shoes. 'I need to get out of here,' I mumble to no one in particular. Somewhere in the distance Gerry's voice echoes, 'Clay! Come back!'

Once outside, I stumble toward the disused car park adjoining the club and reach for the dirty wall, hands outstretched like something from *Hammer Horror*. As I slowly slip down it in a crumpled heap, I think, I wonder if I'll need to boil-wash this T-shirt tomorrow.

I'm now in a small ball, stroking my head and rocking, aware that this probably isn't the prettiest I've ever looked. My fingers and arms are tingling, the tingling feeling racing through my body. My mind's racing too. I feel like I've just spent an evening with the most creative people this world has to offer, thinking about everything I can learn from them, and how Manchester is the most creative place on Earth. Strangely, simultaneously, I'm also aware that whatever's going through my mind is utter bollocks. So I try to ease myself back to normality by breathing deeply. Deep breaths. In and out. Faster and faster.

It's not working. I picture myself looking like a crouched, panting sumo wrestler. And then my mind starts racing again: one minute pleasurable, the next frightening. A drug roller coaster. Except each minute feels like 10. Suddenly, someone, from somewhere in the universe, says, 'Are you all right, mate?' and pats me on the head.

I look up. 'I'm fine,' I reply, though judging by the look on Mr Someone's face *fine* is probably not quite the right word to use. At this point it crosses my mind that actually I'm a complete mess and, given my age, should really be tucked up in bed with a mug of hot Ovaltine.

A minute later (or is it an hour?), another voice. Another strong Mancunian accent. Another tap on the head.

'You all right, pet?'

I'm now seriously thinking that the entire cast of *Coronation Street* is lining up and taking turns to try to pull me through. All it needs is for Betty Turpin to rush forward with a reviving hotpot and a barm cake.

I look up again. 'Look, I'm fine. Honestly. I was just thinking whether I should boil-wash this T-shirt.'

Understandably, the vision looks puzzled and edges away. But then, fortunately, Martin comes to the rescue, revives me, and whisks me back to his home, tucking me safely in bed.

The next morning, after I apologise profusely for my

behaviour, we take a lovely stroll down to the river and have lunch. Then, chatting about the delights of tattooed straight boys, we take the canal route back to the railway station, and a few hours later I'm back in Soho, wondering how I managed to pack so much into one night.

May 10th, 2008: The 'Be Back'

Sunday afternoon. Jorge's reading the papers. I'm by the window, laptop open, gazing outside for inspiration.

A swarthy raven-haired guy swaggers in. He's thickset, square jaw, prominent chin and two-day stubble, dressed in sweatshirt and jeans, though the downbeat attire only adds to his 'top male model on a day off' kind of look. Jorge notes his arrival, pushes his paper to one side. My eyes peep above my laptop like a crocodile in an African river. And we watch as he peruses the rails. He stops by the T-shirts.

'Do you have these in XL?' he asks in a clipped Eastern European accent, holding up an Ed Hardy tee.

'We have them in all sizes,' Jorge replies.

'Can I try…'—he pulls one from the racks—'this one. And…this one. And, er…yes. I will try this one.'

Jorge fetches the stepladders, pulls down the appropriate sizes and the guy saunters off to the dressing room.

'I *lohve heem*,' Jorge whispers in a thick Cuban accent once he's out of earshot. Two minutes later the guy returns.

'They are all nice,' he says in a monosyllabic manner, draping them over the counter. He scratches his stubble and thinks. This is usually the point when they decide not to buy. If they have to think, it usually means the answer's going to be 'no.'

'I will think about it—I need to bring my girlfriend back in with me,' he says. (We call this customer a 'BB': an 'I'll Be Back.' They rarely do.)

'Does she buy all your clothes?' Jorge asks casually, making small talk as he refolds the T-shirts.

157

'Not usually,' the guy replies. 'Because I live in Lithuania.'

Lithuania?

'So is this your first time in London?' Jorge asks.

'No, I have been here once before. I came into your shop. I told my girlfriend all about it.'

'Oh, is she here on holiday with you?'

'No. Valdemara lives here in London.'

Valdemara! Does he mean Valda? From upstairs? Didn't she say her boyfriend was Lithuanian? Oh my God, and she's working today! I saw her heading upstairs an hour ago.

The Lithuanian guy continues, 'But she does not know that I am here. It is going to be a surprise.'

I gasp. Too right it is!

Jorge and the Lithuanian guy turn around. Jorge frowns, then addresses the guy again. 'So do you want us to put these T-shirts to one side?'

'Yes, please. I will be back in a while.' He makes a motion to leave. Gets as far as the door. Stops. 'Do you know what that sign that says "Model" means?' he says, pointing to the yellow neon sign.

I jump in. 'That's a, er…Internet café!'

Jorge looks at me, puzzled. 'Clay, don't be silly!' He addresses the guy again. 'It's a brothel.'

The guy smiles, sneakily. 'What are the girls like?'

'Oh, you wouldn't like them. They're not very nice. They—'

'Clay, that's not true!' interrupts Jorge, pulling a face. 'Some of them are really beautiful.' And he describes for the now very attentive Lithuanian guy the types of girls who work up there: small, large, pretty, not so pretty, how there's all types of nationalities up there and how all tastes are catered for. The guy seems really intrigued now. I have to do something. So I shut my laptop and, while Jorge and the Lithuanian are chatting about prices, I dart out the door, sneak past the window and run up the brothel stairway.

Knock! Knock! Knock!

The door opens. It's Maggie.

'Maggie, I have to speak to Valda!'

'Wot's the matter?'

'I just need to speak with her!'

'She's wiv a customer. D'ya wanna come in?'

I rush inside, trying to catch my breath. 'How long will she be?'

'Dunno, luv,' says Maggie, confused. 'It's 'ard to say. 'E asked for twenty minutes but sometimes it's all over in two. Ya nah wot I mean?' She grins. 'Wot's it 'bout, anyway?'

'Valda's boyfriend! He's downstairs. In the shop!'

Maggie covers her mouth with her hand. 'Oh, she told me 'bout 'im! Look, don't worry, luv. 'E'll never catch her up 'ere.'

'But—' (Oh, God, should I say this?) 'he's been asking about the prices!'

Now Maggie gasps. 'Well, we can't 'ave 'im up 'ere. Wot did you tell 'im?

'I told him this was a, er, Internet café.'

'An Internet café?"

'I couldn't think what else to say!'

'Is he comin' up?'

'I don't know. Jorge's chatting to him. But you mustn't tell Valda. I mean, we have to tell her he's here—but not that he's been asking about the place.'

'Oh, God, no! We can't do that.'

'Look, I've gotta get back to the shop. But can you tell Valda he's been in?'

'All right, luv. If anything 'appens, let me know.'

I fly downstairs again. I'm just about to step outside when I see him walking across Dean Street. He reaches the pillar box and stops. I duck back inside. Did he see me? I peep outside again. He's standing just outside Soho Books, staring at the brothel doorway. Now what? I get down on my knees and peer from the bottom of the doorway. Two women walk past, give me a strange look. Oh, no! Now he's walking this way!

I run back upstairs.

'Maggie! Let me in!'

The door opens.

'He's outside! I think he might be coming up!'

'Quick—get in!' she hisses.

I follow her to the main room. She turns on the TV. A black-and-white picture flickers on: the view outside, onto the street. There's a man loitering there. He's looking through the doorway.

'That's him!'

'Well, if he comes up, we just won't let 'im in!' Maggie says, a slight panic in her voice. We look back to the screen. Someone's standing next to him. A Tesco's bag in one hand, a bottle of Lucozade in the other, large matronly breasts. Oh, shit. Sue! They're talking and they're—entering the building!

Maggie gulps. 'Oh, fuck!'

Suddenly there's the creaking sound of a bedroom door opening. We rush to the hallway. A businessman in a pin-striped suit walks briskly out, thanking someone inside. He reaches for the front door.

'STOP!' yells Maggie.

The man freezes. 'Is there a problem?'

The sound of a key turning in a lock. The front door handle rattles. Maggie rushes toward the bedroom door. 'Stay in there!' she shouts to whoever's inside (Valda?) and slams the door.

'Sorry 'bout that,' Maggie says sweetly to the businessman, pulling the front door open. The businessman makes a move to leave, perplexed. But, blocking his path just outside the doorway are Sue and the Lithuanian guy. I immediately duck behind the wall.

Sue's voice: 'Wot's Clay doin' 'ere?'

Maggie's voice: 'What d'ya mean?

Sue: 'I jus' saw Clay!'

Maggie: 'Er... I need a quick word.'

Sue: 'Wot?'

Maggie: 'In private.'

Sue: 'Let me just see to this guy first.' She says something to him, I can't quite hear what. Then: 'Who's workin' today?'

Maggie's voice: 'No one! Er, I mean, just Eileen.'

Sue: 'Not the bleedin' maid! I mean, whose workin'? I thought we 'ad—'

Maggie: 'No! It's 'er day off!'

There's a knock from inside one of the bedrooms. Valda? I bite my lip. Then Sue's voice again: 'Who's in the bedroom?'

Maggie: 'Rita!'

Sue: 'Why's she knockin'?'

Maggie struggles to come up with an answer. I imagine Sue reaching for the bedroom door, Valda lying there, her boyfriend stepping in. I have to do something. I step out from behind the wall.

'Hi, Sue!'

Sure enough, Sue's reaching for the bedroom door. Maggie's face is panic-stricken. The Lithuanian guy spots me and grins. Sue spots me too.

'You just can't keep away, can ya, Clay? Ain't you gettin' enuf downstairs?'

There's another knock from the bedroom. Valda's voice shouts out something. Will the Lithuanian recognise it? Sue's hand reaches toward the bedroom door again.

Maggie jumps in between, glares at her. 'We 'ave to close! Summat's happened!'

'Wot?'

'I'll tell you in a minute!' Maggie looks over Sue's shoulder at the Lithuanian guy. 'You're gonna 'ave to leave, mate. We've got an emergency.' And she pushes the guy out the door. Slams it and locks it.

'Wot's going on?' asks Sue, annoyed now.

Maggie opens the bedroom door. 'Stay in there a minute, luv. Me 'n Sue 'ave gotta deal wiv summat.'

She shuts the door again without waiting for a reply, drags Sue into the front room, points to the TV screen and the image of a man leaving. 'That's Valda's boyfriend!'

The penny drops. Sue's mouth is agape. She stares at Maggie, at me and back at Maggie again. 'Well, 'e can't come in 'ere!'

'Well, o' course 'e can't!' Maggie insists. 'An' Valda don't know 'e's 'ere either!'

'And he doesn't know she's here!' I add.

Sue looks back at the front door. 'FUCK! That wuz close, then!'

'Exactly!' agrees Maggie. 'Now what we gonna do?'

'Well, you keep Valda inside, an' I'll make sure 'e's gone.'

Maggie leaves the room. I hear the bedroom door opening, Maggie stepping in, then the door closing carefully behind her. Meanwhile Sue opens the front door, slowly, sticks her head out, then looks back over her shoulder and whispers, ''E's gone!'

'Are you sure?'

She steps out and peers down the stairway. 'There's no one 'ere.'

'Okay. I'd better get back. Jorge'll be wondering where I am.'

So I tiptoe back down the stairway and slip back into the shop, taking a seat again on my little red chair.

Jorge looks up from his paper. 'Where've you been?'

'You *don't* want to know.'

May 12th, 2008: An Interview

Sitting quietly in the shop this afternoon, minding my own business (as you know I always do), I am suddenly confronted by two men: one with a clipboard and another who appears to have a video camera for a face.

'We're from Birmingham City Council and we're filming a safer-sex video for schoolchildren. Would you mind if we interviewed you?' says Mr Clipboard.

I am tempted to say, 'Do I look like Joe Public?' but instead what comes out is a rather feeble 'Okay, then.'

'Now, we're going to ask you a set of questions. Just answer as honestly as you can,' he says, pen poised. 'So—how important has safe sex been in your life?'

Wow! What a question. Out the window goes any idea of answering each one with a plug: "We at Dirty White Boy on 50 Old Compton Street think…" How do you answer a question like that, especially when it will be watched by kids?

I think for a few seconds. Then decide to just tell it as it is. Since I don't anticipate drawing breath again for a good few minutes, I take a big deep lungful of air and begin.

'Safe sex has been important to me for as long as I can remember. Nearly every gay friend I have is positive. Sometimes I feel like I'm the odd one out: I'm the only one who hasn't been ill. I'm the only one whose weight hasn't fluctuated. Despite combination therapy, I'm the only one who doesn't have the constant fear of ill health hanging over me. I don't have to deal with other people's prejudices and paranoia. I don't have to worry about how to break the news to my employers, or my family, or potential partners. I've had to watch friends and lovers get seriously ill. I've watched them go from being very healthy to being at death's door in a matter of days. I've cared for them. Nursed them. And, in some cases, it's taken years for them to become healthy again. But I still worry about what might happen tomorrow. I worry, perhaps selfishly, about how I'm going to cope if they go. They're my family. I can't imagine being left here without them.'

I pause for a moment as a gay couple walk past, hand in hand.

'But if you ask any gay man on this street the same question he'll tell you a similar story. Mine, unfortunately, is far from unique.'

Whether this is the answer Mr Clipboard was looking for I am not sure, as by now he is just staring at me. But with a quick nudge from Mr Video Face, he comes out of his coma and continues. 'So, you obviously always have safe sex?'

My immediate thought is to say, "Yes.' But then I decide to be as honest as I can.

'You know what? I would say I nearly always do. And, with everything I've just told you, I'd be stupid not to. But there are times, when you're in a relationship—this is difficult to explain—but if you're negative and your partner's positive, then sometimes, in the heat of the moment, despite everything you know to be right, you can, momentarily, drop your guard.'

By now, Mr Clipboard has stopped writing and is listening intently.

'What I mean is, when you're with a partner you love, you share everything. You don't want to treat HIV as an issue, because you don't want a relationship which is based on that. You want a relationship that's based on sharing. And, sometimes, that total acceptance, that love, it can take it all away—that barrier between what you should and shouldn't do. I've felt that barrier come down a few times, and if that happens to me, with everything I've experienced, then…'

No one speaks for a few seconds. Then the men thank me and pack up their equipment. I stand on the doorstep and watch them as they make their way back down the street.

What parts will they use for their video? How will the school kids react to a middle-aged gay man telling them about safe sex?

And as I think back to everything I've just said—all the memories, the friends, lovers, partners—I'm suddenly close to tears. Thinking about everything my friends have been through. Everything I've been through. And the thought of everything that is yet to come.

May 12th, 2008: Two Old Queens

It's 9 pm. Closing time. I'm outside, pulling down the grates to the shop, popping the bolts into the metal catches.

'Well, 'ave a vada at that one!' giggles a camp voice behind me. 'She looks like a right Dirty White Boy.'

'Wash your mouth out! We'll have none of that filthy muck tonight, thank you very much!'

I turn around. It's Leslie and Dolly. Beaming away. Both dressed to the nines. Scarves, hats, suits and ties. Like a drag-less Hinge and Brackett.

'Now, ducky, we'll have no mention of Roslyn's party,' warns Leslie, eyebrow arched to the point of snapping.

'That's right!' Dolly adds with a knowing wink.

'Because we've come to take you to dinner.'

'Yes. An' we'll 'ave no excuses!'

They grin at me expectantly, like two maiden aunts.

'Ahhh, how lovely,' I reply, genuinely touched. 'Come on inside a minute while I get changed.'

I hold the door open. They step inside. Then I rush downstairs and ask Jorge if he'll be OK, which, as he's absorbed in watching the tennis, appears to be the case. Two minutes later I'm back upstairs. 'Right, where are we going, then?'

'I thought—'

'Dolly, we're not going there!'

'You don't know where—'

'I know exactly where—'

'Why don't we just ask Clayton?'

I clear my throat. 'Jorge and I usually go to The Stockpot.'

'Not that workman's caff!' shrieks Leslie in horror. 'Ducky, the last time we ate there I 'ad indigestion for a week!'

'You only had a chopped salad!'

'Well, I think it sounds delightful,' says Dolly mischievously. Then he turns to face Leslie. 'Now, you just stop all your ditherin'! This isn't about you!'

A few seconds later we're making our way slowly down Old Compton Street, a sulking Leslie on one side, a smiling Dolly on the other, the crowds, tourists, queens and Dagenham hen nights all stepping aside as we pass first Janus, then Caffè Nero, the Prince Edward Theatre, until we were standing outside the glass-fronted restaurant.

I reach for the door. Dolly's face drops.

Leslie steps forward. 'Now, what did I tell—'

'It looks lovely,' interrupts Dolly and he leads us in.

Inside, we scan the oblong restaurant for a free table. They all appear to be taken. Then I spot one at the back and we head toward it. It has a 'reserved' card on it. Leslie picks it up and drops it into the hand of the surprised waitress. 'Your nine-fifteen has arrived!' he says, squeezing around the triangular table and plonking himself down on the plastic seating. I throw the waitress an apologetic look and squeeze around next, followed by Dolly.

'This isn't so bad,' Dolly says reassuringly, removing his beret and smoothing his hair back into a side parting. He leans forward to address Leslie. 'What do you think, dear?'

Leslie removes his safari-style fedora, placing it on his lap, without answering.

'Oh, she's still sulkin',' Dolly says to me in a low voice, but still within earshot. 'She'll snap out of it.'

While I'm examining the menu Dolly nods toward the young gay couple on the next table. 'Now, that's somethin' we couldn't do back in my day,' he says, his eyes lingering on their linked hands.

'Really?'

'Oh, 'eavens no! It was all straight sex round 'ere back then. Prostitutes everywhere, there was.' He leans forward again. 'Leslie, dear, do you remember that dirty bookshop? Sold all those physique books?'

'Er...n-no. No, I d-don't,' Leslie stutters, staring intently at the menu.

Dolly nudges me. I grin back. 'So, when did it all change?'

'In the seventies,' Dolly replies. 'Mary Whitehouse and her

brigade. That's what did it. But, you see, all it did was drive it underground. I remember one day I was walkin' down here an' a dead body got thrown out the window. Landed right at my feet, it did. A young girl. I can still see her face, shocking it was. O' course there was a lot more rent on the street back then. But we didn't 'ave the freedom, you see.' He rests his hand on my arm, eyes sparkling. 'Do you know, I once walked all the way from Tottenham Court Road to Marble Arch, all the way down Oxford Street, holding my boyfriend's hand. I must have been about nineteen. An' we were spat at. People shoutin'. But we did it,' he says proudly. 'We got to the end of the street.'

I catch Leslie's eye. He's looking at his friend with admiration. 'Was that with Gary?' I ask.

Dolly doesn't answer. He stares down at his plate. I feel like I've just intruded on a still delicate subject and for a full minute no one speaks. Leslie scans the restaurant. I stare at the out-of-date theatre posters Sellotaped to the wall, embarrassed. Then the waitress walks over. We order drinks and food from the specials menu. Another minute passes.

'You know what upset me?'

We both look in Dolly's direction.

'The way that nurse looked at me when I held him in my arms.' He pauses, the corners of his eyes glistening with tears. 'I said to her, I said, "Do you mind! We've been together for forty-two years!"'

Leslie reaches across the table and pats Dolly's hand. 'I know, dear... I know.' He rummages in his pocket, pulls out a hanky and hands it to his friend.

'But you know what?' Dolly says, blowing his nose.

We don't answer; stare at the table, out of respect, waiting for him to finish.

'He 'ad one of the biggest cocks in Soho!'

'Dolly!' Leslie covers his mouth with his hand. 'I don't think Clayton—'

I laugh. 'Oh, don't worry about me.'

'Well, there's no point in skirtin' round the issue!' Dolly replies indignantly. 'It was part of who he was! First time I saw him he was leanin' against the jukebox in The Golden Lion an' the vibration was making it bounce all over the place.'

I'm still laughing when the waitress arrives with the drinks.

'So when did you move in with each other?' I ask.

'Oh, not for a long while, dear. Boyfriends never lived together back then. Oh, no. Well you couldn't get a mortgage, for a start. Livin' with yer man is a modern thing. Because it was the double bed, you see. That was the problem. Especially with family.'

Leslie leans forward. 'Tell Clayton about that man.'

'What man?'

'Michael.'

'Oh, him...'

'Who's Michael?'

'A married man I used to work with at British Telecom,' Dolly explains, reaching for his drink. 'We've been friends for years. Since the seventies.' He takes a sip. 'Got three kids now, he has. Although he split from his wife a couple of years back.'

Leslie taps Dolly on the arm. 'Tell him about the—'

'I'm just gettin' to that bit!' Dolly snaps back.

'Gawd 'elp us!' Leslie huffs.

'So, when Gary died, apart from Leslie here, Michael was only one who phoned. An' he called me up one day an' he asked me if I was okay. An' I said, "To be honest, Michael, I'm not copin' very well at all." An' he said, "Well, I'm outside." An' he was. Driven all the way from London, he had.'

The waitress walks back over, carrying three bowls of soup. The infamous Leek and Potato. Leslie looks down at his and grimaces while Dolly reaches for the pepper.

'So anyway, he came in an' he said, "I've got feelin's for you." An' I said, "What do you mean, you've got feelin's for me?" An' he said, "I think about you all the time." An' I said, "Oh, pull yourself together! I'm seventy-five an' you're twenty years younger! With three young sons, I might add!"'

I clear my throat. 'So, are you seeing him now?'

'Oh, no, dear!' Dolly replies, pulling a face as he reaches for his spoon. 'I mean we see each other. But nothing more. I can't 'ave a relationship. Not with Gary only being dead a year an' Michael havin' kids 'n all.'

We carry on chatting. Finish our soups. The waitress brings over our main courses and we finish them. And then I decide to bring something up. Something that could go either way...

'You two are very alike.'

'Do you think so?' chirps Dolly, readjusting his red-striped tie.

Leslie nods in agreement. 'Well, I suppose when you've been friends for as long as we have.'

'Yes, you're very alike...'

They look at each other, back at me again. Pleased with themselves.

'Because you're both wasting your lives.'

The sentence hangs in the air for a second, though it feels longer. Then Leslie clutches his shirt collar. Dolly grabs the table and leans back in his seat. They both turn to face me, faces wrinkled up like gargoyles, about to explode.

'And let me tell you why,' I add quickly, before they get the chance. 'I've got a friend in hospital called Chico and he's dying. He's got a boyfriend called Maz. And if they're lucky they'll probably only get to see each other one more time. For an hour. If they're lucky. While you two have years ahead of you.' I look from Leslie to Dolly. Their faces are frozen. 'You could have what my friend Chico will never have. But neither of you will take a risk. And I think that's really sad.'

I reach for my napkin, wipe my mouth, lean back in my seat, prepared for the onslaught. But—nothing. We're in a noisy restaurant, but it's as if everything's gone quiet.

The waitress arrives. 'Anyone for coffee?' she asks cheerfully, directing her question at Leslie.

'A gin and tonic!'

'Make that two,' adds Dolly. 'Doubles!'

May 12th, 2008: Imagining...

Two old queens walking down Old Compton Street, arm in arm.

They walk in silence, past customers with takeaway bags spilling out of Ed's Diner, past dinner tables laden with baskets of bread and olive oil on Moor Street, past the pub that is The Spice of Life, witness to decades of musical greats, until they're standing amongst the bustling crowd outside the Palace Theatre, the grand and imposing red brick building on Cambridge Circus.

'I'm not quite sure what to say,' says the queen with the pinched face, knowing full well what he will say.

'Me neither,' replies the smaller, squatter one.

'I mean, it's very easy to pass judgment when you're middle-aged, but wait until you're our age.'

'But the question is,' his friend says, 'what if he's right?'

'What do you mean, what if he's right?'

'What I mean is—what if we are wastin' our lives?'

'You were the one who said—'

'I know what I said!' interrupts his friend. He takes the other's hand and looks directly into his eyes. 'But what if I was wrong?'

May 13th, 2008: Lunch Break

1:20 pm.

I'm sitting in Mr Topper's, staring into the mirror while the platinum-blonde assistant clippers my hair.

'I got a friend stayin' with me next week,' she says cheerfully. ''E's from Croydon.'

I carry on staring at my reflection.

'Not our Croydon. The one near Sydney.'

I smile.

'It's a shithole, though. Same as ours.' She catches my eye in the mirror. 'Me an' 'im are both from Croydon. In't that funny?'

'Yes, very.'

'He's comin' over with 'is parents. Eight thirty on Wednesday, they get 'ere. An' he wants me to take 'im out to the clubs.' She switches to a smaller blade. 'I'm a bit worried, though. He's only jus' got outta rehab. He wuz addicted to crystal meth 'n GHB. 'E 'ad that fing—wot's it called?' She stops clippering, resting the clippers on my head. 'Drug psychosis! That's wot 'e 'ad.'

'Oh, dear.'

'So I'm a bit nervous 'bout takin' 'im out. Youknowwhattamean?'

I throw her a look that says, I sympathise, but can you take the clippers off my head?

She carries on. 'I was finkin' of takin' 'im to see a musical. That *Woman in Black*. It's 'bout a woman who 'as a miscarriage an' it comes back to haunt 'er. But I fort that might be a bit deep. So I'm gonna take 'im to see *Wicked*.'

'That's a good idea.'

'Anyway…' she sings, as if about to move the conversation on to something more upbeat, 'you bin out this weekend?'

Before I have chance to answer, she continues.

'I went to me mate's house on Saturday. She wuz 'aving a Hawaiian party. It was really great. All me friends wuz there. An' they'd stuck all these sheets of blue paper on the walls with fish on 'em. It looked just like the sea.'

I carry on smiling into the mirror while she clippers around my ears.

'An' they 'ad this inflatable palm tree that they put the beers in. An' everyone wuz dressed up. I wuz the only one that din't bother. But when I got there they said, "We got a spare grass skirt if you wan' it." So I put that on. The only problem wuz every time I went to the loo I kept pissing on it an' it stuck to me legs. Do you want me to thin it out on top?'

'Er, yes, please.'

'An' me mate Mark wuz there... That wuz weird.'

I think she's expecting me to ask why, so I do.

'Well, he's a soldier in Afghanistan an' he said he's bin gettin' blow jobs from the other soldiers. He said they all do it.'

She stops clippering again. This time she rests them on my ear. 'Do you think he's gay?'

'Well, it certainly sounds—'

'That's wot I said! I said, "You're gay, Mark." An' he said, "No I'm not! I jus' let 'em do it 'cos I'm bored." He gets posted to Cyprus next, Ayia Napa.'

'Well, I'm sure he'll get his money's worth there.'

'There!' she says, holding up a small mirror behind me, showing me the cut from all angles. ''Ow's that?'

'Great. Thank you.'

'Next!'

* * *

It's a warm afternoon and the street's gone through a metamorphosis.

Fashion queens are strutting, burly bears are bumping, Brazilian hookers, twinks 'n lookers, iPods 'n sports bags, Celtic tattoos 'n fag hags, gayers 'n lezzas, bi's 'n transers, everyone competing for that all-time achievement, Soho's Next Top Model.

I stop at the little coffee shop on the corner of Frith Street. Order a cappuccino (decide against a cake). Take my usual spot, tucked up in the corner by the window, watching the madness flow by.

Two minutes later Pam shuffles in. 'Gotta gold one for me?' she mumbles. 'That's all I need, then I can go 'ome.'

I hand her a pound coin. She squints at it through her thick NHS glasses. She doesn't seem impressed.

'It's all I've got, Pam!'

Then she wraps her arms around me, snuffling into my T-shirt. 'Thank you... Luv you!'

And out she trundles, like something from Beatrix Potter. Pam the Fag Lady. The hardest worker on Old Compton Street.

I stir my coffee. Carry on gazing out the window. A glam middle-aged woman glides by, Faye Dunaway hair, tweed suit and a stare; haughty hauteur, dripping couture; surgically enhanced, coy sideways glance. And then, walking past Aware, an old gentleman with a stick, a porkpie hat which he tips. Faces from the past. 1950s class.

I look below me, at the packed coffee tables: tourists chattering, guys cruising and at the end table a star from my New Romantic past, Pete Burns, sipping coffee with a friend. Like geisha girls, with their ghostly white inflated lips, black weave and painted brows. He's spun 'right round baby right round'—all the way round to a new androgyny for a new Soho century.

I check my watch. Twenty-five minutes left of my lunch break. I knock back my coffee, nod at the waitress and head down Frith Street for Soho Square. Kirsty MacColl's bench. Stretching out and letting the sun wash over me. *"On an empty bench in Soho Square. If you'd have come you'd have found me there."*

May 16th, 2008: Lavinia Co-Op

Although it's dark, the gentleman sitting in front of me shines.

The most striking feature is his eyebrows, which are thick, black and heavily pencilled. They rise and fall as he talks, arch and straighten, like bat wings, framing his white, heavily powdered face. And it's this whiteness which contrasts with his crimson lips, the lipstick expertly applied, outlined, suggesting years of practise, transforming the thinness into something more becoming. Then it's his nose. It's long, aquiline, holding a pair of spectacles which cling for dear life to the tip as if hanging from the edge of a cliff. As he talks he tilts his head back, partly to see through the spectacles but also, it appears, to stop them from falling.

His hair is thin with a slight curl (the bit I can see that's not hidden beneath his cap) and he's wearing a grey jacket and holding a pen and clipboard. The overall effect is that of an aging schoolmistress, reminding me of my first teacher, Mrs Evans, who, I would imagine, if she's still alive, would be in her nineties by now. *Clayton is a quiet boy*, she wrote in my school report, *and excels at English and History although he needs to try a lot harder in his maths lessons*. Something like that, anyway. Haven't thought of her for years. It's strange how these memories are flooding back.

We're in the Soho Revue Bar, in Walkers Court. And we've come to see the legendary Lavinia Co-Op from the seminal performance troupe Bloolips, a collective of radical drag performers who formed in the 1970s. I'm with my friend David Parker (aka Marmite Madge) and we're chatting with Lavinia, seated around one of the tables near the stage.

For someone who doesn't know us, Lavinia is remarkably friendly and relaxed. I've been watching him as he's circled the room, spending a few minutes with each group, chatting away as if they're old friends. He peers at me from beneath his glasses, extends a hand, smiles and asks my name. I ask him about his show, the stage direction, his past work. I'm throwing questions at him, really to give myself time to study him. His accent is thick Cockney and he's very polite. And witty. He has a sparkle in his eyes. I try to guess his age, picture what he must look like out of drag. It's hard.

After a few minutes he's drawn into a conversation with a group of people, and as he chats their voices fade into the background, gradually, ever so gradually, until it all goes quiet. And then a memory emerges...

* * *

I'm alone. I'm in my parent's bedroom. Their clothes strewn

across the floor: pleated trousers, sky-blue cotton shirts, tartan skirts, stilettos, brogues. There's the comforting smell of stale tobacco, Old Spice and freshly washed bedding. There's a wardrobe in front of me, my mum's clothes on one side, my dad's on the other, a huge mirror affixed in the centre.

I step forward cautiously and look down at the shoes. It's my mum's that I'm drawn to. I think I'm 11 or 12. But even so, I know that I'm about to do something that's not right, that I'd get into trouble if anyone walked in. Like the time I smoked one of my dad's Slim Panatellas in the bathroom, watching myself in the mirror as I blew the smoke upwards. It doesn't stop me, though. The urge is too strong.

I take another step forward. I'm not just nervous now, I'm excited.

I stretch one foot forward into a patent-leather stiletto. Fasten the buckle at the back. Quickly. Then the other. I instantly feel frightened. I shut my eyes, tightly, then open them, slowly. Look straight ahead, in the mirror.

I reach down again, for a skirt. It's black, flowing, and I wrap it around my waist. There's a small jacket to go with it. I'm almost there now, there's just one thing missing. It's on the dressing table, the long beech dressing table that takes up the length of the whole wall. Past the inlaid jewelry box, the tights, the polystyrene wig stand. There it is: the makeup box.

I hobble unsteadily toward it, gripping the dressing table as I edge past the unmade bed. The window's half open, the net curtains blowing inward, a warm breeze that blends with the acrid smell of the room. Outside, kids are playing, shrieking. The ice cream van's musical jingle somewhere in the distance. I touch the box. Hesitate. Then slowly lift the lid. My eyes widen at the treasure trove of mascara pencils, eye-shadow trays, powders. Shimmering. Greens. Blues. A square mirror. A plastic comb. It's like my sister's Girl's World.

'Clay!'

My heart stops.

'Clay!'

Then it all happens really quickly. I pull the stilettos off, the jacket, the skirt. Throw them on the floor in a pile. I get as far as the door and look back. Panicking. I feel like I'm going to be sick, like the time that kid was chasing me on the way home from school. I readjust the skirt on the floor. Is that how it was? I rush to my room, grab a book, pretend to be reading. And that's where the memory fades. Just there. There is no more. Just the voice, shouting, 'Clay! Clay!'

* * *

'Clay!'

I look across the table. It's Madge. 'Do you want a drink?'

'Er… Yes. Thanks. A coke.'

Then the show begins. I'm mesmerised. Transfixed, until the very end.

May 18th, 2008: Nobody Really Knows

Since I've been blogging about the shop I've met a number of interesting people on MySpace, and because of the shop's location these people have popped in to say hello. I've met singers, actors, writers, artists. It's been one of the advantages of having a shop here, meeting so many creative people.

One of them was a musician. The friendship began in cyberspace. He'd send me long emails about my writing, books that I should read about Soho, so that I could immerse myself in the history. I suppose there was a mutual admiration thing going on as I was equally drawn to his music, beautifully haunting music, with interesting lyrics that really spoke to me, accompanied by videos, some of which were shot just outside the shop.

He would visit us two or three times a week, always with a bottle of champagne, and, once we'd closed, we'd go downstairs and chat until the early hours.

Although he was happily settled down with a boyfriend of over 20 years, living in the country, he seemed starved of friendship. And despite his visits becoming a bit too regular, I enjoyed his company. I was in awe of his musical ability. I would listen to his music late at night sitting here by the window and his poetic lyrics would seep into my blogs.

But then something changed.

It's hard to put my finger on when it started—it was quite subtle at first. He'd pass a comment about Jorge, or about me, nothing to fall out over, but enough to make me uneasy. But then the compliments turned into digs. It was as if, once the friendship was established, he had to kill it. I knew enough about his family history to understand why he was doing it, but, even so, he was pushing the friendship to the limit. Then, one night at the shop, he went too far and I asked him to leave, and the friendship ended.

I'm listening to his music in my headphones now as I write this. I often do. It's inspiring. I go back to it again and again. Is it possible to like the art but not the artist? Yes, it is. In fact, now I know him, the anger behind the lyrics has resonance. And though it's sad that the friendship ended, I know that when I look back on our time here in years to come, it will be his music that I listen to, his music that provides the soundtrack to our brief Soho life.

May 18th, 2008: A Soho Scar

Ben's outside.

But it's a different Ben tonight. He's less confident. Wary. And there's something different about his face too, though it's hard to see because of the crowds: couples holding hands, queens too high to land, cans of beer, drunken cheers, two men dancing, two fighting, and all the time Ben's head moving from side to side, watching it all.

Then he stops. And now I see it. The bruise. The swollen face. His right eye, purple, yellow. And framing his brow, a cut. A

Soho scar. It's the ultimate street hustler look. A nod to the Dilly Boys of old.

How did it happen? An angry pimp? A violent punter? I don't think I'll ever know, because I have a strange, unexplainable feeling that, just like Chico, after tonight, I'll never see Ben in Soho again.

May 20th, 2008: Soho Square

I'm walking down Dean Street.

So, what have I got to do? Collect the repairs from Pino, our Italian tailor. Pick up the dry cleaning. Do the banking. OK. Which first? The banking!

I take a right at the crossroads and head toward Soho Square.

It's a warm summer morning. Pigeons gliding from tree to tree, the sun filtering through the branches. Rays of sunlight bathing a mix of road workers, office staff and a couple of drunks sprawled across the grass. A little patch of tranquillity in a sea of urban madness.

I pass the 20th Century Fox building. Then Frith Street. Glance at the square again, at an old man walking past the Elizabethan-style gardener's hut, taking a seat on one of the benches.

Did I bring the paying-in book? I reach into my pocket. Yes. Here it is. Then I stop. Hold on—was that Leslie?

I cross the road. Peer through the railings. It is Leslie! As I walk through the park gates, he immediately looks up in my direction and our eyes lock.

'Hello, ducky,' he says as I approach.

'I should've known you'd be here on a day like this.'

'Beautiful, isn't it?' he says, admiring the view.

I follow his gaze. 'It's lovely. Can I join you?'

'Of course!' He pulls an ironed white hanky from the breast pocket of his blazer and flicks at the space on the bench next to him. 'Not working today, then?' he asks as I take a seat.

'Yeah, later. I've got a few things to do first.' As I reel off the list of errands, two pigeons land near our feet, stepping cautiously toward us. Leslie shoos them away with his hand. 'What about you?' I ask. 'What brings you here so early?'

He leans back. 'Dolly. She's at the clinic.' He nods toward the NHS building on the corner of Frith Street.

'Anything wrong?'

'Nothing serious,' he says with a shake of his head. 'Just her waterworks.'

There's a few seconds of silence. I lean back too. Close my eyes, trying to clear my head of the errands, feeling the heat from the sun on my forehead.

'Talking of which...' Leslie says carefully, as if there's something on his mind and he's been waiting for an opening. 'This friend of yours...'

'Chico?'

'Yes. How is he?'

I open my eyes. 'Not good.'

'Was he a customer?'

'Yes.'

'That bleedin' shop...' he mutters.

There's another pause. Separate thoughts, separate worlds. Then Leslie asks, again carefully, 'How long does he have?'

'He could go at any time.'

'And his partner? Have they'—he clears his throat—'said goodbye?'

'Yes. The chaplain called me a few days ago. Imagine never seeing the person you love ever again.'

The sentence resonates, though it wasn't intentional. Leslie looks at me expectantly, as if waiting to hear more. So I lean forward, staring at the pigeons pecking at the grass nearby, and recount yesterday's visit.

* * *

I'm in Cambridge Hospital.

Chico's on the bed in front of me, asleep. Next to him sits a prison guard who flicks through a magazine with one hand, linked by handcuffs to Chico with the other. The only sound is the whir of a machine above Chico's head and muffled voices from the TV.

My eyes travel to the window: trees, hedgerows, acres of green fields, a man running with his dog, throwing a ball, the dog barking excitedly, snapping at his heels.

I look down at Chico. He's lost weight. A lot of weight. His lips are parched, his complexion pale and mottled, his arms limp and thin. Even his pyjamas (his clothes have been confiscated in case he tries to escape) appear lifeless, empty, covering his still body like a shroud.

My first thought is, it shouldn't have been like this. This should have been a gradual friendship. We'd have met at the shop, gone for drinks, got to know each other, slowly, the way you do, becoming involved in each others lives, sharing good times, bad times. But not like this. Not just thrown together. Although—it must be just as strange for him.

A nurse walks past the open door. Stops. Peers inside. Glances up at the clock, down at her clipboard. Then walks on. The click-clack of her heels on the polished floor like the click-clack of the keyboard as I type this.

How long have I been here? A few minutes? An hour? A shadow inches its way across Chico's bed like the Grim Reaper. Outside, the sun sinks behind a hedgerow, lighting it up like a pathway to Heaven.

Not that any of this is new. I went through this years ago with my first partner. Watching him sleep, stroking his arm, whispering in his ear. In that ward in the Chelsea and Westminster Hospital, on the second floor. And here I am, years later—another hospital, another friend. Only this one won't pull through.

Then he stirs. The prison guard, absorbed in his magazine, is oblivious to the chain pulling taut across the bed. Chico blinks. Once. Twice. Trying to focus, rubbing his eyes. Forgetting the handcuffs. Then an awkward few seconds as he remembers, as his eyes move from puzzled to sad.

It just doesn't seem fair. I've got a book coming out while Chico's just lying here. And to make matters worse, I'm still writing about him. As if I'm using his misfortune. Just yesterday a friend hinted at the very same thing. And though I argued that I've just been following his life as I have everybody else's, he hit a nerve.

I like to think I'm writing about Chico for the right reasons, trying to keep his name alive, trying to tell his version of events. But, at the same time, there's no getting away from the fact that he's handing me a story. Am I exploiting it? I suppose, if I'm honest, I am. But then again, I have told Chico everything, so it's not as if I'm doing any of this behind his back. Still, I can't shake off the feeling that somehow what I'm doing is not right.

'Honey? Is that you?'

'Yeah, it's me.'

He reaches for my hand. 'Clay, there's something I have to tell you.'

I have a feeling I know what he's going to say.

'The doctors have stopped the chemo.'

Silence.

'You know what this means, don't you?'

I nod.

'It's just a few weeks now.'

'Chico. We're going get you out of here! We're going get you back home with your sisters. I'm going speak to the governor tomorrow. We'll fly back with you if we have to. But we're going get you out of here. I promise!'

He squeezes my hand, a feeble squeeze. 'Honey... I may not get released in time.'

He's right. I look at him. And I'm at a loss.

* * *

Leslie stares ahead, beyond the grass, past slumbering bodies, past the weather-beaten statue of King Charles ll, as if he's gazing into some far distant place—or the past. A full minute passes. I'm just about to tell him I have to leave when he says, barely above a whisper, 'Maybe it should've been like this.'

'What do you mean?'

He looks at me intently. 'You. Writing about him. Telling his story. Us, here. Maybe this *is* the way it was always meant to be.'

I'm not sure how to answer this. So I don't. We sit there in silence for another minute, children playing nearby, the bells of St Patrick's chiming the hour, as I think about the implications of what he's just said. Then Leslie grips the bench rests, whimpers slightly as he stands and says, 'It's strange, how someone I've never met—how they can put everything in perspective.'

I lean up and kiss him on the cheek, then watch as he walks through the gates, crossing the road, turning into Frith Street—the sun in his hair, the moon in his eyes and a head full of memories.

May 24th, 2008: The End Is Nigh

Things aren't going well at the shop. The credit crunch is really crunching now and takings have plummeted.

On Tuesday we made £25. On Wednesday, £65. We need to take at least a thousand a day just to break even. Every night Jorge checks the figures, sighs, closes his black book and hangs his head. It's set to be our worst month ever. So on Thursday Jorge met with an insolvency solicitor, whose advice to us was 'Leave now.'

'Leave now.' It's such an easy thing to say, but we've devoted more than two years trying to make this little shop work. Ploughing in every bit of money we had. Working seven days a week. Never taking a day off. We've survived gang attacks, credit card fraud, a mafia landlady, leaks from the brothel, Thames Water. But the economy—it's beaten us. We were hoping that my newspaper column would help bring more customers in. But it hasn't. People come in just to say they've read it. Crazy people mainly. But none of them have bought anything. All the plans we had for opening a string of shops, all come to nothing.

But we have to close—the strain is just getting too much. We're trying to hold it together but it's becoming increasingly hard. We're not sleeping properly; we're taking sleeping pills. I've started scratching my head in bed at night. I haven't done that for years—I dig my nails into the skin and scratch. God, I'm doing it now as I write this. My face is breaking out in spots— Jorge's too. And I seem to have lost the will to write. Nothing seems that funny to me anymore. The excitement of living here long since drained away. And the stress is affecting our relationship too; I can't remember when we last had sex. We just fall into bed, cuddle up, exhausted, completely drained.

So tonight we started packing all our personal effects: clothes, the daybed, pictures, ornaments, dismantling the home we've made below the shop, just in case the bailiffs arrive unexpectedly. It's really sad, because despite everything, I've come to love this place. It feels like Soho's in my blood.

I'm upstairs as I type this. In my usual spot by the window. Looking outside, watching the crowds. I'm really going to miss this little spot.

May 25th, 2008: A Late-Night Call

Midnight.

I'm sitting by the window, typing away. The only light, my laptop screen.

I reach for my juice, take a sip, glance outside. It's the usual Soho crowd. Danny and David, the local pimps, hustling customers for Sunset Strip. A smattering of dealers. Cruising queens. Drunken stag nights. Bewildered straight couples. And just outside the brothel doorway, inches from where I sit, three straight men loitering, trying to pluck up courage to go in. One of them says, 'You fuck her first and then

I'll have her.' It's about as near to man-to-man sex as their manliness will allow.

I place my drink back on the counter. Go back to the screen, my finger tracing the last line. OK. Now, where was I? Oh, yes…

The phone rings. I reach for the handset.

'Hello.'

'Clay?'

'Chico?'

'Darlin'. Is that you?'

I notice that his speech is slurred. 'Yeah. It's me.'

'Oh, honey…'

'Chico, is everything all right?'

'Chest infection,' he mumbles, as if even saying the words is sapping his energy.

'Oh, no… Are you okay?'

There's a rasping coughing sound.

'Chico?'

'I don't want you runnin' out the next time you see me.'

'Oh, Chico. Why would I do that?'

'Because I look terrible.' He starts to sob. *'Honey… You know I told you I thought the tumour had gone down a bit?'*

'Yes.'

'It's come back.'

Oh, God. What do you say at times like this?

'An' I've lost so much weight. I was forty-seven kilos yesterday. I'm forty-four today.'

'Are you still bringing your food up?'

'Uh-huh. I jus' can't keep it down. I've tried.' Then his voice turns into a raspy mumble. The medication taking its toll.

'Chico?'

Silence.

'Chico?'

'Yes?'

'Are you still taking the nausea tablets?'

'They don't...'

'They don't work?'

'No.'

'Stay strong, Chico.'

'I'm tryin', honey,' he sobs. 'I'm tryin'.'

'Chico, I'll come and visit you tomorrow. Okay?'

'Don't be shocked.'

'Oh, it doesn't matter what you look like.'

'I gotta go now, honey,' he sniffs. 'Give my love to Jorge.'

We say our goodbyes. I put the phone back on the stand. Rest my fingers on the keyboard. Wipe away a tear and start typing.

May 26ᵗʰ, 2008: Room 34

I catch my breath. It's a shock. It's only been a week, but he's like a different person. It's not Chico at all, it's like that Benetton ad. The one of the dying man surrounded by his loved ones. He has the same skeletal look: skin stretched across bone, mouth slightly open, teeth protruding. His breathing is slow, laboured.

I wait for him to draw his next breath. Eventually it comes, through his mouth, a rasping, dry, painful intake of breath. A death rattle.

'Chico.'

Now it's those news reports of starving people in Africa I'm seeing. Pencil-thin arms. Legs that barely make a ripple in his pyjamas.

'Chico, it's Clay.' I stroke his arm, punctured with track marks from the cannula. 'Remember me?'

He doesn't respond. Not a stir.

'Chico, it's me.'

Nothing.

I watch him closely, waiting. Then slowly, slowly, his eyelids move and his eyes flicker open. They stare straight ahead, at the white light emanating from the TV screen above his head, as if hypnotised. Then I notice the smell. A smell I haven't smelt before.

'I love you, Chico.'

His lips move, slightly, ever so slightly.

'Chico, it's Clay.'

They tremble, as if words are about to come out if he can just summon up the energy.

'I've brought your cigarettes. And your magazines. And your—'

I can feel myself choking up, as if I'm about to burst into tears. The prison guard must sense this: through the reflection in the window I see him leave the room.

Then Chico speaks. Something. I can't quite make it out.

'Chico? What is it?'

'Ahhhhh.'

'What is it, Chico? I'm here.'

'Ian.'

'No, Chico. It's me. Clay!'

Then I remember. His last boyfriend. The one who died just months before Chico got caught up in all this—mess.

He tries to push his head forward. Straining toward the light from the TV screen. Staring at the light. His lips trembling, trembling.

'It's okay, Chico,' I reassure him, stroking a pencil-thin arm, trying not to show how upset I feel. 'It's Ian... Ian's here.'

Then he relaxes. His head touches the pillow. His eyes roll to the back of his sockets. The lids close. His mouth closes. And then a faint look of contentment.

I stay with him for an hour, whispering Ian's name.

Then I catch the train back to London. The underground. Back to Soho. The shop. I open my laptop and start writing: about the debts, when we should leave. And then I stop and think about the hospital. The ward, the room. I reach for the Delete button and press firmly, until all the words are gone, realising how meaningless they are. And then I start typing again: about my visit to a dying friend.

May 27th, 2008: The Laundrette

I've just walked into the run-down launderette just off Endell Street.

There's a faded patterned mat at the entrance, bags of clothes spilling over on the floor, a faint smell of washing powder. There's heat in the air, an old man nodding off, slumped in a chair.

I walk to the back of the room to collect my service wash. There's a notice pinned to the door: 'Back in 30 mins!' Thirty minutes from when? I contemplate what to do. Decide that as I'm down to my last pair of clean pants I should wait. I take a seat on the wooden bench.

Outside, a bedraggled homeless man rummages through a bin. He pulls out a Tesco's bag, looks inside, drops it back in again. A young couple walk past. The boy holds on to the girl, her head nestled into his chest. She's sobbing uncontrollably.

I stare at the washing machine in front of me. Feeling apathetic—like a drugs downer without the drugs. The cylinder spins anti-clockwise. Stops, momentarily. Then clockwise. The nameplate on it reads 'Speed Queen.' Reminds me of a guy I knew in the 80s.

Someone walks in. It's Maggie. We chat for while. She asks me how business is going. I tell her—but cut the conversation short. She tells me that business is just as tough for her and that she saw the sign in our window: 'Buy Two Items: Get the Second Half Price.' She says she's considering doing the same. "Buy two blow jobs, get one free!" We joke about her launching a loyalty card. Blow Miles. Then she kisses me on each cheek and leaves.

A few minutes crawl by. The door squeaks opens. I make a move to stand. But it's not Tina, the shop assistant, it's the guy who walks up and down Old Compton Street with his headphones on, singing to Britney at the top of his voice. A few off-key blasts of "Toxic" fill the room, the tumble dryers adding musical accompaniment.

"*With a taste of a poison paradise,*" he sings. He checks his washing, then warbles his way back out. *"I'm addicted to you. Don't you know that you're toxic?"* It crosses my mind that in terms of mental health, he and his idol share common ground.

I look at my watch. I've been here for 20 minutes now. Decide to give it another five, worried about leaving Jorge in the shop on his own, remembering the 12 gang attacks we've had since we've opened. The perpetrators all black. I mull over the idea of writing a column for *The London Paper* about this, imagining the stick I'd get, however I positioned it. A topic political correctness can't quite get to grips with, it seems.

There's another squeak from the door and the old Chinese woman with the limp hobbles in. She's dressed in a waist-length blue denim jacket and brown nylon trousers. Her white hair's slightly curled and her face is very white, devoid of expression, reminding me of a painting I once saw of the Dowager Empress of China, Tzu Hsi.

She takes a seat on the bench next to me, unzips her tartan plaid shopping trolley and takes out a Tupperware container of washing powder, a white shirt and a pair of grey trousers. She places the clothes carefully in a machine, adds the powder, inserts the coins and closes the door. She takes a seat next to me again. I feel her head turn to look at me.

'My husband suit,' she says, her face crinkled up, eyes all but disappearing.

'Okay,' I reply, not really sure what else I can add.

'I wash once week.'

I smile.

The only noise the whir of the machines. We both stare ahead. I look at my watch. I can't wait here much longer.

'He dead.'

Her words, though softly spoken, reverberate. Like an echo in a bottomless cave. Yet still she watches the cylinder go round and round and round, in her own world. It's an uncomfortable moment. Uncomfortable and sad. As I watch her I wonder how long she's been hanging on to her husband's clothes. Weeks? Months? Years? Why does she do it? But then I think, well, maybe Jorge and I have been hanging on to the clothes in the shop for too long, and it's time to let them go too.

Finally the assistant walks in. 'Sorry, luv. You bin 'ere long?'

I stand up. Shrug. 'No. Not really.'

I pay for my washing, make my way outside and head back to the shop, down the back streets of Covent Garden, pulling the rickety suitcase behind me, rushing to avoid the onset of rain.

May 28th, 2008: An Explanation

3 pm. A subdued and tired-looking Wolfy has just walked in. He stumbles up to the counter and hangs his head.

'Wolfy, are you okay?' Jorge asks.

'No.'

'Why?'

He rests his hands on the glass, staring down at the ties. 'I have been off crack for two days.'

'Crack?' Jorge says incredulously.

I stop typing. The manic, hyperactive visits starting to make sense.

'Yes,' Wolfy replies mournfully. 'That is the reason my boyfriend left me... But I do not need to go into a rehab,' he adds quickly, 'because I am clean. I am going to stay clean. My boyfriend said he would come back if I stay clean. And I want to have a beautiful dinner party.' He looks at Jorge despairingly. 'Are you my friend?'

'Er—'

'Can you tell me something?'

'Yes.'

'Am I too fat for black and fitted?'

'No! Not at all. Why do you say that?'

'Because that is why I took crack. I wanted to stay slim for my boyfriend... And now he has gone.'

189

The logic behind this and the outcome are so fucked up I try to shake it off. Maybe Wolfy senses this, because after reminding us again about his dinner party, he leaves.

* * *

11 pm.

Jorge's downstairs watching the sports on TV. I'm sitting by the window, laptop open, watching the pimps fighting for customers. Then I spot Wolfy. He's outside Soho Books, scanning the street nervously, checking his watch every few seconds. What's he doing here?

A tattooed guy in a dark-blue tracksuit ambles by. He stops. They talk, though neither looks at the other. Wolfy digs into his pocket and pulls something out. He hands it to the tattooed guy, who hands him something back and leaves, hurriedly.

Wolfy stares down at his clasped hand. His eyes travel toward the shop. I know he can't see me because the lights are off. But what is he thinking? He looks tense. Then he shoves his clasped hand deep into his pocket again, crosses the street and walks away. Thinking about a dinner party that he'll never get to see.

May 29th, 2008: A Conversation

I'm running down Frith Street, heading toward the Soho Clinic, rushing so fast I bump straight into an old man on his way out.

'Oooppps! Sorry!'

'Well, I never!' he says, and he grabs my hands. 'An' what're you doing round here?'

'Me? What are *you* doing round here?'

'Picking up a prescription,' we both say in unison. We laugh. Then Dolly says, 'Shouldn't you be in the shop sellin' undies?'

'I will be in a few minutes.'

'Gorgeous day for it,' he beams, taking in the cloudless blue sky.

'Yeah. It's lovely, isn't it?'

'I was jus' gonna have a little sit in the sun. Do you want to join me for a natter?'

'Well, I—'

'Oh, don't let me stop you!' He releases my hands. 'Not if you're busy.'

I look at my watch. 'No. It's okay. I've got a few minutes.'

So we link arms and walk through the gates of the square.

'What 'bout over there?' says Dolly, pointing to a nearby bench.

We walk the few steps. Dolly lowers himself, removing his beret and placing it on his lap.

'Such a lovely day,' he says, admiring the surroundings once he's settled. 'Don't often get days like this.' He nods at an old woman on the next bench. 'Oh, by the way,'—he taps me on the arm—'I really enjoyed our dinner the other night.'

'You did?'

'Oh, yessss! Brought back all the old memories, it did.'

I think back to the dinner's last few awkward minutes. Fortunately Dolly's either forgotten them or he's being tactful and he continues talking—about his new flat, his friends in Brighton, 60s Soho. 'Anyway, enough of me,' he says eventually. 'How're things at the shop?'

I pull a face.

'No one buyin'?'

'No. It's dead.'

'It must be quite stressful for that boyfriend of yours. What's his name? George?'

'That's the English translation but he prefers Jorge.'

'Jorggggeeeee,' he says, dragging the word out as if trying to work out its meaning. 'How long have you been together?'

'Ummm...about four years now.'

'Four years!' he sings. He crosses his legs. 'Still in love, then?'

'Yeah...'

He frowns and cocks his head, so I continue. 'Well... You know what it's like. Relationships change.'

'That they do.'

'But we've been through such a lot together. A long-distance relationship. Getting him over here. The shop...'

'These things can bring you together.'

'Oh, they have! Jorge's changed my life. He's taught me so much. About art, clothes. His mother was a master tailor so he knows everything about menswear—the tailoring, the textile manufacturing, fashion trends, designers. He's even designed his own collection.'

'He sounds like a hard worker.'

'Yeah. He is. He's working round the clock to try to keep the shop open. I think it stems from his childhood.'

'His childhood?'

'He had to leave Cuba when he was a small boy. When Castro came to power.' And I explain how Jorge's family left behind houses, money and other family members, arriving in the States with literally only the clothes on their back. 'Jorge was the only family member who could speak English—so he had to become the father.' And as I'm telling Dolly this, I realise that it was probably that experience that made Jorge so driven. 'But anyway, to answer your original question, yes, we're still in love.'

Dolly's watches me closely. 'But...'

'Well. You know...'

'You mean the physical?'

I nod.

'Doesn't last forever, does it?' He edges closer. 'Now, when I first met Gary it was fireworks every night. Had to fight 'im off, I did! Three or four times a night 'e wanted it. Oh, it were scandalous.' He smirks. 'Well, he was such a sexual man, see— what with his, er...' He catches me grinning and laughs. 'Oh, he had 'em queuin' up, he did! All the queens fightin' to get at 'im. An' o' course, well, eventually, he strayed.'

'Did it bother you?'

He fiddles with a button on his jacket. 'There was one time... But it were always me he came home to.'

'But you didn't mind him—'

'You just learn to accept, don't you? Took me a while, mind... Anyway, what about you, dear? Are you both...what's the word?'

'Monogamous?'

'That's the one!'

'You know what, if someone had said to me when I first moved to London, Would you ever have an open relationship? I'd have said, No way! But the older you get, I suppose you become less precious about these things.'

'I know what you mean. Although me and Gary never spoke about it.'

'Every straight couple I've met—whenever they've faced an issue like that, they've just got divorced. Which always seems like such a waste to me.'

Dolly nods.

'But with gay men... I think there's something about two men together that goes beyond just sex. It like there's a bond there that survives these things.'

'Oh, I think you're right, dear,' agrees Dolly. 'It's that shared experience thing.'

The old lady on the next bench stands, using her walking stick as a support, and hobbles past. She's wearing a racing-green skirt and a matching jacket and her still chestnut hair is stylishly bobbed. She smiles warmly as she passes. Dolly returns her smile.

I decide to switch the conversation. 'Anyway, what about this man of yours?'

'Who, Michael?'

'Yes.'

Dolly watches a couple of guys walking across the grass. 'Oh,

I don't know… I'm seventy-five an' he's in his fifties. An' it's such a long time since I've…you know.' He glances in my direction and covers his mouth with his hand, feigning modesty.

'There's always Viagra.'

'At my age!' he shrieks, slapping me on the leg playfully. 'I'd have a stroke!' Then he says; 'What would you do?'

'It's hard to say… Do you like him?'

'I think so…' He looks down at the ring on his finger. Twirls it, contemplating. 'Listen to me. There's me, tellin' you to stop encouragin' Leslie, an'…well…who'd have thought I'd be havin' this conversation at my age.'

'I hope I'm having this conversation at your age!'

We smile. Stay silent for a few seconds. Then Dolly says, 'What about Jorge? Is he your first boyfriend?'

'Second.'

'And the first?'

'He's still around. And we've been friends for—God—twenty-five years!' But just recently, since I've met Jorge, we hardly see each other. It feels a bit like a bereavement.' I stare across the square, just as Leslie did a few days before, past slumbering bodies, the gardener's hut, the trees, to that far distant place—where memories linger.

Dolly reaches for my hand. 'Maybe it's good to let go of the past.'

I turn to face him again. 'Hey, I thought I was giving you the advice!'

'Actually, my dear,' he says, squeezing my hand, 'you just did.'

May 30th, 2008: A Present

It's 9 pm and we're getting ready to close. Jorge's cashing up and I'm pulling down the grates.

Behind me the street's awash with energy: a Christian group are offering to save our souls, tuk-tuks are weaving in and out of the crowds, taxi horns and car stereos are honking and thumping, crowds spilling out onto the street outside The

Admiral Duncan. Everyone making the most of a beautiful May evening. Then a voice cries out:

'Claytee!'

I shove the last bolt in the lock and turn around. Even from this distance, amongst all this madness, he stands out, like a peacock, a multitude of rainbow colours, patterns and fabrics, with a scarf trailing along the street behind him.

He rushes toward me, reaching for my hands. 'Claytee! Sweets! Are you still open, my dear? Say that you are!'

'Raqib! How are you?'

'I'm not intruding, am I?'

'No, of course not!'

'Are you, are, are you sure?' he stutters in his endearing manner.

'I'm sure!' I push the door open, call Jorge and usher him in.

I've never seen anyone wear the kind of outfits Raqib wears and carry them off the way he does. Alexander McQueen bondage boots, Dior grey pin-striped high-waisted jodhpurs, a Costume National waistcoat on top of a Cavalli flower-print turquoise silk shirt, a floor-length embroidered silk kimono draped over his shoulders and the scarf, an eight-foot, multi-striped number by Missoni (which I carry into the shop, like a bridesmaid, to prevent the crowds outside stepping on it).

'Oh, it's so good to be back at Dirty White Boy!' he says, twirling, his scarf and kimono flying around, while his flower-patterned trilby remains perfectly in place, perched on the side of his head.

Jorge rushes over. He greets Raqib with a hug and a kiss, they exchange a few pleasantries and then Raqib announces: 'Now, Jorge-san! I need clothes. I have nothing from your new collections!'

'Raqib, that's not true,' Jorge replies. 'You already have everything!'

'Oh, I can't wear last season's hand-me-downs! Please take me through the rails, Jorge-san. Please! You must have something new for me.'

'Raqib, honestly, you've bought everything!'

'Jorge-san!' Raqib says, with a wag of his finger, feigning anger. 'Please!'

Then Jorge has a thought. 'Actually, I do have a little something. I don't think it'll fit, but you might as well see it anyway.'

'What is it? Will I like it? Will I? Oh, please fetch it for me. Please!'

'Hold on a sec.'

Two minutes later, Jorge walks back up the stairway carrying a black, custom-made, Thierry Mugler dinner jacket, layered with bird feathers. Raqib's face lights up. He quickly steps out of his layers of clothing and slips into it. It's a perfect fit. He spins around again. 'It's gorgey, Jorge-san! Gorgey!' He drapes it over the counter. Then he spies our hat collection. 'Oh! And what are these? You haven't shown me these before!'

Jorge steps forward and blocks his path. 'Now, Raqib, you do not need another hat! You must have about a hundred hats already.' And he's right. They're all lined up, on little hatstands, in his walk-in dressing room.

Raqib gently sweeps Jorge aside and inspects each one. Nodding. Lips pursed. Tiptoeing down the rail like a ballerina. 'Okay. I'll have that one,' he says, completely ignoring what Jorge's just said. 'And...this one.' Then he tries on an Angora rabbit fur top hat. 'And this one.' In then end he takes every hat we have. 'Honestly, you two,' he tuts, opening his Dior purse. 'No wonder you're shop's doing so badly—you never let me buy anything!'

And it's true. As badly off as we are, we're reluctant to sell him too many clothes. We think he buys so many not because he needs them (or he'll ever wear them—after all, he hardly ever leaves his studio), it's because he's trying to help us out.

'Raqib. Please don't buy anything else,' Jorge says firmly, as Raqib starts to run a finger along the trouser rail. 'Come on downstairs and let's have some champagne.'

Raqib squeals with delight. 'Fabulous! Champagne at Dirty White Boy!' Then he picks up the folder he brought in with him and he gives Jorge a crafty wink. 'And presents.'

Once we're seated, clinked glasses and nibbled on some Cuban food, we discuss Raqib's upcoming show at the Metropolitan Museum of Art in New York.

'Of course I won't go. I'll send Yoko. I don't mix in those circles—as you know.' He laughs, for no apparent reason, the way he does, 'HA! HA! HA! HA! HA! HA! That macaw-like laugh of his echoing around the basement. 'The art world's about to collapse anyway. The financial collapse is about to hit us all! And I predict that there will be weeds growing in galleries round the world by the end of the year.' He lights a cigarette. 'Actually, I'm looking forward to a period of calm and silence. Then maybe I can do things that I like as far as my happiness is concerned—away from all the professional madness.' He takes a drag, the cigarette propped delicately between the tips of his paint-smeared fingers. 'But tell me—what of you two? How is the shop doing, if one may ask?'

Jorge tells him we'll be closing soon, for good.

He shakes his head and looks down sadly at the table in front of us. 'Ah, sweets!' He reflects for a few seconds, the mood somber. Then he looks up and he's smiling. 'You know... Visiting you two has rekindled so many memories from my St Martin's days. The recklessness. The absurdity. The magic of it all. And Soho will not be the same without you. But have no fear, my dears—Dirty White Boy will be forever woven within the fabric of the soul of Soho and we shall treasure it as a glorious bloom in our basket of memories.' He reaches for his folder on the floor and places it on the table in front of us. 'Anyway—a little something to take your mind off it all.'

He opens the folder carefully, removing bubble wrap, wrapping paper, tissue paper, placing each sheet carefully on the floor. Then the last sheet is removed and there lies one of his paintings. A half-human figure imploding on a sea of blood with a hypodermic needle centre stage, signed, *To Jorge, Clayton and all the Dirty White, Green, Red, Yellow and Cobalt Blue Boys of this world. Love Raqib.*

Considering his stature in the art world, it's like being presented a piece of work from a young Francis Bacon. Jorge's eyes meet mine, and we thank Raqib profusely.

It's hard to believe what Raqib's achieved. He gave up a luxurious life in Kashmir, born into one of the richest families in the region, to become a penniless art student in London, living in a squat, struggling to get himself through university (where one lecturer told him that his work would only be good enough for decorative throw cushions), hooked on heroin at one point (hence the hypodermic needle in the painting), to become, at the age of 32, one of the country's leading artists. And one of its most publicity-shy.

'You must get John Jones to frame it. I'll give you his number. He is the only one who does museum-quality frames. Now,' he says dismissively, as if he wants no further talk about the painting, 'what are you doing next week? Because I want you to come to the studio. To the Faraway Tree in the Enchanted Forest. It'll be my craziest flower installation to date. As everything else is heading toward absolute shit, let us enjoy the last masquerade. It'll be a swan song to remember. And I shall wear the perfect outfit—an old family friend from Kashmir is designing it. I'm sure you will approve, Jorge-san. It has shades of bright-blue embroidery on white silk. And it's inspired by the Taj Mahal.'

The conversation continues, about art, history, love, sex, until, hours later, with the approach of dawn, champagne long gone, we call him a cab and he leaves. One of the most eccentric and talented artists this century is likely to see.

June 2008

June 3rd, 2008: Packing

We get up early and move another vanload of furniture back to our run-down flat in Holland Road. The Mies Van der Rohe daybed, the antique Chinese armoire, all the artwork; the Picasso drawing, the Dalí woodcuts, the Braque serigraph, the 18th-century Persian primitive on ivory, and the nudes of Jorge that he was given as gifts in Provincetown when he had his *Naked Civil Servant* moment. And, of course, the pièce de résistance, Raqib's painting.

It's quite ironic—we're penniless, and we've been living in a damp, gloomy, rat-infested basement, emptying buckets full of water from two dehumidifiers every day, falling asleep to the sound of the madam screaming down the stairway, in an apartment with no windows, bath or shower, with just a one-ring stove in the dilapidated kitchen, yet we've been surrounded by all this beautiful artwork, work that Jorge refuses to sell because it was left to him by a friend who passed away and he feels to sell it would be bad karma. Well, at least it's out of here now, away from the bailiffs.

We're still living below the shop, but with just the basic necessities now, ready to make a quick getaway should we need to. The main room is almost empty. Our little palace is dismantled and there's an echo, as empty rooms have, the smell of damp really noticeable, almost unbearable, drips running down the walls in the toilet and the kitchen, mould spreading over the ceiling, puddles in the caves under the streets getting bigger by the day.

It's almost as if the building has been trying to keep itself together while we were here but is getting ready to collapse the day we finally leave.

June 4th, 2008: From Bad to Better?

Wake up this morning to drilling inches from my head. Thames Water digging up the street—again! And to add to the mayhem, just outside the Old Compton Street window, Westminster Council decide that now is the perfect time to lay new pavements. Great! Just as we're trying to make our last few pennies, the shop's now completely blocked off.

So I insert a knitting needle into the bottom of a voodoo doll dressed as a workman, sit down, take a deep breath and try to calm myself. Then I open my laptop and log onto AOL. The first email I open is from *The London Paper*. It says: *We're not going to use your column anymore*. They don't give a reason. How polite. I sink into my seat, feeling like a complete failure. First the shop, then the radio show and now this. Could it get any worse? I contemplate lying on the road, my diaries clasped across my chest, asking the workmen to pour tarmac over me and roll me into the ground. But, thinking that might a bit painful (after all, I am a big queen), I decide to have a good cry instead.

Three boxes of tissues later, and with no one in the shop paying any attention to my pitiful sobs, it crosses my mind that writing about my feelings might be a bit more constructive. So I start by describing how I felt the night we made the decision to close.

How weird. I can write again!

It's been so stressful the last few months—not knowing if we were going to close—that I'd virtually stopped writing. But now, now I know we're definitely going, it's as if the pipes have suddenly unblocked and my head's clear again.

I sit back down and start spewing it out. It's as if I'm suddenly aware again. I look out the window, start typing. Watch people on the street, typing, typing. It's pouring out of me. As if I've suddenly been given this powerful closure, setting all this madness into a wonderful little time capsule.

Then my literary agent calls. Oh, no. Please. Not more bad news. I tell him about the shop, worried that he might drop me. But he tells me not to worry—he's going to send a film crew around to capture our last few days. I put the phone down and thank You Know Who.

Now I just have to keep writing. Document these last few days. This is an important chapter in my life drawing to a close and I've got to get it all down before we leave—get it out of my head and onto the page, before the next chapter can begin.

June 7th, 2008: Goodbye to a Dandy

I've known Sebastian for more than a year now, but, strangely, though we're neighbours, it's through email that we've really got to know each other. So when he gave me a quote for my book ("not nearly as bad as I was hoping, you cunt") I thought I should thank him by taking him out to dinner.

I shall start getting ready now, he wrote, two days before we were due to meet. *Inform the media!*

The next day the plan changed.

I am going to a book launch called 'In Search of the British Eccentric.' I am a chapter in the book along with Pete Doherty and Chris Eubank. Why don't you come?

P.S. Oh, and before you start, I'm not a fucking eccentric! Eccentrics are but weeds in a garden whose flowers are dandies.

* * *

6:30 pm. He should be here any minute.

I look down at my outfit. Black CNC jeans, zebra-skin belt, fitted Iceberg shirt. Hmmm. Am I dressed suitably enough to dine with a dandy? I glance at my watch again. The second hand hits the 12. Suddenly, a face appears in the window. A black sequined suit, a sparkling red tie, slicked-back hair, rouged cheeks, a flash of painted fingernails.

He bursts into the shop. 'Darling! I've just had the hair cut. What do you think?'

'It's er, very—'

'It looks like I had it done at a pet shop, doesn't it?'

'No, not at all!'

'Yes it does!' he moans, scrunching up his face. 'Come on— let's pop back to Horsley Towers so I can get my top hat.' He reaches for my hand. 'Oh, by the way, I should tell you. I'm in a terrible mood.'

As we make our way down Dean Street I ask him why.

'Oh, I don't know,' he sighs. 'I feel like such a failure. Like I've wasted my life. And everything feels so pointless. I'd commit suicide if I wasn't such a pansy. Do you ever feel like that?'

I nod. 'I feel like that at the moment, actually.'

'Oh, thank God I'm not alone,' He sighs again. 'Shall we be miserable together, my love?'

As we turn into Meard Street I tell him about the troubles at the shop. He immediately stops and clasps his face with his hands. 'Oh, lord, another part of Soho lost forever. Another friend. Another death.' He stares straight ahead, into the distance. 'Everything we see disperses and vanishes, does it not? Something that is looked at for any length of time is as elusive as if seen for an instant.' He turns to face me again. 'Darling, is there anything I can do to help?'

'No, I don't think so. But thank you anyway. We're in the middle of moving our stuff back to our flat in Holland Park. But hopefully we'll be able to sell up and move back pretty quickly.'

'Move back? But you mustn't leave! Ever! I won't allow it! We need you here! Even if the shop goes, you must not. Anybody who has endured Holland Park will admit that even suicide has its brighter aspects.'

I giggle, but stop when I notice that he's close to tears. He pulls a handkerchief from his breast pocket and uses it to dab at his eyes. 'Oh, I can't bear the thought of you not being here,' he sniffs. 'Soho's being destroyed. First Thames Water digging up our streets. Then the brothels in Peter Street knocked down. The Soho Revue Bar's closing. The Colony's closing. And now you! It'll be like Covent Garden in ten years. If this is the future, I am only delighted that I shall not be here for it.'

We walk on in silence. He pulls open the metal gate at number 7, puts the key in the lock, opens the door and we trudge up the stairway, still in silence, until we reach his first-floor flat.

'Make yourself at home, my love,' he says, ushering me in. 'I'll just go and prepare the face.' He's about to leave the room when he stops. 'Clayton?'

'Yes?'

He pauses. 'You know... I have so enjoyed our gradual friendship. In the old days I liked everything quick—drink, drugs, in bed, in court, all within a week. But there is something to be said for a long, slow burn.' He gazes at me affectionately for a moment and leaves the room.

While he's getting ready I take a seat on the gilt-edged red velvet throne. A woman's voice calls my name from the bedroom. It's Rachel 2, Sebastian's beautiful girlfriend.

She glides into the room. 'What do you think?' she asks, trying on first one and then a second pair of black stilettos. I point out my favourite, help her position her hat, adjusting the spray of black horsehair, just as Sebastian reenters in his stovepipe top hat, his face even more rouged.

'Shall we depart?' he purrs, reaching for my hand, and the three of us make our way out, all in black, like the Addams Family on their way to a midnight funeral.

The walk to Albemarle Street is surreal. I have Rachel 2 on one arm and Sebastian on the other. To say that people are staring is an understatement. People are pointing. A few are abusive. A young guy almost falls off his bike and lands in the gutter. But Sebastian ignores them and walks on with his head held high. St Quentin would've been proud.

The book launch is being held in a very grand publisher's offices, in a room filled with old paintings. There's a huge one of Lord Byron on the wall just above the author, who thanks everyone for attending and gives a speech that I can't quite hear.

After Sebastian's been greeted and air-kissed by half the room, we retreat to a nearby Italian restaurant, accompanied by a friend of Rachel's, an attractive young girl by the name of Katie.

The restaurant is busy and we're seated on a circular table by the entrance. I've got Rachel 2 on one side and there's a spare place next to me for Katie's ex-boyfriend, who apparently is just about to join us. After a few minutes he arrives. He takes a seat. I catch my breath. Oh my God—it's Bryan Ferry!

'Bryan, darling!' Sebastian says, greeting his friend. 'Here, take a seat. Meet Clayton. He's just written a book about Soho.' Sebastian reaches across to stroke my hand. 'Tell him all about your book, my dear.'

Oh, no! What am I going to say? I grew up to this guy's music. How can I possibly talk about my poxy book with this rock icon?

He looks at me, waiting for me to say something. I try to think of something, anything. What comes out is 'Do you like singing your old numbers?' ("Yes.") 'Which is your favourite country to perform in?' ("Many.") Luckily, just as I'm about to ask him if he sees anything of Jerry, he steers the conversation away from my *Heat* magazine line of questioning and asks me about Soho and I relax, though his conversation appears to be more out of politeness than interest. He seems withdrawn, his voice is quiet, his answers short—not that I'm expecting him to burst into "Virginia Plain" or anything, but still. Then I remember the conversation with Katie earlier about how she's just ended their affair.

Across the table, Katie's laughing, looking radiant, while Bryan tries to catch her eye. Looking subdued, pensive, a broken man. It's very sad—though no one appears to notice. It seems that all the money and fame in the world can't shield you from a broken heart.

The evening over, we pay our bill and say our goodbyes. As we turn to leave I overhear Bryan asking Katie to come home with him. She declines. He wanders off, rejected and dejected. Then Sebastian, Rachel 2 and I make our way slowly back down Piccadilly, ignoring the taunts as we hit Brewer Street. Back through the bustling streets of Soho. Back to my crumbling underground home. And back to my equally subdued boyfriend packing up the last of our possessions.

June 8th, 2008: Daniella

We're in a private hospital, walking down a hallway. We pass oxygen tanks, auxiliary nurses pushing medicine cabinets, rota boards, a visitors' room, until we reach the final door at the end, by the fire exit.

Jorge's by my side. 'I think it's this one,' he says, and follows me in.

It's a large, bright room and the sun is streaming through the blinds, bathing the sleeping patient in glorious sunlight. We step closer. An eye opens.

'You got my text, then.'

'Sorry we're late.'

Angie sits up, reaches for her handbag and rummages inside, pulling out a compact and a lipstick, which she applies in one quick movement. She moistens her lips and removes a smudge from the corner of her mouth with a red painted fingernail. Then she checks her hair. Satisfied, she snaps the compact shut. Finally she greets us. 'Better late than never, innit!' she scolds, and she pats the bed, inviting Jorge to take a seat while I take the bedside chair.

'So how'd it go?' Jorge asks.

'Well, it wasn't pretty.' She peers down her nightgown, pulls a face. 'Last night, Katie Price. Today Kate Moss.' She pats her chest. Winces. 'Oh, well. Maybe it'll start a trend an' Posh'll have hers off.'

Jorge's holding a bouquet of white roses. He hands them to Angie. 'Here y'go.'

'Ahhhh... Pop 'em over there, would ya?'

As he arranges them in a vase, she tells us about her visitors, the staff, the food, everything but how she's feeling. The mask never slipping. The mask that keeps her intact.

''Ere, 'ow's that friend of yours?' she asks.

'Which one?'

'The one in hospital?'

Jorge glances in my direction. When you've known each other for this long, words aren't required. I take his look to mean that he wants me to recount our last visit. So I do...

* * *

'Chico!'

His eyes flicker open. Slowly. Halfway.

'Chico, it's us!'

Then his mouth opens. But no words come out. He wets his lips and tries again. 'It's Daniella,' he croaks, his voice barely above a whisper.

'Daniella?'

He nods.

We take seats near the bed. 'Was that your drag name?' asks Jorge quietly.

He nods again. Then closes his eyes. Jorge mouths, 'Say something.' I look down at the bundle of bones lying on the bed, all that's left of our friend.

'So, Chico...' I say, trying to sound cheerful but close to tears. 'When did you start doing drag?'

There's a pause. Then his eyes gradually flicker open again.

'Sixteen.'

'Sixteen?'

'Uh-huh.' He attempts to take a deep breath. 'I put my first dress on at sixteen.'

'Wow! You were an early starter!'

'Hairdressin' in the day an' drag at night. An' the drag just took over.'

There's a soap playing on the TV fixed to the wall. Chico stares at it. The sound's turned down but he looks at peace, as if reminiscing. Jorge looks across at me to continue.

'What kind of drag was it, Chico?'

'Oh, merciful drag, honey!' he replies, more animated now, as if he's slowly coming back to life. 'It wuz merciful. We had eye sequins. Makeup. I mean, serious makeup. Glamour makeup.'

'I bet all the men were after you.'

'Oh, child! They wuz sniffin' round my pussy like hotcakes!'

'All you needed was maple syrup!' Jorge chips in.

'An' butter!'

We all laugh, the mood in the room suddenly lighter. Then Jorge grabs a pillow from the end of the bed and places it behind Chico's head.

'Ahh...those were the days, honey,' Chico sighs, as he rests his head back. 'All gone now. All we wanted wuz to be Miss Continental.'

'You entered Miss Continental?' Jorge asks in amazement.

'Oh, yeah! We had to do interview, swimwear, talent, evening gown, and then the finalists got an onstage question. An' that's when it all took off.' A skeletal hand reaches out for Jorge's hand. 'Oh, I was doin' all the shows back then, honey. Oh, yes. Tourin' round. 'Cos you had to have the backdrops. You couldn't just come out on stage like Pretty Miss Lulu. No way. You had to lick ass for a year to get those sponsors. An' then once you were signed, you had to work it. An' I'd rise outta that floor. With dancers. And outfits. And lights streamin'. An' then

I'd step down an' I'd sing my little black ass off.' He starts to sing, quietly. *"Do you know...where you're going to?"*

'Where was this, Chico?'

'What?' he replies, momentarily lost.

'Where was this?

'Oh, all over, honey... The Fontainebleau in Miami Beach, La Cage aux Folles in Chicago, Copa in Fort Lauderdale, San Antonio, Parliament House. Three shows a night, six nights a week. An' it was hard, honey. All those rehearsals. An' the choreographer would hit me on the legs with a stick an' she'd say, "One. Two. Three. Four. Daniella!"' Cos that was my name back then. Daniella. She'd say, "Can't you fuckin' count, queen?" She made me feel like such an idiot. An' I'd think, 'course I can fuckin' count, bitch! But I just kept missin' that darn four step. That was always my problem. That darn four step.'

'Were you on your own?'

'Oh, no, sugar. There was a few of us. But those Cuban drag queens. Lord, they could be vicious. They'd put Visine in your drink so you'd get diarrhea on stage.' His head moves slowly in my direction. 'Say, are you taking notes?'

'Yes. You don't mind, do you?'

He waves his hand. 'Write it all down, honey. Just keep on writin' 'til I stop breathin'.'

I smile warmly. 'So, when did you start doing Diana Ross?'

'*Mahogany* onwards. When *Mahogany* came out I never looked back. I painted my nails and I was Miss Ross when I stepped outta the car and Dorothy Dandridge when I opened the hotel door. Sometimes Whitney, off season, or Donna Summer for holidays but otherwise it was Miss Ross twenty-four/seven.' He reaches toward his protein drink on the side table. Takes a sip with a trembling hand. 'Oh, I lived in drag, honey! For twenty-five years. I even *travelled* in drag. In the later years I was pretty much livin' my whole life as Miss Ross. I had trunks full of dresses. I remember one time I went through customs as Miss Ross an' I had all my bags round me, an' this big ol' butch guard said, "Where you goin', girl?" An' I said, "I'm moving to the UK, Big Daddy."'

'You moved over here dressed as Diana Ross?'

'Of course, child!'

'To be with Ian?'

'Uh-huh. We met on holiday. An' that was it. I just packed my pantyhose and moved right on over. I remember on our wedding night he said, "I can't believe I've married a drag queen." An' I said, "Well, you married a good one, so shut the fuck up!" He takes another sip of his drink and his eyes move toward the ceiling. 'I jus' hope he's waitin' up there for me.' Then the mood in the room drops. 'You know what…' he says, finally, 'my sisters flew over last week. An' they didn't even wait…' He leaves the sentence unfinished, although it's clear what was meant. 'An' they took Ian's ring. I left it on the table over there an' they just took it. It's the only thing of his I had left. I've been real upset 'bout that.'

Jorge, sensing the change in the mood, tries to keep the conversation upbeat. 'So when did you stop, Chico?'

'Stop?' he replies, drifting off.

'Being Miss Ross?'

'My last Miss Ross was a memorial for a friend. As a favor for a friend who died of AIDS. After that I could never do Miss Ross again. She died that night an' she never came back.' He leans back on the pillow. 'Honey?'

'Yes?'

'Before you go, could you write a letter for me?'

'Sure.'

'It's to Maz.'

I find a clean page in my notebook. 'Okay, fire away.'

He coughs. A dry racking cough that appears to sap him. Jorge holds a glass of water to his lips and he takes two sips.

Then he tries to take a deep breath again and continues, but now his voice is wavering, fading to barely a whisper.

'Dear Maz, thank you for your letters... I'm so sorry I haven't written back... It's been very difficult for me to motivate my hands or speak correctly and that is the reason I haven't written... As soon as I get better I will return your letters... Clayton and Jorge came to visit me today and they were able to write this letter for me... I love you, baby. You hang in there. And take care and don't forget me... Just because I don't write don't mean I don't care... Love you dearly... Chico. P.S.... Please don't forget me.'

* * *

'But you know what? By the time we left he was smiling. I'm so glad we did that trip... Angie? Angie, are you okay?'

'Well, you certainly know how to take me on a roller coaster,' she sniffs, dabbing at her eyes with a bent forefinger. 'You know I won't sleep tonight, don't ya?'

'Sorry, I didn't mean to—'

'Oh, it's nothin'.' She brushes off my apology with a wave of her hand. 'I've been a stupid bitch.'

'What do you mean?'

'All this worryin' 'bout this op and whether I should call Robert. Chico is a lesson to us all.' She opens her handbag again and pulls out a tissue. 'I know I don't know him,'—she touches the corners of her eyes with the tissue—'but will you give him my love?'

I tell her I will. And for the next hour the atmosphere is lively again. We catch up. We gossip. We laugh. Forgetting about our troubles and our stresses. Making the most of our friendship in the only way that we can.

June 9th, 2008: Patisserie Valerie

I browse the menu. Hmmm. Should I go for the eggs or the... I try to attract the waiter's attention. And that's when I spot her: Michele. One of Soho's ancient trannies. Standing by the doorway in a fur coat and matching hat, scanning the room, from table to table, until her eyes rest on the one spare seat, next to me. Here she comes now.

As she walks over I pretend to be absorbed in the menu, and as she nears I look up, feigning surprise. (I can't be the only one who does this.)

'Is there anyone sitting here, dear?'

'No! Go ahead!'

She grins, pulls up the chair and takes a seat, placing her hand-bag on the floor and her hat on the table, revealing disheveled white hair. Like a windswept Golden Girl.

The first time I met Michele was, let me see, about two years ago. It was just outside the shop. She was quite chatty back then. But ever since, it's as if time has taken its toll and whenever I see her she appears to be in her own world—standing on the corner opposite Costa, reliving old memories, tucked away on a leafy corner bench in Soho Square, humming softly, walking slowly down Old Compton Street, ignored by passersby. I wonder if she'll remember me today.

'We've met before,' I say.

She tilts her head back, confused, looking at me as you would an overhyped art installation (a Damien Hirst, perhaps).

'Are you the one that writes about Soho?'

'Yes, that's me.'

Gradually her face breaks into a crooked smile, a mischievous smile, her eyes twinkle and she starts to rock gently in her seat. It's a bit unnerving and I signal the waiter, who, surprisingly, walks straight over.

'Could I have the scrambled eggs and a cappuccino? And, er...' I nod at Michele. 'Would you like something?'

She hasn't heard me. Or if she has, it hasn't registered. She reaches inside her handbag and removes a small chipped gold tube, which she twists until a stub of red lipstick emerges. She draws it awkwardly across her lips. The Italian waiter looks from Michele to me and back to Michele again, tapping his pencil impatiently on his notebook. 'Tea or coffee?'

Michele takes a moment to answer. 'A tea, please.'

'Make that a pot,' I tell the waiter, and he minces off with barely a glance.

A few seconds tick by. Michele fishes into her bag again, this time pulling out a cracked mirror, which she uses to check her lips. And I notice, for the first time, a musty smell about her, a smell that takes me back to my dad's antique shop when I was a kid: of cabinets peppered with woodworm holes, long dead, of drawers lined with yellowing newspapers, long read.

'I'm a witch, you know,' she croaks in a suitably witchy voice.

'Yes. I remember you telling me.'

'A pagan witch.'

I'm tempted to ask her if she can wiggle her nose but decide against it.

'But don't worry,' she says, dropping the mirror back in her bag and smirking. 'I won't put a spell on you.'

Now she's watching me, twirling her necklace around a finger so that the single pearl bounces against her breasts in a strangely hypnotic fashion.

'So, er, what are you up to today, then?' I ask, trying to tear my eyes away and stop myself tumbling into her wrinkled bosom.

'Just passing through…'

'You come here a lot, don't you?'

'Oh, I like to walk in Soho.' Then she leans forward and whispers, 'I never had it done.'

'What?'

She points below the table, looks around to make sure no one is listening, then leans closer still.

'We didn't have it back then, you know.'

Fortunately, just as a vision of her ancient pagan willy nestled inside a pair of old ladies' knickers pops up, the waiter returns with the drinks. He eyes Michele's hat on the table and raises an excessively plucked eyebrow. I signal to Michele. She places it on her lap and we sit in silence until the waiter leaves.

'So would you have had it done if you could have?'

'There was a man once…' she says, but she leaves the sentence unfinished and starts to rock again, backwards and forwards, backwards and forwards, her mind somewhere in the past.

'Did he want you to have it done?'

She stops rocking. 'Oh, yes,' she cackles, reaching for her tea. 'But I'm old now. Very old. I'm not a pretty young thing anymore. It's too late now.' And she recounts a story she's told me once before, about a man in an Earls Court pub called The Coleherne who turned her down when she was a boy. 'He had such big strong arms.'

And as I listen, letting her strange story unravel, I wonder why I find myself drawn to people like this, or why they appear to be drawn to me.

June 10th, 2008: The Girls to the Rescue!

It's a lovely summer afternoon. The street is heaving with gay life. Khaki shorts and sandals, mustaches shaped like handles, G.A.Y. teens, Vauxhall queens, Candy Bar dykes, muscle marys on bikes and Abercrombie tees in a sea of LGBTs.

Valda crosses the street. I wave. She walks toward me.

'Hi, Clay!'

'Hi, Valda!'

I step aside to let her in.

'How's it going?'

She looks downbeat. 'Okay… I guess.'

'Are you sure? You don't look too happy.'

'My boyfriend.'

Uh-oh.

She leans against the counter, brushes her blonde fringe from her eyes and looks toward me with downcast eyes. 'He came over a few weeks ago—as a surprise.'

'Oh, okay!' I try to sound cheerful and surprised. 'How'd it go?'

She gazes out the window, forlorn. 'I'm not sure... I was working but Sue told me to take the night off—luckily.' She glances back. 'He was waiting for me at home.' She looks outside again, watching the Hare Krishnas singing and dancing, tapping their tambourines. 'He said something really strange...'

'What?'

'He said he'd just been to Soho and it was really sleazy. With all the brothels. And he said, "What kind of girl does that type of thing?" He was being...what's the word?'

'Judgmental?'

'Yes.' She bites her lip. 'I've been thinking—maybe I should go back to Lithuania. I can't keep lying to him. He's going to find out one day.'

No kidding.

'And if that's what he thinks, then...'

Two young black youths saunter in, eyeing me suspiciously as they pass.

'Have you spoken to Sue and Maggie?'

'Yes.'

'What did they say?'

She picks at a cuticle. 'That I should follow my heart.'

'It must be difficult.'

Another black guy walks in.

'Do you love him?'

'I think so,' she replies.

'Does he love you?'

'Yes...but... Well, I don't know if I can trust him. But then, look at me.'

Two more black guys enter.

'Hmmm... Have you thought of telling him?'

'I was going to, but—'

'CLAY!' Jorge jumps from behind the counter.

Suddenly everything's a blur. Guys are grabbing clothes. Jorge rushes forward. 'WHAT'RE YOU DOING?' he screams. He snatches an Iceberg jacket from one of them.

'FUCK. YOU. QUEER!' screams one. He's holding something. A knife?

Valda gasps and runs out.

I rush forward.

'CLAY, CALL THE POLICE!'

I grab the phone. A snarling face.

'FUCKIN' BATTY BOYS!'

I dial. Shout, 'POLICE!'

Two guys run down the aisles with Iceberg trainers. Two more. Trying to distract us.

'PUT THAT BACK!' Jorge cries.

I shout down the phone, 'YES! FIFTY OLD COMPTON STREET.' Heart pounding, adrenaline flowing—anything could happen. Where's the metal pole? Should I use it? One guy grabs a handful of jeans. Clothes are ripped. Another guy behind us. Everything's in fast motion. Violence about to erupt at any moment.

Then a woman's voice screams: 'GET THE FUCK OUTTA 'ERE!'

Everyone stops. We all look around. Sue and Maggie are in the doorway, Valda behind them.

'I SAID, GET THE FUCK OUTTA HERE!' bellows Sue.

Maggie steps forward. 'NOW!'

Then, amazingly, one by one, our attackers all slink out. Shouting. Jeering. But leaving, nonetheless!

'GO ON!' shouts Maggie, and she pushes the last one onto the street. He shouts something abusive. And then he's gone.

Jorge rushes to the rails. 'Fuck! The Iceberg jacket!'

I spot an empty shelf. 'And the trainers!'

'Bastards!'

Sue flies outside, frantically looking up and down the street. Then she steps back in. 'They've gone.'

The room stops spinning. Everything slows down and a gradual calm prevails. Jorge sighs. 'Oh, well.' He runs his fingers through his hair. 'I s'pose it could've been worse.'

I walk over to the girls. 'Thank you.'

Maggie reaches for my hand. 'No worries, luv.'

'No one messes on our patch,' adds Sue, with a camp flick of a bleached lock of hair.

Jorge joins us. 'You got here just in time.' He gives them both a hug.

'Did you call the police?' Sue asks.

'Yes, they should be here any minute.'

'Come on, Maggie,' says Sue. 'We better go.'

'Thanks again, girls.'

'Bye, fellas!' They leave. Then Sue pops her head back around the door and winks. 'You owe us one!'

Now it's just the two of us. I take my seat by the window and watch Jorge, checking the rails to see what else has been taken. I can tell he's still shaken, and I know from experience that it'll be a good few days before he calms down again, before he's able to sleep properly. He walks back to the counter, head bowed. He's about to lose it. I can tell.

I stand up. Put my arms around him and we cling to each other for a full minute.

'Clay, I can't take it much longer,' he sobs.

'I know... I know.'

June 11th, 2008: Double Dates

We've started our 50% off sale, so it's a busy afternoon. Guys changing. Music flowing. Till ringing. It's all too little, too late. But we have to grab the cash while we can. So while Jorge's hemming, I'm taking credit cards and swiping. Then, amidst all this fashion drama, an old man totters in: tweed jacket, brown corduroys, a small porkpie hat.

'Charlie!' shouts Jorge from the back of the shop. 'How nice to see you!'

He waves. 'Como estás?'

'Muy bien, gracias.'

As I'm in the middle of serving, he takes a seat and I acknowledge him with a raise of my eyebrows. Then, once the last of the customers have left, I walk over.

'Looking for some thongs?

Charlie laughs. 'No, dear, not today. Actually, I've come to invite you both to Leslie's for dinner.'

'Leslie's?'

'Yes,' he says, beaming. 'We met up last week.'

'Oh, you did? That's great!'

'It is, isn't it?' he says with glee. 'He was very apologetic. He didn't say anything to you, did he?'

'Not in so many words.'

'Well, we had a lovely time. We went to L'Escargot. Have you ever been?'

'Yes, it's very glamorous.'

'Oh, Clayton, it was very romantic. Anyway, he's invited you both round next Friday. Are you free?'

He looks at me expectantly.

'Hmmm... Can I let you know in a day or two? I don't mean to be impolite, but we're going through a tough time at the moment. And I really don't know what's happening from day to day. We're about to close.'

He looks crestfallen. 'For good?'

I nod.

'Oh, how awful. I knew you were struggling, but I didn't realise it was that bad. I bet Jorge's very upset.'

'He is,' I whisper, watching him straighten the clothes at the far end of the shop. 'This shop's been his life.'

'Do you know what you'll do next?'

'No. We can't even think straight at the moment.'

'I can imagine.'

'So if you want any thongs—now's the time.'

Suddenly a voice shouts, 'I KNOW YOU!' We both turn around. It's Angie! She makes a beeline for Charlie. 'You're in Clay's blog!'

'I'm sorry,' Charlie answers. He looks confused.

'You're the Thong Man!'

'I don't quite—'

Jorge walks over and mouths 'Ssshhhh!' to Angie and quickly changes the subject. 'When did you get out of hospital?'

'Yesterday,' she replies. Then she says in a low voice, 'I knew it was 'im. It was the bushy eyebrows that gave it away.'

Charlie overhears us and says to Angie, 'Are you Italian by any chance?'

'Yes, signore!' Angie sings, spinning around, pouting as she twirls. 'Madonna mia!'

'I thought as much. It's a pleasure to meet you, Miss Madonna.'

She offers Charlie her hand and he brings it to his lips.

'You must be so glad to be out,' I say to Angie.

'Oh, God, yeah! Oh, and by the way...' She removes her sunglasses. 'I've got a date!'

'Really? Who with?'

'Robert.'

I gasp.

Angie seems unsure. 'Do you think I'm doin' the right thing?'

I think back to Michele, the chances she never had; Chico, the chances taken away from him. 'Yes. I do.'

Charlie says to Angie, 'Is Robert your boyfriend?'

'You never know!'

'And where did you meet him, if you don't mind me asking?' Charlie asks.

'Here, at the shop.'

'Oh, dear.'

I glance in Angie's direction. 'It's a long story.'

'Anyway, I must be going,' Charlie says, rising from his seat. 'Please let Leslie know about the dinner date, won't you?'

'I will.'

Then Jorge has a thought. 'Wait a sec, Charlie—I've got something for you!' He reaches behind the counter and hands Charlie a Dirty White Boy bag.

'For me?'

'Yes!'

'What is it?'

'Well, open it and see.'

Charlie rips open the packaging and his face lights up as he glimpses the black-and-white fabric inside. 'Is it the—'

'Simulated-sequin, high-gloss, zebra-print thong!'

Charlie covers his mouth with his hand. 'Oh, my! I've read so much about it! Oh, thank you, Jorge,' he gushes, kissing him on each cheek. 'I'll rush home now and try it on. Oh! I just thought! Perhaps I could wear it to Leslie's. Yes. Yes. That's what I'll do,' he says, all in a fluster. 'Goodbye, Jorge. Goodbye, Clayton. And goodbye to you, too, Miss Madonna.'

And we watch as he totters back down the street, clutching the wrapped thong so tightly to his chest you would think it contained the crown jewels, which, a few hours from now, it undoubtedly will.

June 12th, 2008: Money

Our 50% off sale is a hit and the clothes are flying off the racks. Money pouring in. At last! Which is just as well—the bill from the insolvency solicitor is £8,800.

Who would have thought that you'd have to rake up so much money just to prove that you have no money?

June 12th, 2008: More Natural?

I'm being filmed by a TV crew as I type this. They're here to capture our last few days and they're asking me to interact with the world outside the window—just as I would if writing a blog.

It's strange. I do this all the time, but now I'm asked to do it I'm really conscious of what I'm doing.

Oh, God. Now they're doing a close-up.

Wait a minute—five guys have just walked in, looking very suspicious. Oh, great. Now we're going to get raided. What perfect timing.

I stand up. They leave. I sit back down.

This is slightly surreal. Now the TV crew are asking me to look more natural. More natural? Hmmm… What would I normally be doing if I were sitting here waiting for something to write about? So I dig my hand in my pocket and start scratching my balls.

June 12th, 2008: Auntie Beeb

Received an email from BBC Radio inviting me back to plug my book. It said: *We do need you to be more sensitive as to terminology and the descriptions that you use in future. When you were in before, you referred to sodomy on air. We did receive complaints about that. So we would prefer that you use more 'listener friendly' and less graphic terms this time, please.*

Let's see… How does *fudgepacking* sound? Does *fudgepacking* work for you?

June 12th, 2008: I Thought You Were My Friends

3 pm.

I'm typing away, on a bit of a roll, when, all of a sudden, a feeling of being watched creeps up on me. I stop, halfway through a sentence. Wolfy's standing in the doorway.

'I thought you were my friends!'

Jorge looks up from his newspaper. 'We are, Wolfy,' he says. 'But—you don't even know our names.'

'Is it Joe?'

'No, it's Jorge.'

'Jor-ge.'

'That's it.'

'Jorge?'

'What?'

'You missed my dinner party.'

I glance in Jorge's direction. He's staring at me, wide-eyed. How could we forget? We look back toward the doorway. But Wolfy's already gone, walking unsteadily down Old Compton Street, head lowered, running his hand through his tousled hair, oblivious to the jostling crowds.

June 13th, 2008: A Phone Call

'*Yes!*' says the voice at the other end of the phone.

'Leslie?'

'*Yes!*'

'It's me! Clay!'

'*Oh, 'ello, ducky! I was just sayin' to Dolly, "Fancy seein' you mincin' through Soho Square the other day."*'

'How is Dolly?'

'*Oh, she's fine, dear.*'

A voice in the background shouts, '*It's flowin' lovely now.*'

'*Dolly, please!*' says Leslie with great distaste. Then he addresses me. '*She's 'ad problems with 'er waterworks for years… Haven't you, Dolly, dear?*'

'*Years, dear!*' confirms Dolly.

'*She's gettin' on a bit,*' Leslie whispers.

'*What did you just say?*' Dolly snaps back.

'*I was just tellin' Clayton you've got a date next week!*'

'Oh, did he call Michael, then?' I ask.

'*Yes, he—*'

'*Tryin' to get me married off, the two of you!*' shouts Dolly. '*Don't think I don't know!*'

I laugh. 'Oh, by the way, Charlie came into the shop. He said you've invited us to dinner.'

'Well, ducky, I've been promisin' you one of me pot roasts for so long an' I thought—'

'So you called Charlie, then.'

'Yes. Well,' he says briskly. *'I thought it was time to draw a line under it all.'*

'You did the right thing.'

'Thank you, dear,' he says quietly.

It's a golden moment. First Angie, then Dolly and now Leslie. It's as if everything's been leading up to this moment. 'So,' I add, moving quickly on, knowing that Leslie isn't one for sentimentality. 'What time do you want us round?'

'Dinner will be served at eight o'clock. And not a minute later. So don't be late!'

June 20th, 2008: Goodbye to Leslie and Charlie

'My juices have all dried up!' Leslie fumes, looking down at the tray he's just removed from the oven, eyebrow arched so high it's almost hitting his hairline. He spins around and glares at me. 'An' it's all your fault!'

We're in Leslie's flat, sitting around the dinner table; Jorge's on my right and Charlie's on the left. Just minutes earlier, Jorge and I were standing outside Leslie's apartment block in Bloomsbury...

* * *

'This looks like it,' I said, pressing the buzzer labelled 'Flat 3'.

A voice crackled through the intercom. *'You're late!'* The intercom immediately clicked off. The door clicked open. And we stepped cautiously inside.

The entrance hall was dominated by two large mirrors, the corridor carpeted and tastefully decorated, if somewhat old-fashioned. And at the end, a lift, which we took to the 3rd floor. No sooner had we stepped out than a door opened in front of us. Leslie was standing there in a pinny, waving an oven glove.

'Listen, ducky! When I said eight, I meant eight! Not eight ten or eight fifteen.'

'Sorry we're—'

'And do you know why I said eight?' Leslie fired back, trying to peer over my shoulder at Jorge, who was giggling behind. 'Because that's when the cuisine is taken out the oven!'

I mumbled an apology.

'So why are you late?' he snapped.

'Well, we set off—'

'Oh, you lying little minx!' And he flounced back inside. I turned to face Jorge, who shrugged and threw me a look as if to say, *Well, you wanted to come.* I gave him one back that said, *Well, we're here now!*

So in we walked.

* * *

'It's ruined!' Leslie shrieks, slamming the oven tray on the wooden dining table.

Silence. No one dares breathe.

Leslie picks up a fork and prods at the brown lump nestling unappealingly on the tray. 'Look at it! It looks like a sun-dried dog turd!'

'Leslie, dear—' Charlie says.

'Don't you Leslie, dear me!' Leslie spits, pointing the fork at him.

'I'm sure it'll be—'

'It's ruined and that's that!' he cries, hurling the fork into the sink, smashing a wine glass, redefining the term 'kitchen sink drama.'

Jorge and I glance at each other, expressionless. We both look at Charlie, who slinks down in his seat.

I clear my throat—from nerves more than need. OK. Here goes. 'I'm sorry we're late, Leslie. It was just that—'

'The evening's over!'

'I'm sorry?'

Leslie points to the door, his nostrils flaring like a panting racehorse. 'You 'eard!'

'You want us to go?'

'Do you want it in Braille?'

Charlie sits up. 'Leslie! Please! There's no need for—'

Leslie spins around on one heel like an aging ballerina. 'Two weeks I've been preparin' this meal.'

'I know, but—'

'Last Saturday, the meat. Tuesday, the market,' he counts, using his fingers to go through the list. 'I've steamed the tablecloth. The doily. And who do you think polished the silverware all the way through *Gardener's Question Time*? Me! That's who!'

Charlie stands up and edges toward Leslie. 'I really think you should calm down a—'

'Oh, you do, do you?' Leslie snaps, removing his pinny and shoving it in the drawer of a nearby Welsh dresser. 'Well, why don't you bleedin' well go, 'n all!'

'Leslie! Really!'

'Go on! All of you! Get out!' He slams the drawer shut, his pinny getting stuck inside so it doesn't quite close. He tries to close it again, to no avail. Charlie reaches over to help but Leslie steps in front, his face now taking on the pinched appearance of someone who's just smelt something unpleasant.

'Come on,' I whisper to Jorge, and we stand, placing our chairs back under the table.

There's an uncomfortable few seconds while we collect our jackets from the coat stand in the hallway and try to open the latch on the front door. Then Charlie appears behind us. Scarf, hat and coat in hand. He holds the door handle and pulls the lock and the catch releases with a click. One by one, we look back down the hallway toward the kitchen, where Leslie, a hand covering his face, is leaning against the Welsh dresser.

The door clicks shut. I press the button for the lift. No one speaks. Charlie stares at the floor, Jorge at the lift numbers flashing on an LED display, while I dig my hand into my pocket and pinch my left testicle. I always do that in times of stress.

'I'm sorry about that,' Charlie sighs, breaking the silence, once we're outside. 'But you know how he can be.'

'I suppose it was our fault.'

'Actually,' adds Charlie softly, looking me in the eye, 'it was. But not because you were late.'

'What do you mean?'

He pauses. 'I told him a few minutes before you arrived that you were about to close. In hindsight it probably wasn't the best thing to do.'

'How did he react?'

'Not too well, my dear.' Charlie sighs again. 'You see... Leslie has so many memories attached to your shop—*we* have so many memories attached to your shop—and meeting you, well, he would never admit this, but he's grown very attached to you both.'

'So that's why he threw us out? Because we're leaving?'

'I think so.' We walk on in silence, past the British Museum, waiting for Charlie to continue. Eventually he says, 'I think...with you leaving, it's a reminder of when I left him, all those years ago.'

'But we'll be back,' Jorge says. 'It's not as if we're leaving the country!'

Charlie nods. 'I know. I know. It's hard to explain. He just needs time to think it through. Leslie's not quite as tough as he would have you believe.'

We walk down Bloomsbury Street onto New Oxford Street, making our way slowly back to Soho.

'Charlie, would you like to join us for dinner?'

'Oh, that would be lovely.'

'How about the French House?'

'Oh, yes, I haven't been there for years,' Charlie replies. 'Not since Gaston left.'

So we make our way down Moor Street, past the Prince Edward Theatre, tuk-tuks lined up outside, raucous crowds, laughing and jeering, Italians celebrating their win over France at football, Bar Italia a mass of flags, Thames Water barricades forcing people to squeeze along the Old Compton Street pavement, past Pulcinella diners with plates piled high with spaghetti, turning into Dean Street, to the little restaurant above one of Soho's most famous pubs, where Hilary greets us at the bar.

'Hullo, Clay!' she says, kissing me on each cheek. 'Table for three?'

'Yes, please. Can we have that one over there?' I point to an empty table, with the famous black-and-white painting above it depicting Soho characters through the years.

Suddenly a voice shouts, 'Make that four, ducky!'

We all look around.

'Well, you didn't think I was going to let you troll off without moi, did you?' Leslie smirks as he flicks his silk scarf dramatically over a shoulder.

So after hugs, kisses and a few queeny tears, we take our seats and order champagne.

Leslie raises his glass. 'To the end of Dirty White Boy. To the start of your new lives. And'—he grins as he clinks my glass—'to a friendship that will never end!'

June 21st, 2008: Goodbye to Chico

We're in a prison hospice in Norwich. There are three people in this small, dingy room. Me, Jorge and, propped up on the bed, Chico.

Jorge and I have just arrived. After a four-hour journey we were told by the blonde girl in the Visitors' Centre that we could only stay for 20 minutes, ''cos I don't get paid no overtime.'

From the Visitors' Centre we were led through one, two, three padlocked doors, through a courtyard, to the hospice, then down a shabby corridor to Chico's room.

And now we're by his side.

It's hard to believe that it's him. That he's still alive. Long brown poles for legs. Sticks that look like they're about to snap for arms. Deep holes in his cheeks. And sad, haunted eyes. I'll never forget his eyes.

'I wanna go home,' he whimpers. 'I just wanna go home.'

We don't answer. Knowing it won't happen. Not now. Jorge catches my eye, bites his lip as if he's about to cry. I lower my head, aware that he could slip away at any minute.

I try to think of something to say. Anything to take his mind off what he's going through. But I can't. All the way here I'd planned what I was going to say, but now we're here, I just can't think of anything. I feel as if I'm letting him down, just when he needs me most. And the longer the silence goes on, the more deafening it becomes.

But then a strange thing happens...

Jorge starts talking. Chatting. Normally. Recounting stories. And Chico—he starts to smile. The corners of his mouth rise. His eyes sparkle. And just for a few seconds, for a few magic seconds, none of this has happened and we're back at the shop again. Jorge's handing him a pair of jeans, the Iceberg ones, and the matching padded jacket that he's had his eye on. And Chico's joking, telling us how he's going to have to avoid our shop for the next few weeks, stroking my arm as he talks, affectionately, unconsciously, his tactile nature drawing me closer, and I'm thinking that this person is so full of warmth, so full of love, calling us 'honey', exchanging phone numbers, that he's someone I want to get to know, to become friends with, someone to include in my circle. He says something funny as he picks up his shopping bags, his Gucci bag slung over one shoulder, and walks toward the doorway, waving. I'm standing by the doorway, smiling, watching him sashay down the street toward Wardour Street, until he's finally out of sight.

Now it's Jorge I'm looking at, sitting at the other end of the hospital bed. I suddenly feel so proud of him for making this moment happen, for turning our last few precious seconds into something so special. And even though the nurses are here now and they're telling us we have to leave, everyone's in good spirits, and we say goodbyes and kiss him.

Then everyone leaves. Everyone except me. I get as far as the door and stop. I look back, one more time.

'I love you, Chico.'

It's a scene that'll never leave me: the courtyard outside the window; the single bed; his face as he tries to speak.

'I love you too.'

I pause. Close the door. Leave.

Jorge and I walk back down the corridor to the Visitors' Centre. We take a cab to the station. Then the long journey back to London, hardly speaking, in our own worlds, thinking about the awful two years he's had and just wanting him to go now, quietly, quietly and in peace.

June 25th, 2008: Goodbye to Dirty White Boy

7 pm. I'm sitting by the window, on my little red chair, looking out onto Old Compton Street—for the very last time.

For the past two years, this is where I've written my diary, my Soho diary, and this window has been my cinema screen: the car headlights whizzing around the shop, the projector beam; the noise from the street, the soundtrack; the people outside, the actors. And every night I've sat here, waiting for their stories to unfold.

When anything significant has happened in my life I've always written it down: a friend's death, a partner's illness, the end of a relationship. Whenever something's taken place that I thought might change me in some way—something that I might want to look back on—that's when I've written. So having a shop here, and posting these blogs—it's just an extension of what I've always done.

But the last posting from Dirty White Boy: This is difficult to write, because the shop has changed my life in so many ways. It's opened me up creatively; I've met so many interesting people. But by the time you read this, Dirty White Boy will be no more. The last vanload of furniture will be gone and our little shop will be bare. Well, almost bare. Should an over-enthusiastic workman (or robot), be digging in the basement sometime in the next century, he or it may well find a decaying book hidden in one of the caves with a little note attached. My little time capsule to Soho.

* * *

The shop's empty. Jorge's waiting outside and I'm standing by the doorway, key in the door, looking around the shop for the very last time. Finally my eyes rest on an empty space just by the window, where my little red chair once stood. Suddenly, a line from a book titled *Soho in the Fifties* pops into my head: *The day arrives when one must make the return to normalcy with sore mouth and sore conscience and break the dependence on Soho.*

I smile and close the door, and we walk slowly down Old Compton Street, the next chapter of our lives about to begin.

A Few Months Later...

We held the book launch for my book *Dirty White Boy: Tales of Soho* at The Colony, the last event held there before it closed, and we packed the place full of artists, hookers, trannies and pimps. The reviews came out—and they were quite good. We even received a call from Elton John! But then, one afternoon, I received a call that made everything else pale in comparison...

'Hello, Clayton speaking.'

'*Clay, it's Sue.*'

'Sue?'

'*From the brothel. Clay, I 'ope you don't mind me callin' but I need a favour. An' you do owe us one.*'

'Sure! What is it?'

'*The police have shut us down.*'

'Yeah, I read about it in the paper.'

'*We wuz never any trouble, wuz we?*'

'No. Not at all!'

'*Well, someone's made a complaint 'bout us an' we gotta go to court on Monday. An' we wuz wonderin'... Would you and Jorge be our character witnesses?*'

'Of course!'

'*Oh, great!*' she said excitedly. '*Okay, it's at Horseferry Road Magistrate's Court. I'll call you later wiv all the details. Oh, an' thank you, my luv. We really 'preciate this.*'

* * *

The day started ominously.

We were due at the court at 1:30 pm and Jorge thought it'd be a good idea to catch the bus. So we boarded the C1 in plenty of time and took seats at the back, just in front of two large Vicky Pollard–like girls. This proved to be quite amusing, as the 'Vickier' of the two girls kept referring to the dirty old men who were ogling her rather, it has to be said, ample bosom.

'I can't 'elp it if me tits are big. I've bin breast-feedin', innit!' she proclaimed in deepest Essexonian.

It was only as they were leaving, and Miss Bosom muttered 'bleedin' perverts' as she brushed past, that we realised she'd been referring to us! The phrase 'barking up the wrong...' came to mind.

'She thought we were straight,' Jorge said with glee as we walked toward the court. Then I reminded him she also thought we were old.

Heads bowed (in case anyone else accused us of being lecherous old men), we arrived at the court at 1:30 pm dead-on, followed closely by Hilary from The French House, David the Rector from St Anne's church, Niki from the local unit of Legal Action for Working Girls and Juliet from The Soho Society.

'But where are the girls?' I asked.

'They should be here any minute,' Niki replied. 'They're just parking the minibus.'

The minibus?

Then they arrived. All 35 of them. I kid you not. There were Italian girls. Croatian girls. Romanian girls. Middle-aged dykes with crew cuts. Overweight, bleached blonde, Pat from Eastenders–type girls. Girls with long hair. Girls with short hair. Well-dressed girls. Badly dressed girls. Beautiful girls. Not so beautiful girls. Every nationality, sexuality. It was like a United Nations hooker convention. By 2 pm, the entrance to the court looked like an overflowing whore house.

Suddenly a voice screamed, 'THERE THEY ARE!' and a huge

apparition with cannon-like breasts came hurtling toward me. Oh, no! Was it Miss Pollard from the C1? I took a deep breath and prepared to say, 'Listen here! I didn't even look at your bloody tits! Just 'cos my eyes happened to linger in the general proximity of your mammaries didn't mean that I wanted to put my head between them!' But, it wasn't Miss Pollard at all—it was Sue!

'Oh, fanks so much for comin!' she said. 'We knew you wouldn't let us down!'

'Sue, we've just been accused of being perverts by a girl who said we were staring at her tits!' Jorge exclaimed.

'Well, we all know about Clay's obsession with big tits, don't we? He married you, din't he, luv?'

Then Maggie came running over, hair flying behind her, arms outstretched, 'Oh my God! We miss you two so much!'

One of the girls' maids rushed over. Then one of the girls. Then another. And another. Within seconds we were surrounded by them, all telling us how much they'd missed us, thanking us for being here. It was really touching. Like being at a school reunion (for wayward girls).

'Where's Valda?' I asked, looking around.

'Oh, she went back to Lithuania to be with 'er boyfriend.'

'Oh—poor Valda.'

'Anyway, I shunt be talkin' to you!' Sue said with a grin. 'Not after wot you wrote 'bout me in your book.'

'Why, have you read it?'

''Course I 'ave!' She grinned and adjusted her headband. 'We bin sending all the girls down to Foyles to git a copy! They've nearly sold out, fanks to us! An' you even put that bit 'bout me 'avin' me stomach bypass, dintcha, you naughty boy.'

'Er...'

'Why did you 'ave a stomach bypass, Sue?' said one of the girls.

'To stop me puttin' fings in me gob.'

'Isn't that yer job?' cackled Eileen, one of the elderly toothless maids.

'Eileen, wot you brought your luggage for?' said Sue, looking at the huge bin bag upon which Eileen was sitting.

'I'm gonna tell the judge if they kick us owt, I got nowhere to live!' Eileen replied defiantly, 'An' I'll 'ave to start swattin'!'

'Eileen, I fink the word's squattin'!' said Sue quietly. And just for a second, the all-powerful Sue, Sue the Invincible, Sue who has never taken any crap from anyone, Sue who rules the Dean Street crossroads with an iron fist—looked like she was about to cry. It was an extraordinary moment. Like watching a watery-eyed Anne Widdecombe. For a few seconds no one spoke. Everything went quiet. A whole street of madams, maids and hookers and you could have heard a pin drop.

Then the Court Usher walked over and broke the spell. 'Ladies, can we have you all inside now, please. Seventh floor. Court number two.'

So in we piled. All 40 of us...

* * *

'All rise!' shouted the Court Usher.

A mass scrambling of bodies trying to get to their feet as the Judge entered the room. Maggie grabbed my hand as we stood and whispered, 'Oh, 'e looks really mean!' And he did. He was scowling. It made for a tense atmosphere. All very high drama. Girls seated on one side, police on the other. And somewhere in the middle, surrounded by a sea of Nike tracksuits and Argos jewellery, Jorge and I, head to toe in Gianfranco Ferre Black Label.

'Anyone want a barley sugar?' whispered Eileen as she shuffled down the row offering a bag of sweets from her plastic purse.

'No, thanks.' I whispered back.

'I got some Frazzles in me bag if you want!'

'Quiet at the back!' the Judge shouted and Eileen quickly sat back down on her bin bag like a naughty schoolgirl.

First up was the police prosecutor. A pompous, defensive man whose hair looked like it hadn't seen shampoo since God was a lad. To say he was bitchy was an understatement. He delivered lines such as 'Do these women seriously think...' and 'If you can call it work' with as much venom as he could muster. Thirty-five pairs of hooker eyes drilled into him.

The crux of his argument was that the brothel needed to close because it had become a focal point for undesirables, a 'honey pot' for antisocial behaviour. He gave two examples: a person who had been caught with cannabis in the brothel stairway and a person who had been knifed. However, under questioning by the defence barrister, it turned out that both cases were unsubstantiated, not recorded in police files, with no charges brought and no witnesses forthcoming—i.e., dubious.

Then it was the turn of the defence and the first witness called was the Reverend David Gilmore, the Rector from St Anne's, who spoke very eloquently about the drug dealing in the churchyard. His point being, there's a drug problem all over Soho and if you're going to close the girls down for people dealing in their doorway, are you going to close my church down too? He was followed by Niki, who said she'd been helping the girls for five years and had never witnessed any trouble. And then it was Eileen's turn. She told the court that 61 Dean Street was her home, that she needed the tips she earned as a maid to feed her family and if they closed the brothel down, she'd be on the street. I don't think there was a dry eye in the house. This was nail-biting stuff.

Finally it was my turn. Resolving to block out the numerous water leaks we'd suffered in the building, I said that we'd had a great relationship with the girls and they'd never been any trouble at all. I sat back down. Maggie held my hand. Now it was the big one. It was Sue's turn in the witness box.

This was to be the climax of the day. A hush descended on the room. Sue stood up, nodded at her girls and walked leisurely across the room, head held high, proud, without a care in the world. She'd dressed 'full drama' for her starring role: a black headband, tight-fitting black jumper and black polyester leggings tucked into black fur-lined fake Ugg boots. Even her nails were painted black. It was like watching a Bette Davis film (make that Shelley Winters). The maids, the girls, the police, the court officials, everyone watched as Sue made her way casually to the witness box. I squeezed Maggie's hand. Come on, Sue!

Once inside, Sue adjusted her headband, swore on the Bible and, with two meaty hands gripping the railing, she thrust her breasts forward like a ship's carved figurehead, staring at the judge. Amazingly, even he seemed a bit intimidated, and he leant back in his seat and started to fiddle nervously with his glasses. The stage was set. The games were about to begin.

The prosecutor waived his questioning of Sue. The defence barrister approached the witness. 'Ms Smith, can you tell us how long you've been working at 61 Dean Street?'

'Twelve years!'

'I see,' said the defence barrister. 'And in all the time you've worked there, have you ever come across drug dealing in the stairway?'

'Never!'

'And any fights like the one mentioned by the police officer?'

'Not one! Not on my shift.'

'Do you think there may have been a fight when you haven't been there?'

'No!'

'How can you be so sure?'

''Cos we've got CCTV, innit. We got four cameras. One on the street and three on the stairway. No one gets up those stairs without me knowin' 'bout it. An' if there were any trouble, I'd look at the tapes the next day.'

'The police allege that you never cooperate with them and that you never hand over your CCTV tapes.'

Sue glared at the greasy-haired prosecuting officer. He slunk back down in his seat and turned a deep shade of crimson. 'Well, they've made a mistake, 'aven't they? I've been givin' 'em me tapes for years!'

'Hmmm,' said the barrister, leaving enough of a dramatic pause so that we could ponder over the 'evidence' that the police were presenting. 'Now, Ms Smith, did the police ever mention a fight which occurred in the stairway recently?'

'No! Not once!' Sue said, flashing the prosecuting officer another quick glare. 'Look, I get along well with the police. They got their job to do an' I got mine. But let me tell yer this—whenever there's ever bin any trouble on that street, the police always come an' see me first. An' I've always cooperated. I even went to court for 'em once! So do you fink for one minute if they was a fight in the stairway they wouldn't tell me 'bout it? Bollocks! Ooops, sorry, me lud! Wot I mean is, I've always 'elped 'em. I keep a clean, well-run, respectable walk-up, I do.'

'A walk-up?' enquired the judge.

'Yeah, it means the door is always open so you can walk up. It saves havin' the punters hangin' outside. 'Cos no one wants that—you know—punters hangin' out on the street.'

'So—the reports of men lingering by the doorway?' enquired the barrister.

'Well, I can't 'elp that, can I? 'Aven't you ever 'ad someone lingerin' outside your 'ouse?'

'Ms Smith, could you just answer the question, please?' the judge said politely.

'Sorry... Look, if someone hangs round the doorway, we scream down the stairway 'n tell 'em to bugger off!'

'And can you tell the court why don't you call the police?' said the barrister.

'Well we can't keep callin' the police every time a bleedin' man—oh, sorry, me lud!—we can't keep callin' the police every time there's a man standing in the doorway, can we? That'd be stupid. Sometimes we might get three guys come up. An' one might finish a bit quicker than the other two.' A few of the girls started giggling at this point. One whispered, 'Never quick enough in my book!' Sue waited for the laughter to die down before she continued, 'So sometimes 'e might wait outside an' have a fag. You know, an after-sex fag while he waits for his mates. We don't mind men like that standin' there.'

'So, Ms Smith, in all your twelve years of working at 61 Dean Street, you have never witnessed any drug dealing or anyone being knifed?'

'Never! Not in my 'ouse!'

'No further questions, Your Worship.'

'Thank you, Ms Smith,' said the judge. 'You may step down. And thank you for your evidence,' he added with a smile.

'Fank you, me lud.'

With that, Sue left the witness box just as she'd walked in, grinning away, triumphant, head held high. The whole room gazed at her in awe.

'Well, done, girl!' Maggie whispered as Sue swept past, her blonde tresses swishing from side to side. 'They ain't got rid of us yet!'

Then the judge informed the court that he would reach his decision on Wednesday, and the court was adjourned.

We got up to leave. As we were filing out, the Court Usher carried over a box of masks and started handing them out to the girls.

'Wot's that for?' said Sue, trying on a gold masquerade number.

'Well, there'll probably be press outside and we thought you might want to hide your faces,' said the Usher.

'HIDE ME FACE?' Sue fired back, and she threw the mask back in the box. 'I GOT NUFFIN' TO BE ASHAMED ABOUT!'

'Yeah, we got nuffin' to be ashamed about!' said Eileen, taking hers off too.

Suddenly a crescendo of 'YEAH! WE GOT NUFFIN' TO BE ASHAMED ABOUT!' rang out and the girls threw their masks back. It was a real 'I am Spartacus!' moment. Really beautiful. And as the box filled back up, Sue looked around at her girls like a proud mother hen. Then the girls linked arms and, with giggles all around, skipped out the door of the Magistrate's Court, laughing and joking, completely flummoxing the gang of creepy photographers who were waiting tentatively nearby.

***

A few days later, my mobile rang.

'Hello!'

'*Clay?*'

'Yes.'

'*It's Sue!*'

'Hi, Sue, how's it going?'

'*Clay, you're never going to believe it! WE WON!*

Epilogue

A one-man play based on the life of Sebastian Horsley, *Dandy in the Underworld*, opened at the Soho Theatre in London on 15 June 2010. Sebastian was found dead at his London home two days later. He died of a heroin and cocaine overdose. His funeral took place on 1 July 2010, at St James's, Piccadilly, and was attended by more than 400 mourners. He was 47.

To: saintsebastian@talktalk.net
From: clayuk@aol.com
Sent: 19/06/2010
Subject: Goodbye to Soho

Sebastian darling,

I've been trying to write something about you for a couple of days now—but nothing's felt right. It's been really difficult. It could be the last piece I ever write about you ("It'd better bloody not be!" I can hear you cry). Then I was lying in bed this morning when I had an idea. I know! I'll send you an email.

Of course, whenever I send you one you always reply, half an hour later, with a huge email back full of quotes, quips and beautiful phrases. Well, now it's my turn to send you a huge email.

When you came to see my play last month, knowing you were in the audience really lifted me. I felt so much more confident up there. Remember what you said to me afterwards? 'Darling, the people on the stage were making such a racket I could hardly hear what the audience were saying.' You did make me laugh. And when I told you what an inspiration you were to me, you replied, 'You are an inspiration to me too, my dear. I love people who put themselves out there and risk ridicule. It is brave.' Well, now it's my turn to tell you what I thought of *your* play.

Darling, it was a triumph. Although it was very surreal—surreal and sad. Not that Tim Fountain had done anything wrong. Not at all. The script was very good. It was well structured. And your front room was re-created perfectly: the display case full of human skulls, the sunflower painting, the press cuttings, the life-size poster, the bottle of vodka wrapped in the red glittery material (like the one you bought for me and Jorge), the statue of the gold cock that you won at the Erotic Awards (remember the night we went to collect it?) and the velvet-lined window seat where I used to sit.

And I thought the actor playing you, Milo Twomey, was very focused too. It took real guts to get through last night's performance. And Tim did such a heartwarming speech afterwards. How he kept it together I don't know. He did make everyone laugh when he said, 'Sebastian would've been horrified that I'm here on stage wearing double denim.' Because we all know what you thought about denim.

I was sitting next to Jorge and David Benson. (Remember when I brought him around to you and he delivered his Kenneth Williams play in your front room?) Juliette was sitting a few rows in front. (She laid flowers outside your flat before she came.) And there were so many of your friends in the audience last night. There was so much love in that room. Then the scene where you're about to take heroin. Well. The atmosphere was, as you can imagine, heartbreaking. Such poignancy. Jorge was already sniffing quite loudly at that point. (So much for being the butch Cuban, hey?)

No, there was nothing wrong with the play. But all the way through, as I was watching it, I was just—stunned. It was only once it'd ended and I was chatting with Tim at the bar that it all came flooding out. I lost it completely (and I think I left a trail of snot on Tim's shoulder). You see, all I could think about were the times that we'd spent together.

It was weird how we met, wasn't it?

Jorge and I were living below the shop, in that large, damp, rat-infested cellar. And you were living two streets away, in a townhouse on Meard Street ('Horsley Towers' you called it). And do you remember that blog I was writing on MySpace at the time? How I'd always be sitting by the window, tapping away on my laptop, writing about the strange characters on the street? Then one day I spotted you.

The first thing I noticed about you was your clothes. You were dressed like no one I'd ever seen, in your black Victorian-style suit, red velvet waistcoat, white shirt with collars down to your knees and a black tie, the knot the size of a baby's head. And, of course, the top hat. You were quite an imposing figure, gliding past our Dean Street window. With your dyed black hair and your white powered face, you looked like a faded junkie rock star in undertaker drag. So I started to write about you; and Soho being the village that it is, of course, eventually, you got to hear about it.

I don't mind you referencing me at all, my dear was your reply to my first email. *I would only mind if you did not reference me.*

And so our friendship began.

We had a lot in common. Just a year apart in age, you were a Leo dating a Gemini, I'm a Gemini dating a Leo. You loved Marc (Bolan); I love Marc (Almond). You were writing a newspaper column; so was I (before we both got sacked). You'd dreamt of being a rock star and had been in a band; so had I. You described yourself as a 'failed artist'; any artistic field I'd dabbled in, I'd also failed. And we were both on the verge of bankruptcy.

But that period, and the two years that followed, was different. It was an important time for us both. Finally there was a hint of success in the air. You had an autobiography coming out. My 'Soho diary' was about to be published. We came to your book launch/art retrospective and I invited you to join me onstage at my first reading in that Soho basement bar. (I was so proud to have you there. It will always be a highlight of my life.) Do you remember us joking at the time about how, despite promoting our work, our books would both end up in the same remainder bin?

'I wonder who'll be the "top",' you teased.

But of course yours didn't end up in the remainder bin. It sold tens of thousands and you received press all over the world.

Then, the following year, we both took to the stage. Me, at the Trafalgar, and you at The Union on Greek

Street. My performance was a bit shambolic. I missed scenes out. 'Dried' on stage. Mind you, you came across as a bit nervous in yours too. But you know what I regret now? You were so complimentary about mine. (I'll treasure that email, though I think you were just being polite.) Whereas I, thinking I was being helpful, told you everything you did wrong. How insensitive of me. I hope you forgave me.

But then we dusted ourselves down and came back this year: me, back at the Trafalgar last month, and you with a play at the Soho Theatre that opened just last week. The plan was, of course, that we'd attend each other's and compare notes.

I mention all this because, as similar as our lives have been over the past two years, I know I have always been the amateur watching, and being guided by you, the real McCoy. Whether it's been our lives, our books or our plays, you've towered over me. You've become known across the world. With anyone else this could be reason for professional envy. But not with you. I've followed your every move in awe and with total admiration.

You see, Sebastian, as I've told you before, you are a genius. And I don't use that word lightly. I have met three geniuses in my life: Quentin Crisp, Raqib Shaw and you. And one of your most endearing qualities was one you shared with St Quentin: you belonged to everyone. No one could claim you as their own. You corresponded with complete strangers. Met them in Frith Street for coffee. Invited them to your flat. (Probably fucked a few.) Your address was well known and you shared yourself with the world. So my friendship with you has been far from unique. It was one of many. But it's meant a tremendous amount to me. And in the three years that we knew each other you taught me a great deal.

You once said to me, 'The great object of life is sensation, to feel that we exist, even though in pain. You can do anything you want to do. But what is rare is wanting to do a specific thing: wanting it so much that you are practically blind to all other things, that nothing else will satisfy you. Most people go through their lives without ever doing one whole thing they really want to do.'

When I told you that I wanted to write, you said, 'Then remember, my dear, a real artist creates for no other purpose than to please himself. Those who create because they want to please others and have audiences in mind are not artists. There are many people who write but have no real need to. I don't think we should ever feed back to the public its own ignorance and cheap tastes. If one has a heart, one cannot write or paint for the masses. The masses are asses.' This is just one of your pieces of advice which I will take to my grave.

Then, in July 2008, the credit crunch hit and we lost our little shop. Do you remember what you said when I told you? 'If this is the future I am only delighted that I shall not be here for it.'

And now you're not here for it.

Our last meeting was at your after-show party last Tuesday, at St Barnabas, the House For Fallen Women. (How apt.) It was a very glamorous setting and the party was buzzing: media types, agents, artists, Wildean-looking queens. I waved at you when we came in and you waved back, but you were in the middle of being interviewed. So I made my way to the garden outside and chatted with the guests. Then I had one of those strange feelings you get of being watched. I turned around and there you were, looking at me, rather sadly I thought. We sat down and talked, me between you and Rachel 2.

I said: 'What's the matter, Sebastian? Why are you so sad? I thought you'd be happy.'

You replied: 'When John Hurt played Quentin, Quentin's star rose higher. When Peter O'Toole played Jeffrey Bernard, it was O'Toole that shone. I hope I'm not about to be eclipsed.' And then you smiled.

'Didn't you like the play?'

'Oh, I thought it was beautiful. But writing a book is such a personal, solitary thing, as you know. And then having your words thrown back at you like that. Well...'

We stood up and kissed and you said, 'If on Friday night, after you've seen the show, you pass by and my lights are on—please pop up.' I said that I would, but if you were out, I'd 'see you on email.'

Now I'll never see you on email again. And the emails are all I have left: a hundred or so emails, your book and the memories. Memories of you striding down Old Compton Street, the crowds parting as you swept by; memories of your camp little wave as you tapped on our Dean Street window before you burst into the shop full of sparkling wit and repartee; memories of us sitting in your front room while someone was using your bedroom to 'entertain'; memories of our meals in The Ivy and The Mermaid. (We never did make it to The Stockpot, did we?) And of course, memories of your kindness, your gentleness and your politeness, the side of you that your critics didn't get to see. 'Belittling others is no pastime for those convinced of their own standing,' you once said. (Though it did made me laugh when you told me that you'd once shat in a Tiffany box and couriered it over to a critic. "Now the shit has hit the foe!")

Anyway, I'm going to miss you, you old queen. Someone like you comes along once a generation, and I feel honoured to have known you. Now whenever I go to Soho I'll always walk past your flat and gaze upwards (as I do when I walk past Quentin's flat on Beaufort Street), and I'll remember the way you'd lean out of your window, in your long black silk negligee, the one with the marabou feather–lined neck, your face coated in a fine white powder, your eyes caked in last night's mascara, purring, 'Hello Romeo, Juliet here. Welcome to Horsley Towers.' I'll never forget that.

OK. I think I've said everything I wanted to say. It's time to press the Send button, though there'll be no point in checking my inbox later on. No more quivers of excitement when I see the name Saint Sebastian pop up. As you said in your last email, just a few days ago, *I am a peculiarly ill balanced member of the human race who burns a strange meteoric course. A blazing meteor when it descends to Earth is only a stone. The key is to turn the stone into a shooting star on Earth.*

And that is exactly what you did.

Goodbye, sweet man. See you in the next one.

Love,

Clay (and Jorge) x

Acknowledgements

Ever since I was a young boy, drawing strange cartoon-like characters on my bedroom wall, I've tried to create something, to bring it to people's attention, to show that I have something to say, but I always failed. By the time I hit my forties I thought it would never happen. Then one morning, I was sitting by the window of our shop, looking out onto Old Compton Street, when, as if by magic, weird and wonderful characters started to materialise. So I'm going to start by thanking the two characters who most influenced this book.

I would like to thank the irreplaceable and much missed Sebastian Horsley, for his friendship and advice, for throwing down a perfumed gauntlet and revelling in the glory of his own individuality. You were, and will always be, my artistic guiding light. And Chico Thomas—when you swept into our shop that Sunday morning, honey, who could've known what lay in store. But now you're safe and Miss Ross will live forever.

There would not have been a book without the Polari powdered humour of Leslie and Charlie; without the increasingly beautiful and much quoted Angie Pasquale, and, of course, without the Queen of Soho herself, HRH Sue (and her Lady in Waiting, Maggie).

I owe so much to my editors, Juliette Rose, Juliet Pickering and Mark Rhynsburger. With a (large) pinch of fairy dust you've made me sparkle. And for being a faithful agent, Miss Pickering again. One day I'll write a proper book—I promise!

I want to thank Joe Pearson for sticking with me—from Spongefinger, to *Roots*, to *Dirty White Boy: Tales of Soho* and now *Goodbye to Soho*. Maggi Hambling, for bringing Sebastian back to life on the cover (and bringing me to tears). Graham Rees, for additional cover design. Gabriella Meros, photographer of Sebastian's 47. Jamie McLeod, photographer of London's waifs and strays. Dom Agius, photographer of London's underbelly. Claire Thompson and all at Turnaround and CPI. My 'Girls Court' friends, Paul Hunwick and David Masters. Elton Uliana, for being there until the midnight flit. Jacques Humpich and Lidio Netto, for support above and beyond. My girlfriends through the years; Gail 'Penny' Blackburn, Anouk 'Noopie' Cruttenden and Maria 'Pippa' Jarvis. Roger Lloyd-Thompson, aka Dexter Clark Celebrity Hairdresser, for the meeting of the minds. Débora Virumbrales, our favourite Soho waitress. Rachel Garley, the oh so beautiful Rachel 2, girlfriend and muse to a Soho Prince. Jonathan Kemp, for literary advice over steaming Thai dinners. Arthur Wooten, for five years of 'across the pond' support. Lois Froud a.k.a HaLo-iS, London's most glamorous DJ, for love and theatrical videos. Stewart 'multi-media' Who? and the Hospital Club, for rehearsal space. The Polari boys, Christopher Bryant and Bryon Fear. Tim York, for being the original Dirty White Boy. And for helping me bring *Dirty White Boy* to the stage, the multi-talented '6 characters in one show' Edinburgh Festival star and national treasure, Mr B himself, David Benson.

Talking of plays, I am so grateful to the esteemed Nicholas de Jongh, for taking me to see (and patiently explaining) the classics. To Phil Willmott and Katherine Hare, for directing *Dirty White Boy* and turning it into a production that brought the audience to its feet (and I don't mean to leave). To James Seabright and all at Seabright Productions, for time and investment. To Alexis Gerred, for singing his little heart out in the play. To Maggie K De Monde and Martin Watkins, for songs straight from their magical debut album. To Stage Manager Jules Richardson, for being so calm under pressure. And to all at the Trafalgar—I hope to be back one day...

I honour and celebrate my four muses. Marc Almond, the first artist I fell in love with—you have inspired me since I was a spotty teenager, singing Mambas songs into a hairbrush. It was you who brought me to Soho. Quentin Crisp, who taught me to unpack every part of myself until all that was left was me. Sebastian Horsley, for grasping Quentin's baton and waving it aloft for all to see. And of course Soho, for holding me in its embrace for over 30 years.

Bringing up the rear, the Littlewoods. I'm nothing without my Mum and Dad, brother and sisters (Jay, Sara and Tori). You're always there. You're always supportive. You'll never know how much you all mean to me.

And last, but so very far from least, the husband, Jorge Betancourt, who came with a very large dowry. You started Dirty White Boy 16 years ago and it's travelled from shops, to books, to stage. I love you so much. You changed my life and set me on a different path. I owe you everything.

Oh, and I should also thank you, the reader. I hope you've enjoyed my Soho stories and they haven't put you off visiting. There's nowhere like it in the world. And it will rise again. It always does.

Glossary

arse: the bum (similar to the American word *ass*)

Ayia Napa: a tourist resort in the southeast of Cyprus. It is known as a party town

Beeb (or 'Auntie Beeb'): the British Broadcasting Company (BBC)

Bet Lynch: a fictional character from the UK television ITV soap opera *Coronation Street*. She was famous for her leopard-skin style of clothing, considered naughty, racy and very sexy in her character's early days

bin man: garbage collector

Bluewater: a shopping mall close to London's M25 motorway

bollocks: testicles or balls

brolly: umbrella

bugger (verb): a slang word used to describe anal intercourse; or sexual intercourse between a person and an animal

bum: the bottom (again similar to the American word *ass*)

caff: café

Charles Hawtrey: a small, effeminate, English comedy actor

coach: bus

council estate: a collection of local-authority, public, or social houses

Dame Shirley Porter: a former Conservative leader of Westminster City Council in London. She has been described as "the most corrupt British public figure in living memory, with the possible exception of Robert Maxwell". Thankfully she spends most of her time now in Israel

dilly boys: male prostitutes who once frequented Piccadilly Circus in London's West End

dinner lady: a woman who cooks and serves food in a school cafeteria. Since the 1960s, dinner ladies (or 'lunch ladies' in the US) have sometimes been caricatured as overweight, women with hairnets, rubber gloves, glasses and moles

dole queue: a line of unemployed people awaiting state unemployment benefits

donkey jacket: a short buttoned coat typically made of unlined black or dark-blue woollen material. Originally worn as a work jacket. Considered to be cheap

fags: cigarettes

fanny: female genital organs (the American equivalent is 'pussy')

flat: apartment

HMP Littlehey: Her Majesty's Prison in Littlehey

Hola! **magazine:** a Spanish-language celebrity magazine

HRH: Her Royal Highness

knickers: women's underwear

knob: penis

minge: vagina

Nanette Newman: an English actress and author. She was also famous for being the face of the Fairy Liquid advertisements, with the jingle *"Now hands that do dishes can feel soft as your face..."*

natter: to talk idly

NHS: National Health Service

OBE: The Order of the British Empire is an order of chivalry which recognises service to the arts and and sciences, public services outside the Civil Service and work with charitable and welfare organisations

Olive: a rather plain, dull character in the London Weekend Television sitcom *On the Buses,* played by Anna Karen

Oystercard: a plastic smart card you can use to pay on public transport

pinny: a sleeveless garment worn as an apron

posh: rich, aristocratic, wealthy, loaded, fancy, upper crust, well off, well to do

pudding: the British term for all desserts

punter: a paying guest or customer, especially of a brothel or prostitute

queue (noun and verb): a line of people; to form a line

quid: British slang for £1 in currency

QX magazine: a London gay magazine often depicting scenes from gay clubland

remainder bin: the 'leftovers' or sale section

Richard and Judy: Richard Madeley and Judy Finnigan, a married, Middle England, middle-class couple who are British television presenters and columnists

rota (boards): a notice board which sets out employee weekly schedules

Round the Horne: a BBC Radio comedy programme, transmitted in four series of weekly episodes from 1965 until 1968. One of the most popular sketches was Julian and Sandy, featuring Hugh Paddick and Kenneth Williams as two flamboyantly camp out-of-work actors, speaking in the gay slang Polari (see below)

school weed: the child (usually a boy) most likely to get bullied at school

serviette: a napkin or face towel used at the table for wiping the mouth when eating

shag/shagging: sexual intercourse

spot: in this book, either a pimple or a locality
summat: slang for *something*
Tesco's: a global grocery and general merchandise retailer
Toblerone: a triangular Swiss chocolate with honey and almond nougat
trainers: sneakers
Turkish Delight: a chocolate bar. Premium varieties consist largely of chopped dates, pistachios and hazelnuts or walnuts bound by a gel; the cheapest are mostly gel, generally flavored with rosewater, mastic or lemon
VAT: Value Added Tax

A Note on Polari

You will also come across slang language called Polari in this book. Polari (also Palari, Palare or Parlaree) was a coded language spoken in Britain by the gay subculture, particularly in the 1960s. It was also popular with actors, circus and fairground showmen, criminals and prostitutes. There is some debate about its origins, but it can be traced back to at least the 19th century, and possibly as early as the 16th century. It is likely that the word derives from Italian *parlare*, 'to speak.' Here are a few choice terms that appear in this book:

bijou: small
bona: good
cottage: public toilet
eek: the face
lallies: legs
mince/mincing: to walk/walking affectedly
vada/vadering: see/seeing
visage: the face

About the Author

Clayton Littlewood was born in Skegness, England, in 1963 and grew up in Weston-super-Mare.

When he was in his teens he moved to London to join a band called Spongefinger. After being rejected by every record company in town he turned to pirate radio, hosting a comedy show where he posed as a 70-year-old female West Country aromatherapist called Doctor Bunty. This led to an MA in Film and Television and writing comedy scripts (inspiring one agent to say, 'This is the most disgusting piece of filth we've ever read. Do not contact us again!')

In his recent incarnations Clayton has been running the Soho designer menswear store Dirty White Boy with his partner, Jorge Betancourt, writing the "Soho Stories" column for *The London Paper* and contributing regularly to BBC Radio.

His first book, *Dirty White Boy: Tales of Soho*, was published in October 2008, with a book launch at Soho's infamous The Colony Room Club. The book was named the *GT* Book of the Year (2009).

In June 2009 Clayton turned the book into a play and appeared on stage at the Trafalgar Studios in London's West End alongside actor David Benson and singer Maggie K de Monde. The play returned for an extended run in June 2010, Clayton again narrating alongside David and singer Alexis Gerred.

Goodbye to Soho is his follow-up.